"Resources for individuals with bipolar disorder are few and far between, but those for the people who care for them are even scarcer. Julie A. Fast and John D. Preston have put together a valuable resource for families and caregivers of people with bipolar disorder. Taking a holistic perspective, these authors offer advice that will help readers help their loved ones with bipolar disorder. More importantly, this book encourages and helps readers to take good care of themselves and their relationships."

—Sheri Van Dijk, MSW, RSW, psychotherapist and author of *The Dialectical Behavior Therapy Skills Workbook for Bipolar Disorder, The Bipolar Workbook for Teens,* and other books

"Julie A. Fast and John D. Preston have put together an impressive second-edition guide for couples struggling with the reality of bipolar disorder. They strive to decouple the diagnosis from the individual living with it. This premise lays the groundwork for their discussion of compassionate, non-blaming communication combined with effective couples-based solutions for those striving to work through the interpersonal complexities of a relationship impacted by bipolar disorder. *Loving Someone with Bipolar Disorder* really is a must-read for anyone who does."

—Russ Federman, PhD, ABPP, director of counseling and psychological services at the University of Virginia and author of Facing Bipolar

"I am truly impressed with this wonderful book. I will have it in my office and recommend it to patients' partners as a matter of course as they go through the journey with this illness."

—Steven Juergens, MD

"More than an education about bipolar disorder, this is a welcome to the journey, in the kindest language you will find in any such book. Open to any page and you will notice the tone and wisdom of people who've obviously been there. It's a challenge to maintain a relationship with someone who has this illness. You'd do well to have a guide, and you will not find any better than Julie A. Fast and John D. Preston. Nor will you find any clearer advice than that which the authors have laid out. Their book is remarkably emotionally intelligent and a privilege to read."

—James Phelps, MD, mood disorders specialist at Samaritan Mental Health in Corvallis, OR, and author of *Why Am I Still Depressed?*

"This book will help the loved ones of people living with bipolar disorder to better understand its challenges. It provides clear, concrete ways of giving the support needed to keep their loved ones healthy and get them through the rough spots."

—Ruth White, PhD, MPH, MSW, associate professor of social work at Seattle University and author of *Bipolar 101*

loving
someone
with
bipolar
disorder

SECOND EDITION

Understanding & Helping
Your Partner

JULIE A. FAST
JOHN D. PRESTON, PsyD

New Harbinger Publications, Inc.

Publisher's Note

Distributed in Canada by Raincoast Books

Copyright © 2012 by Julie A. Fast and John D. Preston
        New Harbinger Publications, Inc.
        5674 Shattuck Avenue
        Oakland, CA 94609
        www.newharbinger.com

Cover design by Amy Shoup; Text design by Tracy Carlson; Acquired by Melissa Kirk; Edited by Nicola Skidmore

---

Library of Congress Cataloging-in-Publication Data

Fast, Julie A.
  Loving someone with bipolar disorder : understanding and helping your partner / Julie A. Fast and John D. Preston. -- 2nd ed.
    p. cm.
  Includes bibliographical references.
  ISBN 978-1-60882-219-5 (pbk.) -- ISBN 978-1-60882-220-1 (pdf e-book) -- ISBN 978-1-60882-221-8 (epub)
  1. Manic-depressive illness--Popular works. 2. Manic-depressive persons--Family relationships--Popular works. I. Preston, John, 1950- II. Title.
  RC516.F376 2012
  616.89'5--dc23

          2011039637

Printed in the United States of America

16   15   14

10   9   8   7   6   5   4

To Ivan Kanis and Julia Gray Alverson

—J.F.

To Lauren Preston

—J.P.

Contents

Acknowledgments vii

CHAPTER ONE
Getting Started 1

CHAPTER TWO
Treat Bipolar Disorder First 7

CHAPTER THREE
Multipolar Disorder. 18

CHAPTER FOUR
Medication Basics 34

CHAPTER FIVE
The Holistic Treatment Plan. 54

CHAPTER SIX
The "What Works" List 65

CHAPTER SEVEN
Bipolar Disorder Triggers 79

CHAPTER EIGHT
A Couple Takes Charge 102

CHAPTER NINE
The Bipolar Conversation 127

CHAPTER TEN
Your Emotional Response to Bipolar Disorder 144

CHAPTER ELEVEN
Work and Money. 156

CHAPTER TWELVE
S-E-X 172

CHAPTER THIRTEEN
What about You?. 184

CHAPTER FOURTEEN
The Hard Truths about Bipolar Disorder 196

CHAPTER FIFTEEN
How to Create Laughter and Joy in Your Relationship 210

APPENDIX
Quick Reference Guide to Medications 219

Resources. 237

References 239

Acknowledgments

It took more than twenty years of living with bipolar disorder to create a holistic treatment plan that helps keep me stable every day and to give me the knowledge I needed to write this book. Ivan Kanis was with me for the past ten years and I can never thank him enough for his love and support. There were ups and downs, as with any couple where both partners have bipolar disorder, but we made it through. Our relationship is very strong. We are both living examples that people who have been very ill with bipolar disorder can stay healthy and as stable as possible when they use a holistic treatment plan.

I would like to thank my family, especially Rebecca Alverson, Ed Fast, Ellen Schlotfeldt, and David Grayson Fast for letting me live with them while I worked on this book. They didn't always understand me, but they tried. I would like to thank my writer's group in Portland, Oregon, for providing the companionship I needed during the very solitary process of writing so many hours a day. Megan Loomis, Lisa Langford Heron, Liz Nakazawa, Nancy Lapaglia, Jacki Sturkie, and Debra Meadow always understood the fears, struggles, and triumphs that come with writing a book.

I must thank my naturopath, Dr. Cynthia Phillips, for her constant support during the years when I was so ill. She is one of the main reasons I was able to get well enough to live my life again. I would like to thank Dr. Steven Juergens, Suzanne James, and Susan Picard for their excellent help as well. I'm far away from so many friends, but they are always in my heart. Pam Palacios, Suzanne Bibby, Patricia Myung, Marcia Lins, and Teresa Lins Csorba have stuck by me through so many ups and downs I can no longer count them. We've survived mania, depression, anxiety, anger, and psychosis (all on my part of course) but managed to stay friends.

I would like to thank my coauthor John Preston, PsyD, for his support and professionalism. He truly made this book special. He also helped me calm down when I felt overwhelmed with the work of writing while having to deal with constant mood swings. I would also like to thank my acquisitions editor, Jueli Gastwirth, for calling and asking me to write this book. My editor, Kayla Sussell, really polished this manuscript and taught me a great deal about editing.

And most of all, I would like to thank all of the people who have written and supported me through my websites www.juliefast.com and www .bipolarhappens.com/bhblog. There are so many of us with this illness. It's my dream that everyone will find a treatment plan that is right for them as individuals so that they can have happy, healthy, and stable lives. It really is possible.

—Julie A. Fast
2003

CHAPTER ONE

Getting Started

The partners of people with bipolar disorder are very similar. You are the ones who stay in the relationship instead of walking away. You are the main caretakers. When your partner is ill, you hold your lives together. You know the terrible fear of watching the person you love become someone you don't even recognize. When your partner is ill, you take care of the house, the finances, and the children—all the while having to hold your fear inside. Often, your partner is too ill to seek help. You call the doctors and sometimes the police. You make sure the prescriptions are filled and up-to-date and that everything is taken care of. This is a lot to ask of one person—and yet you, as the partner of a person with bipolar disorder, do it all the time. This book is for you.

Are You Tired?

You may be worn-out from playing so many roles in your relationship. The goal of this book is to help you find the right balance between understanding and helping your partner so that you are still able to pursue your own goals and dreams. This book can provide you with the tools you need to be a resource and support for your partner instead of a crisis manager and constant caretaker.

It may be that your partner's bipolar disorder has been in control of your lives for years. You may have created ways of coping that no longer work.

This happens. With this book, however, you are going to learn a holistic treatment plan that can replace crisis control and mere coping. You *can* learn to change what isn't working into something that does. The tools in this book can show you how to best use your own strengths in combination with new techniques. By the time you finish all of the chapters, you will have a foundation for working with your partner to treat bipolar disorder holistically—a foundation that will help you create the stable and loving relationship you deserve.

What Is a Holistic Treatment Plan?

As you undoubtedly know, traditional treatment for bipolar disorder focuses on medications. Certainly, medical treatment is essential and it's assumed that your partner is on medications and under the care of a doctor while you read this book. But, it's also known that many of you have partners who refuse to see their doctors or take medications, while some of you may be reading this book because your partner needs more than medications to achieve stability. The solution lies in a holistic treatment plan in which medications are one part of a plan that includes diet, exercise, sleep regulation, and lifestyle changes, as well as behavior changes and trigger recognition.

Holistic treatment is based on the belief that a person can't change one part of their life without changing all of it. When you use the holistic approach to treating bipolar disorder, your role as a partner becomes as important as any member of your partner's health care team. The good news is that many people with bipolar disorder can achieve stability once they have a treatment plan that helps them prevent the symptoms that characterize the disorder. The key is to have tools you both can use to find relief from the ups and downs of this illness. This book will give you these tools.

The Correct Diagnosis

Loving Someone with Bipolar Disorder is not designed as a diagnostic manual (although diagnosis will be discussed to a degree in chapter 3). Ideally, it is hoped that your partner has been diagnosed by a licensed psychiatrist, although, nowadays, many people are diagnosed by general practitioners or other mental health professionals, who may or may not have the necessary skills to treat the disorder. It is important for you to understand that while some psychotherapists are qualified to diagnose (or treat) bipolar disorder, not all have sufficient training. It is important that your partner is evaluated by a mental health professional who specializes in treating severe mental illnesses. In other words, no matter who has diagnosed your partner, it is essential that the diagnosis be clear and correct.

How to Involve Your Partner

At first, it may be hard for you to get your partner to use the tools in this book. As you probably know, there are many stages to bipolar disorder. It will help if you are clear about where your partner is right now on a stability scale of 1 to 10. If your partner is stable and wants to do this work with you, then the optimum rating of 10 applies, and you can do the work in this book together. If your partner is in the hospital or is otherwise too ill to participate with you, then the minimum rating of 1 applies, and you can use the book yourself and introduce the new techniques when your partner is more stable. If your partner is somewhere in the middle, use your own judgment. It's highly recommended that you read the book and make the changes in yourself first, and then introduce them to your partner at a later time; especially if your partner is not well enough to do the book with you from the beginning.

Crisis Situations

If you are currently in crisis—that is, if your partner has left, is in a severe episode, is in the hospital, has stopped medications, or is refusing your help—naturally, you will use this book in a different way. If you are in this type of crisis, focus on yourself first and make the recommended changes on your own. Then, when things calm down, you can introduce the changes to your partner. If your partner is stable and you plan to work with this book together, celebrate: you have a great start.

The Reality of Bipolar Disorder

Always remember that although bipolar disorder behavior is frustrating and destructive, it's not purposeful, nor is its presence meant to punish you or anyone else. When someone is in the middle of a mood swing, compassion goes a long way. It helps to keep this in mind as you begin working with this book.

Loving Someone with Bipolar Disorder is not a quick fix. It's easy to be hopeful and excited about something new, but when it becomes difficult (or your partner does not respond immediately), it's also easy to revert to old patterns where you alone must do everything to keep your relationship together. Or maybe your partner is too ill to respond. If that is the case, or if your partner is under extreme stress or their thinking is distorted, they may be unable to do the work. Naturally, this will frustrate you. But you are not alone. At first, many partners of those with bipolar disorder must do the work by themselves.

This Work Takes Time

In this book, you will be asked to rethink your current lifestyle and the way you react and respond to your partner when they are ill. You may need some time to adjust to new ideas. In fact, making healthy adjustments and relearning how to live with your partner may take more time than you think it should, but significant change can and often does take place if you are patient.

Go easy on yourself. Many of the techniques discussed here will produce immediate results, especially if your partner is stable and willing to work with you. Others may take many attempts to see tangible results. Your goal is to create a foundation for treating bipolar disorder slowly and calmly; one that focuses on prevention instead of crisis control. Remind yourself to focus on the solution, not the problem. Problems are immediate—solutions take time. Here are some of the qualities you will need while you are creating your holistic treatment plan:

- An open mind and the willingness to try new ideas to treat an old problem.

- Enough time to learn a new way to live with bipolar disorder.

- The courage to grieve the loss of some of the hopes and dreams you had for your relationship, while simultaneously taking decisive action to improve the relationship.

- A journal in which you can explore your ideas, thoughts, and emotions, and in which you will complete the important journal exercises you will find in each chapter.

Why keep a journal? Keeping a journal can seem like a lot of work at first, but it is an essential part of this program. The ideas and lists you write in this journal will become the basis for your treatment plan. Here are some of the many good reasons for using a journal to help you create a new treatment plan for bipolar disorder:

- You are a student and students take notes.

- Writing and drawing in a journal allows you to say things you would never say out loud; journals are private.

- Journals help you get some perspective on what is you and what is bipolar disorder.

- Journals let you cry and complain without bothering other people; journals don't hurt other people's feelings.

- Journals are a very safe place to explore very serious topics.

- Writing things down helps you prevent fires instead of having to put them out all of the time.

- Journals help you create a plan; plans loosen the control bipolar disorder has on your relationship.

- The pen is mightier than the sword and bipolar disorder has a really big sword.

- Your journal can be your friend when your partner is too ill to be the friend you need.

Some Helpful Advice

The odds are very good that you are starting this book with a lot of hope. One reason people frequently don't finish books with the same kind of hopeful enthusiasm they start with is that the reality of their situation starts to weigh them down, and hopelessness creeps in. It helps if you can make a deal with yourself right now that you don't have to practice all of the techniques presented here at once. You simply can't. No one can.

You will probably want to get started immediately and that energy is great, but if you can channel that energy into doing each chapter slowly and thoroughly, one step at a time, you can keep your hope alive. Implement the ideas chapter by chapter. They really do build on each other. Give yourself plenty of time to see the important changes. Use your journal every day.

If you have children, teach them journaling techniques and let them write about their feelings about bipolar disorder. If they are old enough, make sure you include them in your new treatment plan. Children may seem too young to understand what is going on, but you may find that involving them in positive action plans that help your partner get better will also reassure your children. Most of all, keep your hope alive. This is a tough but very treatable illness. With the right combination of medications and a holistic treatment plan, you and your partner can work toward the relationship you wanted when you first got together.

Treating bipolar disorder holistically is not about what is wrong with your relationship. It is about what bipolar disorder has done to your relationship and about creating a treatment plan that takes power away from the disorder. This plan can help you maintain your perspective when your partner is ill. Treating bipolar disorder realistically is about remembering what is good in your relationship and why you began it in the first place.

A Final Note

TREAT BIPOLAR DISORDER FIRST: This is a phrase you will see often in this book. It means that because of the seriousness of the illness, you and your partner must make it your top priority to focus on treating and managing bipolar disorder, so that your relationship can achieve stability. To end the control that the disorder has on your relationship requires that you use all of the tools you can find to prevent bipolar disorder symptoms. Appropriate medical treatment is a big part of treating the disorder first, as are the action plans you will find in each chapter.

You are now ready to get started. The treatment system you are about to create will give you the tools you need to take action and can make a big difference in your life and your partner's. You *can* do it.

CHAPTER TWO

Treat Bipolar Disorder First

*If you want to have a happy, healthy, and stable relationship,
you have to treat bipolar disorder first.*

Bipolar disorder is very predictable. If you are currently in the middle of a stressful situation, this may be impossible to believe, but it really is a predictable and often very treatable illness. Life with bipolar disorder may feel like a roller-coaster ride and it may cause terrible problems in your relationship, but once you learn the patterns of the disorder and specific strategies to treat the mood swings and their symptoms, you have a good chance of creating a stable and healthy relationship based on love, joy, and growth, instead of one based on living from crisis to crisis.

What Does "Treat Bipolar Disorder First" Mean?

When your partner is ill, their beliefs about themselves and the world are often distorted. If you try to talk with them about your relationship, work, or life in general, you often talk to the bipolar disorder instead of to the person you love. When you treat bipolar disorder first, with strategies that help both of you notice and ultimately prevent mood swings, your partner can become more rational and be more of the person you love. Then, you can discuss issues and be assured that your partner is responding from who they are, instead of from what the illness tells them to say (or do). Learning practical strategies to treat bipolar disorder first helps you build a stable foundation that is in place when the next bipolar storm hits. The building of this foundation starts when you examine where your relationship is right now and where you want it to be in the future.

Building a Stable Foundation

Your first goal is to get a clear picture of how bipolar disorder currently affects your relationship. This will help you decide what you want to change initially and recognize what you will need to do to get started. (Your journal will help you with this process, so have it ready.) When you talk honestly with your partner about how bipolar disorder has affected both your relationship and you personally, you set the cornerstone for your new foundation. As with all the suggestions in this book, if you can't talk directly with your partner at first, you can use your journal and trusted friends or a therapist to begin exploring the issues.

Think about Bipolar Disorder Realistically

Have you ever thought rationally about the sacrifices you are willing to make to create the stability your partner needs to treat this illness? Or does it seem that the ups and downs of the disorder only allow you to live day to day? Have you thought about what must change for you to continue in this relationship? Have you ever discussed the main issues you struggle with regarding bipolar disorder?

It helps to get your feelings out in the open and on paper so you can discuss, realistically, the toll this illness has taken on your relationship. It also helps to know how committed you are to helping your partner prevent mood swings in the future. The foundation for healing is based on complete honesty. You will have to ask yourself some tough questions to get started. Then, this book will help you find the tools you need to handle the issues these questions bring up for you. Your first journal exercise will give you an idea of how you are currently feeling about bipolar disorder and the role it plays in your life.

EXERCISE: Bipolar Disorder and Your Relationship

Answer the following questions in your journal: *How has bipolar disorder affected my relationship as a whole? How has it affected me as a person? What is the hardest thing that I face daily regarding this illness? What do I want to see change right now? What do I need in my own life to find happiness? If things stay as they are, where do I see my relationship in the future? What is going well?*

Your answers will help you focus on the areas of your relationship that need immediate help. You can then use the techniques discussed in this book to make the necessary changes to move your relationship where you want it to be in the future. If you feel that your partner is well enough to answer the questions with you, first answer them separately, and then talk about your answers together. This will help you both get started in the direction you want to take while you are working with the book.

What Major Issues Do You Face?

Thinking about the major issues in your relationship that are caused by your partner's bipolar disorder will help you understand what is working and what is not. You can learn to recognize what you can and can't do. When you are clear about what you need, you will be able to talk to your partner rationally and compassionately about a plan that will treat the illness first. You will be able to tell your partner exactly what you need and you will get a realistic picture of what your partner can do on their own.

It helps if you can think of this process as a negotiation between the two of you. Remember, you are reading this book because your partner has an illness that needs treatment. Be gentle. This may be the first time that you have ever really talked with your partner about *your* needs. Talking with your partner about these needs is not about blaming your partner, especially if they are not ready for change. Instead, it is about your needs and the changes you are ready to make. It can be a positive experience.

One way to introduce the subject of your needs to your partner would be to talk about what you personally want to do in the future to treat the illness in order to minimize its impact on your lives. Remember, you must be honest about what you will do and what you would like your partner to do to treat bipolar disorder first. It may help to think of your needs as agreements you can make with yourself and your partner. This can take the pressure off the two of you and may lead to more rational and positive discussions. Here are some positive examples of how to approach discussing what you are willing to do to help your partner find stability:

- I'm willing to learn new techniques to help you get well.

- I understand that bipolar disorder is an illness, and I'm willing to work with you instead of blaming you.

- I agree that I'll have to make some changes in my own lifestyle to help you stay stable (e.g., changes in social obligations, busyness, sleep habits, diet, exercise, and the use of caffeine, alcohol, and drugs such as pot).

- I understand that the cost of not treating bipolar disorder far outweighs the cost of allowing things to stay as they are.

- I'm willing to try out the techniques described in this book for the next six months, and if you are still not ready at that time to make the changes needed, I will reevaluate my approach.

- I agree to examine my own emotional behavior to see what I may be doing to contribute to your bipolar disorder symptoms.

- I understand that you are ill and are not sick on purpose. I agree to remind myself of this when I'm frustrated with your progress.

- I'm willing to be more assertive with your health care team and to let them know that I need help and direction as much as you do.

As a couple, you can talk about what you both want and need from your relationship and what you think you will need to do in the future to treat bipolar disorder first—so that you both can find some stability. You will learn many new techniques in this book, but for the moment your focus should be on what you need for yourself and from each other. Here are some ideas of what you can decide to do together:

- We will learn to work on bipolar disorder together—as a team.

- We agree to use the techniques in this book even when they don't work immediately.

- We know that many positive changes can happen quickly, but we agree that it may take longer than we want to make the big changes.

- We agree that we love each other and we want to our relationship to be healthy and whole once again.

- We agree that we can't continue as we are if our relationship is to survive.

Working Alone

If your partner isn't working with you at first, reading these ideas may be very frustrating (or depressing). This doesn't mean that the situation is hopeless. Being honest with yourself is a very powerful tool. There are many ideas contained within this book that you can use by yourself. You can then introduce these ideas to your partner when they are more stable. If you can't talk with your partner, use your journal to write about what you are willing and able to do. This will help you see where you are in *your* life and also to see what you can realistically give to your partner. Of course, if your partner is currently in the hospital, you will need to allow time before you introduce any new ideas, but you can certainly get started on your new behaviors and be ready when your partner comes home.

Needs, Not Punishment

When you do talk with your partner about your needs and how you feel, be careful not to sound as if you are warning them about the consequences of their actions. That is, don't say, *You better do this or I'm going to leave.* Instead, try to talk to your partner in a loving way and let them know you are trying to take care of yourself and ensure that your relationship will be stronger in the future. When you treat bipolar disorder first, with compassion and the realistic tools you will learn in this book, you can learn to focus on the positive and what works to help your partner stay stable, instead of punishing your partner for their bipolar disorder symptoms. You can then work together to create goals that will help you get to where you want to be in the future.

Setting Goals

In life you are taught to make personal, financial, and physical goals. What no one tells you is that you have to make bipolar disorder goals as well. As the partner of someone with bipolar disorder, you need to create realistic goals that will reflect what you can and cannot do. As a couple, you can set goals that take into account the limitations of the illness. You probably know that untreated bipolar disorder is a goal wrecker. You may have had great plans for your relationship only to have found that the disorder ruined your plans over and over again. To counteract this, you must set clear, attainable, realistic goals that carefully consider the limitations that bipolar disorder puts on your relationship.

What Are Goals?

Goals are realistic: For example, if you don't want to play the caretaker role any longer, this doesn't mean that you have only the choice to leave your partner. Instead, your goal could state that you will begin to set more realistic limits on how much you will do. Of course, it will be important to learn the new tools you will need to stop or diminish your caretaking role and learn to ask for help from others, but such changes start with stating a goal.

Goals have a timeline: For example, you might set a goal that states, "I want to have a more loving and stable relationship that is not controlled by bipolar disorder, and I'm willing to wait six months to see the changes before I make any major relationship decisions." Setting goals is a process, not only a result. The time it takes for you to reach your goal is just as important as reaching the finish line. Set a time limit and remember that all of the time before that time limit is part of the entire process.

Goals can be dreams: As long as you understand the true limitations bipolar disorder places on your partner, and you continue to believe that your relationship is worth the work, your goals can take you where you want to go. They teach you to find success within limitations. So dream big, but dream realistically.

Goals are attainable: Your goals should always take into account the facts of bipolar disorder and not assume that the illness will just vanish one day. (Even though that would be really nice.)

Goals take time: Surely, you have heard the saying "Two steps forward, one step back." When it comes to reaching goals, this is an accurate description. You cannot expect a straight trajectory into positive change. It is fairly certain that you will take a lot of winding roads, but if you are ready for the setbacks and disappointments along the way, you can reach your destination.

One way to reach large goals is to break them into smaller pieces. When something feels like it is too much to do or too hard, or it feels as if it is not working, do only a small part of it. Sometimes, on your path toward your goal you will be like a rocket, but at other times, it will feel as if you are crawling to your goal. This is normal. You can say to yourself, *I may be crawling today, but I'm still on my path.*

Goals are different from plans: Sometimes, a goal may seem impossible because there are so many roadblocks along the way. Many people quit trying to reach their goals when the problems seem impossible to fix. But one way to help yourself stay on track is to remember that it is not the goal that needs to change when things get tough. Instead, it is the plan that needs changing. Maybe you need new tools or a different way of looking at the situation. So remember, when reaching a goal such as achieving a more stable relationship seems difficult or impossible, your plans for how to arrive at your goal may have to change occasionally, but your goal can stay the same.

EXERCISE: Explore Your Goals

Treating bipolar disorder first in your relationship is a lifelong process. In order to decrease the control that bipolar disorder has over your life, your goals can help you to focus on what you need to do immediately. Now, using your journal, write down your goals for your relationship. Here are some examples of the goals you can set for yourself:

- I want a loving relationship where bipolar disorder is just an illness my partner and I manage together. I'm willing to do what it takes to make this happen.

- I want to be in a relationship where we are equal partners and I'm not a caretaker, so I will do whatever it takes to make this happen.

- I want us to travel together in a healthy way. I would like to do this within the next year.

- I want a relationship where out-of-control anger and violence are not options. I will no longer accept out-of-control anger or violence in this relationship. This starts now—today.

- I'm going to learn about the role of diet and exercise in mood swings by educating myself and asking questions.

- I want to learn more about my partner's medications and their side effects.

- I would like to be more assertive with my partner's health care team to let them know what I need from them. I will remind myself not to get intimidated when I see my partner's doctor, and I will have my list of questions ready.

- I want to help my partner find stability by examining our lifestyle.

- I want to understand and accept the fact that my partner cannot work right now, and I want to learn how I can help our family deal with this financially.

- I want my relationship with my partner to be stable for our children. I want to involve them in this healing process.

- I want to spend time with my partner—not with my partner and bipolar disorder.

- I want a normal sex life that is about passion and love, not about bipolar disorder symptoms.

- I want to track our money so that we do not have to go through another financial emergency. I'm going to start educating myself on what I can do to create a financial plan.

- I will not let bipolar disorder make any more decisions in my relationship.

- I'm going to maintain perspective. I may have years and years of old behavior to change and it's going to take time. I give myself that time to reach my goals.

You and your partner both need your own separate goals as well as the goals that you will work on together to make your relationship stronger and more stable. These goals will help you explore the reality of the limitations that the disorder places on your relationship. Create goals that focus on what you *can* do, instead of on what bipolar disorder makes it impossible for you to do.

Project Your Goals into the Future

The next step is to project your goals into the future. For example, if you want to deal with your finances, so you can be safe in case your partner cannot work, look at where you want to be in six months, a year, and five years. Ask yourself, *If I don't make these changes and I'm still in financial trouble in six months, can I live with that?* Or if you want a more loving and stable relationship, project into the future to see where you will be in one year. Ask yourself, *If my relationship is not more loving and stable in one year, can I live with that?* This will help you understand how strong your desire is and will remind you that it will take daily work to meet your future goals. It is really important to examine the cost of not changing—of staying the same. Ask yourself what the cost to you and your family will be in the future if you do not treat bipolar disorder first. Picture yourself five years from now, if things do not change.

You may feel overwhelmed as you contemplate the future. This is normal. Anyone in your situation would feel overwhelmed. When it comes to treating this illness, the secret to dealing with the feeling of being overwhelmed is to let yourself off the hook by saying, *I'll just do what I can do right now. Bit by bit. I don't have to do this book all at once. I just have to do what I can.* You can even create a set response for when you feel overwhelmed by all that you want to change in your relationship. You can say to yourself, *I'm so proud that I'm starting to learn new ways to help myself and my partner. I can give myself the time it takes to make these changes and I accept that this is the first step.*

Then pat yourself on the back for doing whatever you can do, even when you feel overwhelmed. You can also keep a separate section of your journal just to write about your frustrations. Keep this at the back of your journal and let it all out, and then move on. There are always risks and fears in a big change. The secret is to feel the fear, acknowledge the risk, and just move forward anyway.

Think Positively

It is human nature for people who are suffering or overwhelmed to focus primarily on what is negative. Even in the midst of difficult times it is important to focus on the good parts of your relationship as well, especially when your situation may feel hopeless. Before you finish this chapter, think of the good qualities your partner brings to you and your relationship. What do you love about your partner? What potential do you see that you know will bloom once the mood swings and their symptoms have been minimized? Write about these positive aspects of your relationship in your journal and then share them with your partner. This will help you focus on the reason you are reading this book in the first place. You want a happy, healthy, and stable relationship. And you have taken the first step toward reaching this goal.

REALITY CHECK

It is often very sad to face the realities of bipolar disorder. For example, you may be reading this book alone. Your partner may be in the hospital, may have left, or may not be willing to do the work that is needed to change both of your lives. Or, perhaps your partner is willing to do what it takes, but the illness just seems to win every time. This illness can put a terrible strain on a relationship. But instead of focusing on what is going wrong, focus on what can change once you start using the techniques you will learn in this book. When your partner decides to come with you on this journey, it can be a wonderful experience.

HOW TO INVOLVE YOUR PARTNER IN THIS PROCESS

- Start the new plan yourself. As your partner sees you change and become more focused and stable, they will hopefully want the same for themselves.

- Model your new behavior so your partner can follow you. Bipolar disorder takes a lot out of your partner. Sometimes it feels impossible for them to do anything that takes effort. They will appreciate the help.

- Involve your family and friends and teach them the new techniques.

Treating bipolar disorder first means that you do what it takes to stabilize the illness by learning new techniques for treating it, so that you can then move on to more meaningful issues. Treating bipolar disorder first means that before you can enjoy your relationship, you must get bipolar disorder out of the way.

CHAPTER THREE

Multipolar Disorder

Bipolar disorder is not characterized just by mania and depression. In fact, BI-polar disorder is a bit of a misnomer. Yes, people with the illness do go up and down, but doesn't it seem as if they also go sideways or do little corkscrews as well? Maybe if it were called MULTI-polar disorder, people would understand the illness a bit more.

Most people assume that bipolar disorder is only about mania and depression. And to a large extent that's true, but a holistic view understands that the disorder also includes a variety of symptoms in addition to mania and depression that also affect your partner's thinking and behavior. One key to treating the disorder successfully is knowing what you, as the partner of someone with bipolar disorder, are up against. It's very important for you to get a solid handle on the multifaceted nature of this disorder so as not to be surprised by the various and sometimes confusing symptoms of the illness.

Bipolar disorder is complex. These days in the psychiatric literature it's popular to refer to "bipolar spectrum disorders," as there appear to be a number of related conditions that share some common features. All variants of bipolar disorder include the following features:

- Obvious changes in mood.

- These mood changes are *episodic,* meaning that they are generally not continuous but come in fairly separate bouts with measurable time in between. (Rapid cycling is the exception to this and will be defined later in this chapter.)

- Bipolar disorder is due primarily to a biological abnormality involving changes in brain chemistry. The illness is typically lifelong and doesn't simply disappear one day. Without appropriate treatment it can become progressively more severe.

It may be stressful for you to read that the illness is lifelong. Luckily, treatment is possible. This illness *is* predictable. Once you and your partner learn the major symptoms of the disorder that you may deal with regularly, you can learn to treat each symptom individually to create a more stable relationship. Your first step is to learn the different terminology used to diagnose bipolar disorder.

Bipolar Disorders

When people are first evaluated and given a diagnosis, there are often inadequate explanations about what the diagnosis really means. People may leave their health care professional's office with many unanswered questions. It's natural if you and your partner want and need to know more about bipolar disorder and how to treat its symptoms. It helps if you first understand your partner's specific diagnosis. People with bipolar disorder share common symptoms, but there are different forms and the severity of the illness varies.

Bipolar Disorder I

People with bipolar I (one) experience severe depressive and full-blown manic episodes. Some people switch directly from manic to depressive episodes (or vice versa), but many will have times between episodes when there is no apparent mood problem; such times are called *euthymia* (a neutral mood state). Approximately 1 percent of the general population has bipolar I (National Institute of Mental Health 2003).

Bipolar Disorder II

Bipolar II (two) is the most common type of bipolar disorder, seen in about 4 to 5 percent of the general population (Judd and Akiskal 2003). People with bipolar II have a very high frequency of major depressive episodes. Over a lifetime people with bipolar II spend three times as much time in depression as do those with bipolar I (Akiskal et al. 2000). The other primary feature of bipolar II is the absence of full-blown mania; instead, people with bipolar II have episodes of *hypomania*. (See "Hypomania" below for a definition.)

Cyclothymia

Cyclothymia looks like a mild version of bipolar disorder, presenting with episodes of mild depression and hypomania. Such individuals are often seen as being very moody and emotionally reactive people. Cyclothymic mood swings can occur for many years with no evidence of severe depression or mania, but it's now recognized that for the majority of people with cyclothymia the mood swings worsen and they eventually convert to bipolar I or bipolar II (Akiskal et al. 2000).

Rapid Cycling Bipolar Disorder

Among those with bipolar disorder, 10 to 20 percent develop what is known as *rapid cycling* (Bowden 2003; Akiskal et al. 2000). It's seen in bipolar I and II (but is much more common in bipolar II) and is more common in women than men. Rapid cycling is characterized primarily by its high frequency of mood episodes. Technically, people are said to have rapid cycling if they experience four or more episodes of mania and/or depression during a twelve-month period. Some people may have many more than four episodes per year and are said to have *ultra-rapid cycling*. There are those who may cycle monthly, weekly, and even daily. There is also increasing evidence that substance abuse or incorrect use of antidepressants or stimulants may be key factors in causing or aggravating rapid cycling.

The Many Faces of Bipolar Disorder

Now that you have a clearer picture of the way bipolar disorder is diagnosed, the next step is to become more familiar with your partner's individual symptoms. Bipolar disorder can be very confusing. There are so many different symptoms within symptoms that it may seem impossible at first to get a handle on all that is going on with your partner, but it *is* possible.

The next section will help you start to think about the big picture of your partner's bipolar disorder. Once you see the big picture, you will be ready to treat each problem individually so that you are not overwhelmed by trying to treat everything at once. First, you will learn the signs of the typical depression and mania mood swings of the illness and then you will become acquainted with the multifaceted symptoms within these mood swings.

For clarity, this book will refer to depression, mania, and the symptoms associated with these mood swings as *major bipolar disorder symptoms*. Later in this chapter you will be asked to place your partner's major bipolar disorder symptoms into categories. This will help you and your partner in later chapters when you create a separate treatment plan for each major symptom.

Depression

Symptoms of depression (often referred to as "major depression" or "clinical depression") include sadness, unhappiness, or irritability; low self-esteem; a loss of enthusiasm, motivation, or vitality; extremely negative and pessimistic thinking; a range of physical symptoms including disturbances in sleep, appetite, and weight; loss of sex drive; and fatigue. Intense worry, anxiety, agitation, and suicidal thoughts are also common symptoms of major depression. Major depression can dramatically interfere with functioning (e.g., work, school, parenting, relationships).

Depression is disruptive because it affects the mind *and* the body. A depressed person often slows down to the point that nothing can get done. Getting out of bed can feel like a monumental task to the depressed brain. Depression can also cause irritation and unreasonableness. A depressed person may be unhappy and mean, or weepy and clingy. Depression can distort your partner's thoughts to the point that they can say and do very unreasonable things. The duration of a major depressive episode can vary substantially from person to person and often persists for a number of months.

When I'm depressed, my body and mind simply shut down. All tasks become impossible and it feels like I'm living my life in heavy mud. Sometimes my depression tells me that it would just be easier to stay in bed all day. It tells me I'm no good and that everything I do is junk. It's so strong. I just can't fight it. It's as though something has taken over my mind and my body and I'm no longer in control.

Mania (Full-Blown)

People with bipolar I have full-blown mania. This mania is usually described as either *euphoric/expansive* mania or *dysphoric* mania (also referred to as "agitated" or "mixed" mania). Dysphoric mania has none of the pleasure felt in euphoric mania. All manias are accompanied by increased energy, racing thoughts, and a decreased need for sleep. Euphoric/expansive mania includes

- feelings of heightened self-esteem and often grandiosity (for example, thinking *I'm the smartest person in the world*),

- an intense desire to be active (this takes many forms, such as agitation and restlessness, or an urge to be very outgoing and gregarious),

- and often very poor judgment (for example, spending enormous amounts of money and putting one's family in financial jeopardy; sexual promiscuity; reckless behavior, such as driving too fast; and substance abuse).

In the early phases of euphoric/expansive mania, the person may actually experience a tremendous sense of well-being. However, often as energy begins to escalate and thoughts become more rapid, it starts feeling like an engine running out of control. Wildly creative thoughts disintegrate into chaos and confusion, high energy turns to agitation, good judgment is lost, and even very bright individuals can neither think clearly nor recognize that their out-of-control behavior is dangerous to them or to their loved ones. Upbeat moods quickly collapse into intense irritability and the person in the manic episode loses their ability to function normally. Psychosis often may appear when a manic mood swing goes this far.

Dysphoric mania also is characterized by high energy, racing thoughts, poor judgment, and restlessness, but there is no sense of well-being. In the context of the frenzy of high energy, there is a pervasive mood of despair. Just as in major depression, negativity and pessimism dominate. Approximately 60 percent of people with bipolar disorder have euphoric/expansive mania, while 40 percent have dysphoric mania.

The ideas come so fast when I'm manic, I can't keep up with them. They're such good ideas that I know I've just created something to change the world. The last time I was manic I stayed up all night writing a new software system that I was positive would revolutionize the industry. I couldn't sleep and felt so full of this amazing energy. The next morning I was very irritated and snapped at my partner. I tried to fix everybody's problems. I soon had trouble writing. Then, I was no longer in control of my thoughts. I remember thinking, "I'm a genius," and I believed it. Then I started to do dangerous things. I walked across a freeway without looking first for oncoming cars. Mania isn't fun when this starts. Things start to unravel and I have to go to the hospital. My partner had to get a court order to keep me in the hospital because I refused treatment. I was put in restraints because the nurse feared I would hurt her. I was in the hospital for three months before I came down.

Hypomania

Hypomania (both euphoric and dysphoric) is seen in bipolar II and is much less intense than full-blown mania. There is an increase in energy, a decreased need for sleep (but no daytime fatigue), and impaired judgment, though not as serious as that seen in full-blown mania. During euphoric hypomanic episodes, people have a heightened sense of well-being and are very productive and gregarious. During dysphoric episodes, people are agitated, pessimistic, and restless.

This type of mania can last for a few days or go on for months and, although everyone around the person can tell something is wrong, it's very difficult for the person experiencing the hypomania to notice the problem until the episode is over. The person's social life often increases, as can substance abuse and spending. It's hard for friends or family members to do anything about it, as the person is still basically functioning. Often, this is when the person is perceived as "wild" or "irresponsible," causing the family to give up on them.

Major Symptoms of Bipolar Disorder

Beyond the classic presentations of the bipolar disorder mood swings described above, there are a number of symptoms that often accompany bipolar I and II. Technically, these are not mood swings per se, but they are dominant features seen in many cases of bipolar disorder and are important to understand.

These symptoms (along with depression and mania) will also be referred to as *major bipolar disorder symptoms* in order to help you create a separate treatment plan for each major symptom your partner experiences. Here is a list of the symptoms your partner may experience along with mania and depression. Please note that this is not a definitive list. Your partner may have other symptoms as well that will need to be addressed when you create your treatment plans.

MAJOR BIPOLAR DISORDER SYMPTOM PATTERNS

- Depression*

- Mania*

- Hypomania*

- Psychotic symptoms

- Paranoid symptoms

- Intense anger and irritability

- Anxiety

- Feeling overstimulated/overwhelmed

- Problems with maintaining focus, attention, and concentration

- Suicidal thoughts and impulses

- Self-destructive behaviors

- Hypochondria

* Specific symptoms have been described above.

Psychosis

Psychosis is a severe break with reality that can occur with mania or depression (though not with cyclothymia or hypomania). Because there is so much confusion and stigma surrounding psychosis, it helps to know that although psychotic behavior seems totally bizarre, random, and frightening, it's a normal symptom for many people with bipolar disorder. The following information will help you understand some of the psychotic symptoms your partner may experience.

General Psychotic Symptoms

Your partner may experience an intense feeling of unreality where the world seems strange and unfamiliar. Their thinking can become extremely disorganized. This results in very poor judgment and is often accompanied by intense fear or anxiety. During this confused state, the ability to reason is completely lost. Your partner may also have very odd or bizarre thoughts and behaviors. Psychosis can truly impair the way your partner looks at the world. If your partner says or does something that seems completely unrealistic or frightening, it's important that you talk with their doctor about psychosis.

Psychotic Delusions

Delusions are far-fetched, highly unrealistic, even bizarre beliefs—for example, the belief that one has been chosen as a special messenger of God to save the world, or the belief that one has been cursed by Satan. One version of delusions is referred to as somatic delusions (seen more often in severe depression) where the mistaken belief involves the body or one's health, such as believing that one's internal organs are rotting. With delusions, such a belief is unshakable, and the person completely loses the ability to recognize that their thinking is irrational. When delusions are present, it is near to impossible to reason with the person; their capacity for critical thinking is generally quite impaired.

Psychotic Hallucinations

Hallucinations are defined as perceiving something when an actual stimulus is absent, such as hearing voices when no one is present (auditory hallucinations) or seeing visions that have no basis in reality (visual hallucinations). At times, people experiencing a hallucination realize that they are hallucinating, but often they react to the experience as if it were entirely real, having lost the capacity to appreciate the unreality of such experiences. People often confuse hallucinations with negative self-talk. It's important to know that auditory hallucinations can occur in your partner's own internal voice; they don't have to take on an outside voice. It's also important that your partner recognize that what they are experiencing is a symptom of bipolar disorder. Hallucinations can be very frightening, for both you and your partner, but they are a normal part of bipolar disorder if your partner is in a psychotic state.

I have many different types of hallucinations. I often see myself being bitten by a dog or hit by a car. I see my body fly in the air and land on the ground in front of me. I have looked down and seen my wrists cut and bleeding. I smell things more strongly and hear voices that tell me I should not be where I am or that I'm a failure and should die. This can be very scary.

Paranoid Symptoms

When a person is paranoid, they may have completely unrealistic and unsubstantiated beliefs that other people are out to harm them, humiliate them, take advantage of them, or be unfaithful. Often, profound distrust and suspicion is at the heart of paranoia, and this can be very disturbing to family members. To be paranoid means believing that something is happening that isn't happening, such as thinking that everyone at work is talking about you, or that you have no friends. Paranoia is very disruptive because it feels entirely real although it has no basis in reality. The person suffering from severe paranoid symptoms may believe that their spouse is trying to poison them or is in a conspiracy with the local mental hospital to have them permanently committed.

As with other types of psychotic thinking, attempts to reassure the person may be futile; their mistaken beliefs are intense and unshakable. Often a part of the experience of paranoia is believing that certain events or objects in the environment have special meaning. For example, seeing a road sign that says, "Danger, Winding Road Ahead," causes the paranoid person to conclude, *That sign is meant especially for me; I just know that I'm about to be harmed.*

Technically, paranoia is a symptom of psychosis, although many people with bipolar disorder develop a milder form of paranoid thinking. This type of impaired thinking doesn't involve bizarre or unbelievable conclusions; rather it is simply being highly suspicious, mistrusting, and hypervigilant.

I've lost so many friends because of paranoia. I can feel that they're saying things about me and I have to tell them what I feel. It's as though I'm just sitting there and suddenly I have the idea that my friends don't want to be with me and that they're avoiding me. When I'm in a stressful situation such as a classroom, I get the feeling that people are looking at me oddly and that they're all talking about what is wrong with me. When I ask them why they are treating me this way, they truly have no idea what I'm talking about. They then think I'm totally weird and the friendship is over.

PSYCHOSIS IS CONFUSING

Psychotic symptoms can be difficult to understand. Often, people with bipolar disorder keep their psychotic symptoms to themselves because they really don't know what is happening and don't know if their thoughts are normal or a part of the illness. Psychosis can be very subtle and chronic, or it can be profound and sudden and can erupt with little warning. Because psychosis can be a normal symptom of bipolar disorder, the more you know about it, the less frightening it becomes.

The most important thing to know is that psychosis is very disruptive for the person with bipolar disorder. Even a mild psychosis greatly impairs a person's ability to function. It's also important to know that psychosis can be treated and prevented.

Intense Anger and Irritability

Inappropriate and intense anger is often seen as a personality problem instead of as a symptom of bipolar disorder. In fact, unreasonable and frequently violent reactions to events that normally wouldn't cause irritation and anger are commonly seen in both depression and mania. (Even in euphoric mania, the person's upbeat or even jovial mood is easily punctured and anger can quickly flare up.) This irritation and anger is often directed toward people and objects and may include slamming doors, hitting walls, yelling, or physically abusing others. Road rage is also very common. Some people with bipolar disorder end up in jail because of this symptom. During anger outbursts the person may say and do things that ordinarily they wouldn't say or do (for example, saying very hurtful things to one's partner). Later, when the emotions die down, the ill partner may feel remorse for what was said or done. It's very common for partners to become fearful during intense eruptions of anger or to experience hurt feelings when the ill partner says harsh or cruel things.

Sometimes my anger is so strong I feel like I'm going to explode. It feels so good to hit something or yell and start a fight. It's a release from all of the pressure inside. It doesn't even feel wrong at the time. It feels like something I have to do.

Anxiety

Anxiety is a common feature in both mania and depression. It generally emerges in three ways. The first signs of its presence are its physical aspects: muscle tension, jitteriness, restlessness, shortness of breath, rapid heart rate and/or palpitations, tremors, sweating, and sleep disturbances (especially difficulty in falling asleep). Second are anxious thoughts: fretting, worrying that bad things are about to happen, and significant thoughts about being out of control or inadequate to face daily challenges. Third are the emotions of anxiety: intense uneasiness, panic, feeling out of control and overwhelmed, and a sense of impending danger or dread.

Often anxiety symptoms appear to others as extreme overreactions to life's normal daily stresses. And even though people with bipolar disorder may feel anxious about specific matters, it's not uncommon for them to experience what is called *free-floating anxiety*. Here, the anxiety doesn't seem to be attached to any specific event or situation.

When I get anxious, I can feel my pulse pounding in my neck and I know that if I'm asked to do even one more thing I'm going to cry and run from the room and just hide in bed. Anxiety churns in me and makes me feel that I can't go on. It makes it impossible for me to work or talk with people normally. I just feel this whirling feeling of being sucked into something I can't control. I actually wring my hands and lose my breath. I get the feeling that something bad is going to happen to me, but I just don't know what it is. This often stops me from doing things I once enjoyed.

Feeling Overstimulated or Overwhelmed

Many experiences in daily life are stimulating for anyone. At times, this kind of intensity is a source of excitement and enjoyment; at other times the stimulation may just feel overwhelming. With bipolar disorder, however, even ordinary life situations may be experienced as completely overwhelming, which can be hard for others to understand. The sense of being overwhelmed may occur as a response to something as simple as meeting a deadline at a job, going to the supermarket, having to pay bills, or doing the dishes. To complicate matters even further, many people suffering from bipolar disorder often seek out highly stimulating experiences (such as exciting sporting events, movies, parties, vacations, taking on obligations, a heavy workload, or a large course load in school). Then they begin to feel overwhelmed. (They may not have been able to anticipate that so much activity would end up being overwhelming.) It's important to keep in mind that although life's stressful and difficult experiences can, of course, become overwhelming, many apparently pleasant or positive events can overwhelm as well.

When I go to a concert, or a baseball game, or to the mall, I just can't enjoy myself. There are so many people wearing so many colors. They're all talking and making other noises. I worry about where my car is in the parking lot and if I'm going to make it through the evening. I start to feel that something is wrong and that there's too much going on. I feel very pressured. I want to leave and get some peace. This makes people call me negative and a spoilsport, but I just can't help these feelings.

Problems with Focus, Concentration, and Attention

Difficulties with focus, concentration, and attention can accompany all forms of mania and depression. People can become quite distracted and forgetful. It can also be very difficult to stay organized or to stay on track for finishing projects or work assignments. Projects often seem overwhelming and, to the person with bipolar disorder, the brain can feel like it's not making connections or that it's going in all directions at once.

When I look at a project I can't see the steps I need to take to finish it. It just all looks like one big impossible jumble and even when I start with good intentions, I get completely distracted. This has made school and work almost impossible for me.

Suicidal Thoughts and Impulses

Suicidal thoughts and impulses are common symptoms that can be the most worrisome aspect of the disorder for those with the illness and their partners. Sometimes, such impulses arise from feelings of self-hatred and guilt, although, most times, the urge to kill oneself is born of the desire to just stop suffering. Sadly, the suicide rate among those with bipolar disorder is quite high, and thus any suicide threat must be taken seriously.

The best solution for preventing suicide is to get aggressive and appropriate holistic treatment for bipolar disorder and to work together to make life worth living for yourself and your partner. Suicidal thoughts seem so personal and emotional, but it helps if you understand that they are often a normal part of bipolar disorder.

When I'm depressed, I just reach a point where my thoughts take over and tell me that I'd be better off dead. This seems very reasonable, as I'm in so much pain from the depression I can't see any point in staying on this earth. Suicide seems like a solution when I hurt so much. It doesn't matter if I have a lot of people who love me or if I have good things in life. When I'm this sick, it just doesn't matter.

Self-Destructive Behaviors

Self-destructive behaviors can take several forms: severe substance abuse (that is, endangering one's health or safety with drinking or using drugs), very reckless behavior (such as dangerous driving), binge eating (including overeating and purging by vomiting or by using laxatives), and self-mutilation (for example, burning or cutting oneself). It might make sense to you that someone who is suffering would drink alcohol to the point of oblivion, to numb out from the pain. But often some of these other disturbing behaviors are very hard for partners to understand.

Some people who suffer with bipolar disorder experience a rare physical anomaly. When they inflict physical pain on themselves (for example, by burning themselves with a cigarette), they feel an almost instantaneous relief from psychological pain. Typically, this cessation of emotional suffering lasts for about an hour. In addition, they actually feel no physical pain from the burn. This very peculiar phenomenon is seen primarily in those who have bipolar disorder and co-occurring *borderline personality disorder.* Some people also experience a short-lived diminution in suffering from bingeing or reckless behavior.

It's important to know that, most times, self-harm behavior is not motivated by the desire to suffer or to punish oneself; rather it reflects desperate attempts to reduce suffering (although, obviously, such attempts can backfire and cause serious injury or death).

When bipolar disorder gets really bad I feel so much pain inside I have to get some release. The only time I feel okay is when I drink myself to oblivion. At least then I can escape.

Hypochondria

Hypochondria is an intense preoccupation with and worry about one's health even when a physician has provided assurance that there is no evidence of a physical illness. Again, this can be a frustrating experience for partners, who quickly discover that no amount of reassurance or rational argument can free the person with bipolar disorder from intense worry about their health.

Feeling Overwhelmed?

It's okay if you feel scared and overwhelmed just from reading about the many symptoms your partner may experience. Bipolar disorder *is* scary if it's untreated. Recognizing and naming all of your partner's major symptoms is the first important step to take in understanding and beginning to take control over bipolar disorder. When you and your partner know what to expect, the illness can't throw you a curveball anymore. This will help you to predict the future with some accuracy and also help you to feel safer.

Your Partner's Major Symptom Categories

This section asks you to create a list of your partner's major symptoms. Depression and mania will be the first major symptoms on your list. Your eventual goal is to discover all of the major symptoms your partner experiences when ill. Your list will help you to see that bipolar disorder is not one thing one year and something completely different the next year. For each individual, the disorder tends to follow a pattern. At first glance, it may seem like a wild and crazy pattern, but upon closer inspection you'll likely find that it has quite a bit of consistency.

Once you discover that consistency, you will be ready to create a plan that can address each of your partner's major symptoms individually. This book's primary goal is to help your partner reduce these symptoms and to give you the tools you need to help your partner maintain stability. Breaking down your partner's bipolar disorder into its major symptom categories is the first step in this process.

EXERCISE: Break Down Your Partner's Bipolar Disorder into Specific Symptom Categories

1. **Find the consistent problems:** It will help if you can do this exercise with your partner, but it also works if you do it alone. Review your relationship together. What are the main and *consistent* problems your relationship has faced due to bipolar disorder? Is your partner often angry and irritated with you over little things? Does your partner get depressed and talk as though they have never done anything right in their life? Does your partner hop in the car and take a long drive just to see something beautiful? Does your partner spend money like crazy on things they don't need? You are the discoverer here. These consistent patterns are often the manifestations of particular symptoms. Make a list of these problems in your journal and decide what major symptoms they might represent.

2. **Interview your partner:** Ask your partner if they have ever experienced the major symptoms listed in this chapter. (Do this only if you feel your partner is stable enough to help you. Don't do this if your partner is in the hospital.) Ask them about each symptom. Have some questions ready in your journal. Here are some sample interview questions: *What does it feel like to be depressed? What does it feel like to be manic? What psychotic symptoms have you had? When you have suicidal thoughts, what goes through your mind?* You will use this information when you create your final list.

3. **List the categories in your journal:** Using your journal, look over the symptom categories in this chapter and create a list of your partner's major symptoms. You will probably add to this list as you work through the book, but it helps to have a generalized list to get started. You will use these symptom categories as the basis for your treatment plan.

Now that you have separated your partner's bipolar disorder symptoms into major categories, you are ready to move on and create a plan that specifically treats each major symptom. Knowing what major symptoms your partner is experiencing, especially those that don't look like depression or mania, is a vital step toward creating a treatment plan that will help you achieve stability in your relationship.

REALITY CHECK

It may take several months to even begin to put together a comprehensive list of your partner's major bipolar disorder symptoms. Give it time. It helps if you can treat this as an ongoing project and not as a one-time assignment. (Reading this chapter again can also help.) Involve your partner, friends, and family members. This is the time to get all of the bipolar disorder symptoms out into the open, so that they are no longer frightening or controlling. You may meet some resistance to this. There is still a lot of shame associated with having a mental illness in our society. Think carefully about how you want to approach this project. Involve people who are ready to be involved, and always respect your partner's privacy. If you meet resistance from your partner, you will have to find the middle ground because you are also important in this relationship, and if being more open about bipolar disorder and the role it plays in your life is what you need, you will have to find ways to meet this goal.

When you decide to treat bipolar disorder first by thinking about the role it plays in your relationship and you then learn to break down your partner's bipolar disorder into its major symptoms, you are creating a foundation for a healthy and stable relationship. Your role as a partner is important and can truly help your loved one and your relationship find stability.

CHAPTER FOUR

Medication Basics

*As a partner, you need to know as much about medications
as the person with the illness. You are the one who will be
there when the side effects are difficult to tolerate, when the
medications take a long time to work, and possibly when
your partner goes off medications or refuses to take them.*

This chapter speaks honestly regarding the challenges you may experience during your partner's medication journey as well as how the process affects you. The appendix at the back of the book covers all medications used to manage bipolar disorder, how and why they are prescribed, how they work, their possible side effects, and any monitoring needed to make sure the medications are working effectively.

Bipolar disorder is a very complex illness, and medication treatment can be just as complex. The goal of this chapter is to address your concerns directly and help answer your questions so that you can move forward with hope and energy in your relationship with your partner. Your goal can be to use the information in this chapter to help your partner and ultimately help both of you decide what current and future decisions you need to make regarding medications. No matter what the situation, the facts are clear: medications exponentially increase your partner's ability to manage bipolar disorder, and this creates a greater chance for you to have a good relationship. This is great news, since it means there can be very positive outcomes when your partner uses medications as prescribed along with the management plan presented in this book.

EXERCISE: Your Partner's Response to Diagnosis and Attitude toward Medications

In terms of medications, there are a few basic scenarios you and your partner may be experiencing. Look over the list below and see which most closely matches your current situation. Your partner can go in and out of these scenarios—just as people go in and out of mood swings—but it helps to know where you are right now.

- **Your partner accepts the diagnosis and is on medications, but side effects are a problem.**

I watch my wife shuffle around the house like a zombie. She wants to work, but she can't find the energy. She says the meds are killing her and she would rather have mood swings. Her writing is so shaky I can't read it and she is desperately upset about her weight gain. This breaks my heart. There must be a way to find the right medications.

- **Your partner does not accept the diagnosis and thus refuses medications.**

My partner, Adam, was recently diagnosed and is fighting the "label" of bipolar disorder. He refuses to take medications and won't work or help around the house. It's like having a bear in the basement. He is always angry and I can never predict his moods. I'm scared and lonely about our future and what bipolar disorder is doing to our family. I can't talk with his doctors—he won't let me—but I know that he was given meds. My goal is to help him accept the bipolar disorder diagnosis and take his meds, though maybe that's what my friends call wishful (and stupid) thinking. My first goal is to learn all I can about this illness and the medications. Then I can talk with him and let him know my needs.

- **Your partner accepts the diagnosis but goes on and off medications.**

I've been with my boyfriend for ten years and I'm very tired of him going off his meds all the time. When he's manic he thinks he doesn't need them, and when he's depressed he says he's hopeless and doesn't have the energy to take them. I stay because of our kids. I think I have ignored a lot of this just to get by. I am much more aware of the patterns now. I see how I get fooled every year, and it has to stop.

- **Your partner accepts the diagnosis, is taking medications consistently, and would like to know more information about the treatment.**

When my partner, Alex, first got out of the hospital, he was drugged for months. Things are so much better now, but we need more help in understanding why he has to take certain meds and how we can make the process easier. There was never a problem for any of us in terms of accepting the diagnosis. We just need more information on the medications and how they will affect his future. We have done well in the past year. I know we are very lucky.

No wonder bipolar disorder management is so challenging! You may feel alone in many ways, depending on the current state of your partner's illness. People with physically ill partners often face the same challenges. The next step is educating yourself on the topic of bipolar disorder medications and their impact on your partner's health and ultimately your relationship.

Bipolar Disorder Medications

The good news is that there are only four main categories of medications used to treat bipolar disorder, which makes it much easier to understand your partner's medications and why they are prescribed.

- Mood stabilizers

- Antidepressants (used with great caution, since they can cause manic episodes)

- Antipsychotics

- Antianxiety medications

Outside of these categories, there are also a few other medications that are sometimes used to treat bipolar disorder. The appendix provides extensive information on all of the medications used in the treatment of bipolar disorder.

Unfortunately, there is some not-so-great news along with the good news. Isn't that always how it is with bipolar disorder? While it may be simple to understand the four categories, challenges arise when a prescriber must decide which medications to use from each category, how to combine them, whether they will interact negatively with medications taken for other medical or psychological conditions, and which drugs are the most effective with the least side effects. It can't be stressed enough that this is a complicated process, which is why finding a successful medication regimen for your partner may take much longer than you hoped. Most prescribing decisions are based on current research, so it's helpful if you know the basics.

Warning about Stimulants

It is well established that illicit stimulants such as cocaine and methamphetamine are notorious for causing manic episodes. Given this, for a number of years there has been some concern about the use of prescription stimulants to treat attention deficit/hyperactivity disorder (ADHD) in people who have both bipolar disorder and ADHD. It turns out that up to 35 percent of people with bipolar disorder also have ADHD. The most recent consensus is that stimulants such as Ritalin, Adderall, Dexedrine, and Concerta can be safely given to people who have bipolar disorder, but it is important to first get stabilized on bipolar medications before starting a stimulant. If stimulants are prescribed, people must be cautious about taking any of the medications after noon because some of the drug may still be in circulation later that night and interfere with sleep (and getting good sleep is very important in maintaining mood stability).

The STEP-BD Research Project Findings: Structure Equals Stability

In the largest study done on the treatment of bipolar disorder, called the STEP-BD Research Project (STEP-BD stands for Systematic Treatment Enhancement Program for Bipolar Disorder), 58 percent of patients achieved full remission during the research program using state-of-the-art medical treatments (NIMH 2011). But it's very important to note that the 58 percent who did well were treated aggressively using strategies such as sleep monitoring, strict adherence to medications with the least side effects, and a nonstressful and very structured environment. Also, keep in mind that people in research studies are monitored very closely, and side effects and noncompliance issues are dealt with appropriately. What does this mean for you? Though this kind of intense monitoring rarely happens in real-life settings, you can do as much as possible to create a similar situation in your relationship by following the strategies in this book and finding the right medication combination for your partner. In other words, when you and your partner can create a very structured environment around sleep, medications, and relationships, things can truly change for the better. (If you're cynical about this, we understand, but change is possible.)

The lower response rate in the other 42 percent of study participants is likely due to the five factors listed below, which directly reflect the difficulty of managing bipolar disorder in the real world.

1. **Patients stop medications or change dosages because of problematic side effects.** This is never a good choice, as quickly going off medications or reducing the dose without supervision can cause physical withdrawal symptoms as well as lead to the reemergence of serious mood swings.

2. **Patients stop or change medications because they are in denial about bipolar disorder.** It's very natural for anyone affected by bipolar disorder to hope that the illness will just go away one day. Because of this, patients may either refuse medications or go on and off them until they finally accept the diagnosis.

3. **Patients stop or change medications during a mood swing because they lack insight.** This is especially true for those in full-blown mania or a suicidal depression. For example, patients in manic situations often lose the ability to accurately remember past experiences and how destructive they may have been. Thus, the decision to stop medications is based only on present feelings and not on possible future consequences.

4. **Patients rely on medication treatment alone and do not use a management plan such as the one found in this book.** It's essential for all people with bipolar disorder to establish routine lifestyles, take advantage of psychotherapy that specifically addresses life with bipolar disorder, deal actively with relationship problems, and work toward cultivating stronger family relationships and building a supportive treatment team. This isn't easy, but as the chances for success are greater when a person is on medications,

you and your partner are already a step ahead of most and can more smoothly implement the strategies in this book.

5. **Patients perceive a negative stigma attached to the bipolar disorder diagnosis.** It's a very personal decision to tell others about a bipolar disorder diagnosis. Even though the illness is now less stigmatized and is talked about more widely in the media, people may feel shame, fear losing a job, or worry that they will be judged by others for the illness. This desire for privacy and even secrecy can be very hard on the partner, since they may feel there is no one to talk to. If the person with bipolar disorder finds it overwhelming to deal with the diagnosis, it makes sense that they may refuse medication treatment as well.

If you and your partner can recreate the positive factors identified in the study and do all you can to prevent the above behaviors, your chance of a stable relationship increases dramatically.

Need-to-Know Facts about Bipolar Disorder Medication Treatments

It has been said that in psychiatry there are no "home run" pills. Bipolar disorder medications are absolutely necessary and often lifesaving, but it's important to know that they rarely achieve a home run on the first try. Here are some realities about using medication to control bipolar disorder symptoms:

Medication doses are often more aggressive at the beginning of treatment in order to get very severe symptoms (such as suicidal behaviors, extreme manic agitation, or psychosis) under control. If your partner recently had a severe episode, especially if they were (or are) in the hospital, the first line of treatment is to get the episode under control. This can mean some really big doses of medications with some very strong side effects. It helps to know that medication doses can often be reduced, at least to some degree (and thus side effects can greatly diminish) once an initial mood swing is under control. For example, a very high dose of a mood stabilizer and antipsychotic may be needed when someone is in a full-blown manic episode, but once the episode is under control, the medication plan may change significantly.

Most people diagnosed with bipolar disorder will need to try more than one medication in order to find stability. Finding the best medications almost always involves trial and error. It's not a given that the first medications will work. Although first-line medication choices such as mood stabilizers are well established, it's essential to understand that almost all people with bipolar disorder will need to try several drugs or drug combinations in order to find stability. Each person is an individual and it is impossible to know ahead of time which specific medications will be effective. Obviously, efficacy is important, but equally important is finding medications that the patient can tolerate—for instance, medications that have minimal side effects and do not cause allergic reactions. It's essential that you prepare yourself for a prolonged period of medication trial and error, especially when your partner is first diagnosed. Accepting this reality can ease much of your frustration as to why it can take so long to get it right.

The Facts about Side Effects

More than half of those taking bipolar disorder medications will struggle with significant and problematic side effects. We can't stress enough how difficult it can be to experience serious mood swings and then have to deal with medication side effects on top of already being ill. This is especially true in the first year of treatment, when the prescriber may try a number of drugs and drug combinations in order to find a combination that your partner can tolerate and that does a good job of managing the mood swings. In these cases, side effect concerns are often secondary, as the person has to get stabilized first. Unfortunately, problematic side effects may lead to your partner stopping the medication outright or experimenting with different dosages, which can lead to relapse and possible physical reactions. This highlights why finding the right medications is so essential, even when it seems to be taking forever.

It's essential that you know the facts regarding the side effect risks and benefits associated with medication treatments. It's your right, and it's to your advantage, to become knowledgeable about your partner's medication treatment plan. Bipolar disorder medications are among some of the most difficult of all psychiatric medications to prescribe and manage. Two-thirds of bipolar disorder medications cause weight gain, and it has been well established that rates of obesity are higher among bipolar disorder patients. Thus, weight gain side effects can be especially challenging in individuals who are already trying to control their weight. Sleep problems and sexual side effects may also greatly affect a person's comfort level with medications.

It's important to point out that it's usually a tradeoff between side effects and mood swing reduction. As is the case with most medications used to treat serious illnesses, the benefits of the medications can outweigh potentially problematic side effects. The goal is always to find medications that work with the least side effects, but in order to do this, medications must be tried with an open mind and given a chance to work.

A Reasonable Approach to Side Effects

It's essential that all people affected by bipolar disorder be realistic about the side effects listed in the medication information sheet that accompanies all prescription drugs. The drug companies have to list every single possible side effect that could happen to a person, even if just one person in ten thousand experienced that side effect. Side effects are listed in order of occurrence, and it's important to note that very few people experience the less common side effects. Be especially skeptical while reading comments found on the Internet regarding certain medications. Many people refuse medications because they have read extensive side effect lists or sensationalized information on websites. People tend to leave comments on the Internet when they are upset that a medication didn't work. It's quite rare for someone to go online and rave about a medication.

The reality is that all drugs have side effects. The goal is to find those that have the least side effects and work well to manage your partner's mood swings. The need to go through numerous trials of various drugs can be frustrating, but keep in mind that almost everyone who eventually finds lasting stability probably went through this process.

Pharmacotherapy: Using Medications to Treat an Illness

It helps to think of bipolar disorder medication side effects in the same way you would view the side effects associated with medications for the treatment of any serious physical illness. If your partner had heart disease, they likely would be willing to take medications with many side effects in order to stay alive. The same goes for a severe viral infection, cancer, or diabetes. It's often easier to accept these medication side effects because they are treating very tangible illnesses. A person clutching their heart, experiencing kidney failure, or at risk of death from a severe infection has obvious physical symptoms. The problem with bipolar disorder is that for the most part it's physically silent. Because of this, the symptoms that truly need treatment are easier to ignore or to blame on someone else. The goal is for you and your partner to work through any misconceptions about medications and to realize that medications are just as important for managing bipolar disorder as they are for managing any illness. The following scenarios speak directly to this issue.

Scenario One: Stefano's Story

Stefano is forty years old. He's in excellent health, runs every day, and really watches what he eats. One day as he was climbing into the cockpit of the plane he was flying to Mexico on a freight run, he felt a pain in his chest and stumbled down the stairs. His coworkers called an ambulance that transported him directly to a hospital, where he received triple bypass surgery. It was successful. His doctor said he could live an active and productive life but that he would have to stay on his heart and cholesterol medications. Stefano was already in good health, so he needed to keep up the exercise and good eating habits, but if he didn't take the meds he had a high chance of another and possibly more serious heart attack.

Stefano's partner, Margaret, asked, "What are the side effects of the medications?"

The doctor replied, "The first medication has a risk of causing migraines, irritable bowel syndrome, vision problems, and thyroid disease. The second medication can cause vertigo, internal bleeding, and muscle pain." The doctor continued, "I want to stress that though these side effects are possible, they are rare, and without these medications there is a high chance that Stefano won't survive. Once we find the right dosage of these meds, side effects may subside and Stefano can get back to his regular life."

Stefano and Margaret decided that Stefano would not take the medications due to the side effects. Stefano didn't want to risk thyroid disease, even if it was relatively rare. Margaret was really worried about the possibility of internal bleeding. Stefano didn't want his quality of life to be dictated by side effects and agreed that Margaret was right. Medications were too risky and he would probably never have another heart attack anyway.

How do you feel after reading this story? Would you or your partner suggest that Stefano stay on medications? Most people probably would.

Scenario Two: Marsha's Story

At twenty-five, Marsha was diagnosed with bipolar I after a severe manic episode with psychotic symptoms that occurred when she and her partner were traveling in Spain. After a brief stay in a psychiatric hospital, she was flown home and went into a private hospital paid for by her family. Her partner, Roland, was scared and had no idea what bipolar even was. Was it contagious? Could she have children? Would she get better? Would the drugs work? Marsha's doctors gave her lithium, and it worked much more quickly than expected. After a lot of questioning by her doctor, Marsha realized she had been depressed and hypomanic for most of her life, starting at age nineteen when she first tried to kill herself. But this was her first severe manic episode. Her doctor also prescribed an antipsychotic and explained to her that bipolar disorder is a very serious illness that requires lifelong medication treatment in order to manage the mood swings. He said that she was lucky that the combination of lithium and an antipsychotic worked so well.

Marsha asked, "What are the side effects of these drugs?"

The doctor replied, "With lithium: possible low thyroid, excessive thirstiness, sedation, and lack of creativity. It will also be necessary to do frequent blood tests to monitor levels of the drug. The antipsychotic medication has side effects including weight gain, a risk of high cholesterol and triglycerides, and an increased risk of type II diabetes." He then explained, "With the very aggressive form of bipolar disorder that you have, especially with the psychotic symptoms when you were manic and your past suicide attempts, I feel that the combination of lithium and an antipsychotic is your best chance for stability. This combination works well for many people, and I'm pleased to see it work so well for you. You may not have to stay on the antipsychotic, but that will have to be decided in the future. Overall, I'd say you are someone who reacts well to medications and should have an excellent outcome. The side effects usually decrease over time. These medications really can prevent such a serious mood swing from happening again."

Marsha weighed her options and decided not to continue the medications. She said, "I'm not going in for a blood test once a month and there is no way I'm gaining weight after I've worked so hard to stay thin. It's not worth it. I will just deal with this on my own." She believed that the manic episode was simply a stress reaction to traveling and she would remain stable now that she was home. Roland was very upset. He saw the benefits to medications, but there was nothing he could do to change her mind. It was as though she was making decisions for their future without asking his input.

How do you feel after reading this story? It's very eye-opening to think of how differently medications and their side effect tradeoffs are approached in response to a physical illness as compared to a mental illness. The point, of course, is that all pharmacologic treatments have side effects, whether the drugs are being prescribed for heart disease or bipolar disorder. In our society, not taking heart attack prevention medications would be seen as unreasonable. The reality is that it's just as unreasonable not to at least try bipolar disorder medications to manage mood swings.

Can you guess which medication can have the following side effects?

Heartburn, nausea, upset stomach, black or bloody stools, confusion, diarrhea, dizziness, drowsiness, hearing loss, ringing in the ears, severe or persistent stomach pain, unusual bruising, vomiting. And when a severe allergic reaction occurs: rash, hives, itching, difficulty breathing, tightness in the chest, swelling of the mouth, face, lips, or tongue.

The answer is aspirin.

What about You?

Medications can negatively affect you as well. Many bipolar disorder medications cause excessive sedation, decreased sex drive, and weight gain—symptoms that can directly affect you as a partner of someone with the illness. Additionally, you may frequently be the one who has to encourage your partner to stay on medications and deal with the outcome if they refuse to take their medications or don't take them as prescribed. Please note that you always have a choice about what works for yourself instead of focusing only on what works for your partner. You naturally can't always micromanage your partner's medications, but you can help make the process easier. If possible, go to appointments together when medications are first prescribed. You can take notes and ask questions about the medications and why they are being used in your partner's specific case. You can also set up a timer or alarm that goes off each time a medication is needed. Another helpful strategy is a medications chart where you list the medication name and type, when it was prescribed, the symptoms it controls, dosage, when to take the medication, side effects, and whether it works. This will give you great information to use with a prescriber if change is needed.

My husband, Jerry, is getting over a huge manic attack. He had been doing well for years and then the medications just didn't seem to work as well. There were signs he was going into another manic episode, but we both ignored them. Maybe he was finally just happier! Then the shit hit the fan and he went back to the psych ward. When he came home he was a zombie. His moods were definitely stable and he was able to go back to work within a few weeks. But he would come home and pass out in front of the TV. He would wake up for dinner and then go back to bed! We used to have such a great time together—we'd eat out a lot and go to movies. We don't have kids, so he's my best friend. I was upset and lonely because he was always asleep. And I hated seeing him this way. He hated it too. I knew it wasn't his fault, but I just missed him so much. I felt like I'd lost him. I knew that medication side effects can include sexual problems, and he was so tired, we never made love. I finally forced him to go back to his doctor. She agreed that he was way too sedated and she changed his medications. Things are so much better. If I hadn't been there, I think that Jerry would have kept living like a zombie simply because he was too tired to go to the doctor! I always tell Jerry—it's never okay to just put up with difficult side effects. We have to do something!

Six Reasons People with Bipolar Disorder Refuse Medications

People with bipolar disorder usually have a love-hate relationship with medications. Because of this, it's normal for them to go on and off medications or even refuse them altogether. It is beyond the scope of this chapter to go into this topic in detail, but please do know that you have choices when your partner doesn't take medications and that you must think carefully about how a partner who has mood swings and refuses medications affects the relationship and your life, especially if there are children involved. The following information offers insight into the question of why someone who is obviously ill would refuse to take something that could increase quality of life and help you both maintain a stable relationship.

The Person Truly Can't See They Are Ill

It's unfortunately common for people with obvious and often very serious bipolar disorder symptoms to have total lack of insight that they are ill, even when all evidence points to the illness. This sounds impossible, but it's a well-researched and proven fact. It's unlikely that a person would run on a broken leg until it broke in half. But people with bipolar disorder, who are much more ill than someone with a broken leg, will often keep running, wreaking havoc in their lives and the lives of other people, all without realizing they are ill. They *will* run until they break. It's human nature to want to know why a person with bipolar disorder can't see the obvious. The answer is that loss of insight and self-awareness is a part of the illness and has to be treated as a symptom.

Jacob has lost his job, and most of his friends and his family have no idea how to talk with him. He will get manic and tear up the house—he pulled out a sink in our bathroom once, ripping it right out of the wall! There was water everywhere. He said he was just angry. When we talk to him about getting help, he literally says, "Help with what? I'm not sick." I'm watching my beautiful partner disappear in front of me. I know that there are times when I can talk to him, and I now have a plan to use those times to talk about his getting help. He is much more open to it when he's not in a rage. So it's definitely the illness taking him over. It's so weird that he can't see it. Everyone knows it's bipolar—it's all in his family and he has the same symptoms, but he has never been to a doctor and I am not sure he will ever go. It's now time for me to make a decision about what I want.

The Medications Actually Aren't Working

There are many with bipolar disorder who want to get better and do all they can to comply with medication treatment, but it doesn't always work as hoped. This doesn't mean the right combination can't be found, but many people go off their medications in frustration.

My girlfriend, Janelle, has tried eight medications and they haven't helped. She says she is done listening to her doctors when they tell her that they will eventually find something that works! She wants to stop all medications. We have a management plan and that helps so much, but there are still too many mood swings. We need help. Does she keep going? It's not about side effects! The meds actually don't work!

Friends and Family Members Are Unsupportive

Those taking bipolar disorder medications need a lot of support from loved ones, support in taking medications and also understanding how challenging this kind of treatment can be. It is not uncommon for well-intentioned family members to undercut or sabotage treatment because they do not fully appreciate the necessity of medications. It's often those on the periphery who will undermine your plans. Parents, friends, grandparents, or other relatives may say, "Why does he need medications? He just needs to buck up and get a job!" or, "Medications are a crutch. They are too expensive and don't really work. If someone wants to get better, they get better. Those drugs are not needed." And a huge problem is that the person with bipolar disorder is often strongly influenced by these people. Also, if the mood swings are extreme, especially the mania phases where judgment is lost, it's easy for your partner to listen to others and justify stopping medications.

My partner's family will do anything to keep the lie going that their son doesn't have a problem, even though he has been in the hospital three times. Once, they even took him to the hospital! His brothers and friends continue to drink with him when he's manic, and when I try to talk to his mother about his illness, she says I'm overreacting. They see him only when he's doing better (manic!) because he is always at home yelling at me when he's down. And I'm the one who deals with his mania when he goes way up. They don't believe in meds, and his brothers party with him and keep him out late in order to help him feel better. I've never seen anything like it. I said to them, "If he had pneumonia, would you take him skiing? If he had diabetes, would you force him to eat cake? Please listen to me. I need your help. I can't do this on my own anymore." They still think I'm the one with the problem, and I feel very alone in this situation.

The Person with Bipolar Disorder Thinks the Problem Is with Everyone Else

In this situation, the person has usually been diagnosed, is aware of the diagnosis, and has even been in the hospital, but still refuses to accept that bipolar disorder is causing any problems. The person might say, "The doctors were wrong, you are wrong, and everyone is wrong! Leave me alone!" Though this is similar to not realizing the illness is real, this person is actually much more aware of bipolar disorder in general and knows it exists but refuses to believe it's what is going on in their case. "You're the one with the problem" is easier to say than "I need help."

My boyfriend, Kevin, just got out of the hospital a few months ago after he was manic and psychotic and beat up a huge bouncer at a concert. Only a manic person would try to beat up a bouncer and expect to win! It was like he had the strength of five guys. He now stays in our basement, where he drinks beer all day. He yells at me and says I'm a loser. When I try to talk to him about the medications that are literally sitting on our kitchen table, he tells me I am making things worse. I know he smokes pot, too. If I go downstairs he gets very upset. It took me a long time, but I stood up to him and said it's not acceptable. It hurts our kids, and they are scared. He has a choice to make. He can stop thinking I have anything to do with his behavior and take his meds, or I am gone. I am tired of beer bottles and bongs.

The Person with Bipolar Disorder is Self-Medicating

It's amazing how many people use alcohol or drugs such as methamphetamine and pot to deal with mood swings instead of taking medications. When this becomes serious, the term used is *dual diagnosis*, in which the diagnoses are bipolar disorder and addiction.

Axel and I were both in party mode when we met. At the time it was fantastic. Lots of sex, drinking, staying out all night. We decided to move in together, and within a month Axel went so down he would not get out of bed. I had no idea what was going on. He told me he was bipolar. I felt that was information he should have told me before, and I was mad. I now see that he drinks constantly in order to deal with the mood swings. It's easy to miss reality when you're drinking with a manic person and having a great time. You think this is who they are. I can drink a lot, but I always stop when it goes too far. He doesn't stop.

There Are Problematic Side Effects

This is the main reason people with bipolar disorder stop their medications, and it's easy to understand why. The medications affect the very centers of emotions and behaviors, so it's natural they would affect people negatively in the following areas:

Sleep. Medications often affect sleep in one of two ways: either they keep the person up due to agitation, or, more commonly, they create such sedation a person can sleep all night and day. Sleep problems, especially drowsiness, often lead a person to stop the medications in desperation instead of changing to a different medication with fewer side effects.

Fiona works in musical theater, and I'm so proud when she sings in public. I now see that a lot of her success came when she was quite manic. Everyone just considers her a theater type! After she got out of the hospital from her terrible manic episode, the medications took her away, as far as I am concerned. She slept all day and all night. She couldn't work and wasn't able to even sit through a movie, and she certainly couldn't be in a play. I feel really lucky because her side effects got a ton better after a few months of adjusting her meds. I know it was important for her to get stable and keep going with the meds the hospital gave her. I am glad we stuck it out.

Sex Life. Some bipolar disorder medications come with sexual side effects (as explained in the appendix), the most common being the inability for a person to have an orgasm or to ejaculate. The medications can also take away a person's sex drive or make them too tired to be sexual. This is a side effect that certainly affects partners! (Sexual issues are discussed in more depth in chapter 12.)

Roger loved sex when we first met. When he was diagnosed and started meds, he still wanted sex, but he couldn't do it. In other words, the plumbing was not working. He changed meds as quickly as his doctor said he could. The sexual plumbing was fixed.

Weight. This is the side effect that most commonly leads to people stopping their bipolar disorder medications. The weight gain from medications can be so unexpected and so uncomfortable that a person may stop the medications in order to deal with the weight gain without thinking of how this will affect the bipolar disorder symptoms. This weight gain can be far worse for your partner than yourself, so it's important to work together to keep focused on where the weight gain comes from and how to find medications that work with fewer weight-gain side effects.

My partner, Carly, gained sixty pounds from her meds when she was first diagnosed. She was devastated. Especially about what she called the double spare tire around her stomach. No matter how often I told her I was fine with it, she was really mortified and would not take her clothes off in front of me. I love her and want to make love, and she won't because she's embarrassed and upset. This means I'm affected by the side effect of the medications as well! You may not believe this, but the weight gain was not a super-big deal to me. I was upset because she assumed the weight gain that was so terrible for her was just as terrible for me. It wasn't. I knew she needed to lose the weight health-wise, and her nurse practitioner was changing her meds and promised her it would start coming off. But what if her symptoms came back? My message to everyone on bipolar meds is to tell your partner what you are going through and really believe us when we say what we can and can't handle. Carly lost forty pounds of the weight, but the last twenty have stuck around. She eats right and exercises a lot. So what? It's not going to kill her, since her lifestyle is so healthy. She bought new clothes and never stops trying to get the weight off. But she does see that I love her. I wish that women understood that men like their bodies in all shapes and sizes. Carly was so ill for so long. I'll take the weight gain any day. No joking. I mean it! Don't make a problem like bipolar worse than it already is!

Know That People Can Change and Life Gets Better

It is extremely important to know that difficult situations, like the ones in the above scenarios, can and often do improve. As mentioned before, this chapter is an overview of what you may experience, and it's not possible to go into strategies you can use to turn around everything mentioned here, but you now have the basic information you need in order to take the next step in finding out more regarding your partner's medication treatment. You can use the tips from other chapters to create a plan to talk with your partner about medications in the same way that you would talk about a topic such as anger. Yes, it's frustrating to read about why your partner may be having trouble with medications and then not have a quick fix. But please know that it is possible for things to change for the better. It happens all the time. It's possible to find the right combination of medications and move into a stable life. Many, many people with bipolar disorder eventually see the importance of medications and how they can create a more satisfying, loving, and productive life.

Will Your Partner Have to Take Medications Forever?

You may be wondering how long your partner will have to take medications. It depends. On a positive note, new medications may one day be introduced with more successful results and fewer side effects, and there may be new nonmedication treatments in the future. For now, medication use depends on your partner's type of bipolar disorder. For example, those with full-blown mania are more likely to need lifelong preventive mania medications as compared to those with hypomania, who don't necessarily need a strong antimanic medication but may need more protection against depression. In other words, it depends on the specific type of bipolar disorder (bipolar I or bipolar II), current and possible symptoms, your partner's history (for example, past suicide attempts), and an assessment of ongoing risk. A few people go off medications and have years of stability, while others can't stay off medications for even a month without a return to mood swings.

The advent of gene therapy will likely change bipolar disorder management in years to come. For now, it's completely proven through research, and probably your own life experience, that ongoing medication treatment— combined with appropriate daily lifestyle management as discussed in this book—is essential for a good outcome in treating and living with bipolar disorder. This means that for now, staying on medications provides the best chance of staying stable during life's significant ups and downs.

Your Right to Know about and Participate in Your Partner's Treatment

The Health Insurance Portability and Accountability Act (HIPAA) of 1996 was not created to specifically address mental health issues, but there is a provision in the act that does address the need to protect those with illnesses from being exploited through the use of their medical records. It's a pretty simple law: it says that a person with an illness has to authorize another person to see their medical information. Unfortunately, this has had very serious and negative consequences for the loved ones of people with bipolar disorder. The act works well when a person is in their right mind and can rationally think of what information needs to be shared. The problem is that many people with bipolar disorder are often *not* in their right mind when they are faced with a privacy decision, especially during manic and paranoid psychotic episodes. Unless your partner says you can actively participate in their treatment, you will not be able to find out what medications are being prescribed, what specific treatment plan exists, or what the prognosis is. You may not even know where your partner is being treated or by whom. It can be a nightmare for you to hear your partner say that they don't want you to talk to the health care professional or discuss medications.

The only way around this is to have your partner sign a form recognized in your state that allows you right of access to medical information. This can be a medical power of attorney or a release of medical information form or, in some situations, a petition for guardianship. Many partners of people with bipolar disorder consider full access to mental health care information a requirement in order to stay in the relationship. This is essential if your partner has mood swings that affect their judgment. Contact a local mental health organization or visit your state's medical information website to find the correct documents and get one signed as soon as you can. It may seem impossible to get someone in a mood swing to sign, but it does happen. Obviously, if you are currently in more of a crisis situation and your partner refuses access, the best time to fill out a form is the next time the person is more stable and reasonable. If your partner is currently in the hospital and won't give you access to information, you can ask general questions of the staff such as "If a person were in this situation, what would the normal protocol be?" This at least gets you some general information you can use to help your partner or get help for yourself.

Your Partner with Bipolar Disorder Can Get Better

Do people with bipolar disorder get better? Absolutely. The use of medications along with the management plan in this book can lead to stability and a reduction and possible remission of your partner's mood swings. This will take time and good communication skills, but stability is possible.

My partner, Zac, and I no longer have a life dominated by bipolar disorder. He takes his meds, and they have just become a part of our lives. He gets down more than most people, and we are always careful when the summer starts and he is more susceptible to mania, but overall things are pretty normal. Zac was not exactly a model bipolar patient at the beginning. He refused meds for a long time. I finally left and told him I would be back when he got into therapy and took his meds. It was a long time ago, but I remember feeling so hopeless and sad. I could see what his future would be like if he refused to take the meds. And I could see what my future would be like if I stayed with him. I'm proud that I left and took care of myself. He told me later that this scared him so much he felt something shift and he thought for the first time that maybe medications were an answer and not a weakness. I know we're lucky that he had this change, but I'm so glad he did. My message to anyone who loves someone with bipolar disorder is to understand the medications and why they are needed and then set limits on what you can and can't handle. This is how Zac and I saved our relationship and built a life together that is still sexy, fun, and hopeful.

Even someone who has struggled with bipolar disorder for years can find relief. It's also very possible that someone who initially disbelieves the diagnosis or refuses medications can change and take bipolar disorder treatment seriously. (Yes, it does happen.) It takes a lot of work, but it's worth it. Not much is easy when it comes to bipolar disorder management at first, but with practice bipolar disorder can be successfully managed like any chronic illness. People do get better, and good relationships where one person has bipolar disorder are absolutely possible. Your future can be positive. The ultimate goal of this book is to help you and your partner create a loving relationship that recognizes the importance of a lifelong management plan that includes needed medications, but also one that is not controlled by bipolar disorder.

REALITY CHECK

You now know the medications used to treat bipolar disorder and some of the complications that may arise when your partner is put on a specific medication regimen. (Remember that the appendix discusses specific medications in detail.) The hard work begins once you come up against how well the medications work, what side effects are too intense to live with, and the possibility that your partner won't listen when you say you're leaving if they don't take their meds. There are positives and negatives, but the outcome can be good. When you know about medications, you can remind your partner, when they are in a hopeless and worried place, that it takes time to find something that works. And then you can remind them that when the medications work, life can change for the better almost overnight.

Knowledge about medication can improve your life and your relationship. It helps you make decisions that work not only for your partner, but for you as well. If your partner is refusing medications, you can make an informed decision about what you want to do. If your partner is having trouble with medications, you now have enough information to ask the right questions and get help if needed. And if you feel like you're in limbo because a diagnosis has been made but you don't yet know whether the medications are going to work, that's normal. Medications are the first line of treatment of bipolar disorder. It's worth the time it takes to find the ones that work for your partner.

CHAPTER FIVE

The Holistic Treatment Plan

The most effective way to treat bipolar disorder is to have a holistic treatment plan ready and waiting when bipolar disorder symptoms start appearing.

Medications are the backbone of bipolar disorder treatment, but they are only *one* part of a holistic treatment plan. Have you ever noticed that your partner has many symptoms that the medications don't help? Or maybe you've observed that medications take care of the severe symptoms and keep your partner out of the hospital, but there are still many nagging symptoms that your partner must deal with daily. As you read in chapter 1, the solution is a holistic treatment plan that incorporates lifestyle changes, behavior therapies, diet, exercise, *and* medications to create a well-balanced plan that fits into both of your lives.

Now that you have broken your partner's bipolar disorder into major symptom categories, you are ready to create a treatment plan based on the fact that different symptoms need different treatments. This treatment plan will teach you and your partner to *respond* to what the illness says and does instead of *reacting* to the symptoms as though they come out of thin air. You both can learn to predict what is coming and have the tools ready to treat each symptom before it turns into a full-blown episode. As you become more aware of the predictable patterns of your partner's illness, you can learn to help your partner stick to the plan when ill, with the ultimate goal of preventing the symptoms in the future.

Creating Your Holistic Treatment Plan

Creating a holistic treatment plan is a multistep process that you've already begun. The list of major symptom categories you created in chapter 3 was the first step. This chapter will build on that list as you move to the second step: recognizing and creating a list of the particular symptoms within the major categories of your partner's bipolar disorder. Chapter 6 will then teach you the necessary techniques to take action to minimize those symptoms by figuring out which treatments work and which don't work. The process will continue in chapter 7 as you learn to recognize and ultimately prevent the triggers that cause your partner's bipolar disorder symptoms. Chapter 8 will then describe one couple as they work their way through this whole process.

Some Words of Encouragement

Before you move forward, it's a good idea to let go of some of the old behaviors you and your partner may have practiced when bipolar disorder was raging. It may help to know that even really bright, kind, and compassionate people can become unreasonable when faced with bipolar disorder symptoms. The new ways of responding to the disorder that are covered in this book may feel unfamiliar and may even be uncomfortable at first. If you and your partner have said and done things that you regret, now is a good time to let go of the past and focus on the present and the future. You really can learn a new way to live with bipolar disorder.

Discovering the Particular Symptoms within the Categories

If you ever wanted to solve mysteries like Sherlock Holmes, now is your chance. You will become a bipolar disorder detective. You (and eventually your partner) will observe and write down every single specific symptom under your partner's major bipolar disorder categories so that you will become familiar with the pattern of the illness. This is important because knowing the specific symptoms, especially the first symptoms in each major category, teaches you both to notice when mood swings are starting.

Knowing what your partner thinks, says, and does from the very beginning is the only way you can modify and hopefully stop the bipolar disorder symptoms before they become troublesome. This can be an amazing process of discovery for the two of you. You will see that the symptoms that once seemed so random and out of control actually begin with the same small behaviors every time. (Later on you'll be able to use the lists you create in this chapter to help you discover the triggers of bipolar disorder mood swings.) These symptom lists will help you treat bipolar disorder first instead of reacting to the behaviors themselves, and you will learn that symptoms are part of an illness and not something personally directed toward you.

You will find that each major bipolar disorder symptom category is very specific. Depression, for example, uses different language and behavior than psychosis does, just as anger and irritation are different from anxiety. When you both learn and memorize the specific symptoms individually, you will no longer have to wonder constantly, *What is wrong?* Instead, you can look at your symptom list and determine the exact problem your partner is facing and what you both need to do to stop it. Once you begin to notice when a major symptom is starting up, you will no longer feel so lost when your partner starts to change, once again. The symptom list becomes a tool you both can use to separate bipolar disorder from your relationship. The exercise below will guide you in making a symptom list for each of your partner's major bipolar disorder symptom categories.

Discovering the Symptoms

Before starting the exercise, review the following example. There are many elements to consider as you make your symptom lists. The framework used in this book includes the following thirteen categories of symptoms:

- What your partner says

- Relations with others

- What your partner thinks

- Medications
- Work or school obligations
- What your partner does
- Sexual behavior
- Physical signs
- Eating, alcohol, and drugs
- Changes in daily activities
- Spending behavior
- Sleep schedule
- Exercise level

These activities may seem like a lot to observe on a daily basis, but once you become familiar with the system and your partner's behaviors, it becomes much easier. You will see fairly quickly that your partner's behaviors under each of the categories listed above will stay pretty much the same depending on which major symptom is starting. The sample list below is provided as an example of what you might write in your journal as you begin this process. An exercise for you to complete follows this example.

For now, try to think of those symptoms your partner has in common with the following lists. Don't be surprised if your partner's symptoms are quite similar. This may happen because bipolar disorder is a very predictable illness. Its common symptoms are exhibited by everyone who has the illness. This information alone will help you to see that much of your partner's behavior is governed by bipolar disorder and not that something is lacking emotionally or psychologically in your partner's personality. The following sample list is for depression.

EXAMPLE: SYMPTOM LIST FOR DEPRESSION

The following list of depression symptoms uses the twelve categories listed above.

WHAT YOUR PARTNER SAYS

- "I'm bored."

- "You never want to do anything with me."

- "You don't love me."

- "What's the point?"

- "Leave me alone!"

- "I'm such a loser. Why would anyone want to be with me?"

- "I just don't have the energy."

- "I'm sorry I'm such a burden."

- "I don't know what's wrong with me."

- "Things are not right in my life. I need to make some changes."

- "I wish I were dead."

RELATIONS WITH OTHERS

- Is very irritated, snappy, cranky, impatient.

- Has trouble thinking of anyone but themselves.

- Feels that others are judgmental.

- Can't or won't call or see friends.

- Feels unworthy of friendship or love.

- Is unresponsive to suggestions and ideas.

- Is not the partner you know and love.

- Ruins relationships due to neediness.

- Pushes everyone away.

WHAT YOUR PARTNER THINKS

- Nothing I do is right. I've never done anything right.

- I have no friends.

- I'm fat (ugly, skinny, disgusting, and so on).

- Is this all there is?

- Did I do something wrong?

- People are stupid.

- People don't like me.

- Things will never get better—never.

- Things would be easier if I were dead.

- Everything is difficult.

- Projects are overwhelming. I can't do them.

MEDICATIONS

- Says the medications no longer work.

- Stops taking medications.

- Takes more medications to get better. May become overmedicated.

WORK OR SCHOOL OBLIGATIONS

- "Work is boring."

- "I don't want to work anymore."

- "I just can't seem to do a good job at work."

- Says things are "overwhelming" at work or school and does a lot of worrying and talking about work or school.

- Feels unappreciated for what they do.

- Stops going to work or school.

WHAT YOUR PARTNER DOES

- Gives away possessions.

- Complains; becomes very irritated and angry.

- Overanalyzes everything.

- Focuses on the past.

- Withdraws from life.

- Doesn't get excited or enthusiastic about things.

- Stops taking care of personal hygiene.

- Becomes silent.

SEXUAL BEHAVIOR

- Is not sexually responsive.

- Clings or cries.

- Doesn't want to be touched.

- Needs more sex to feel loved.

- Can't meet your needs.

PHYSICAL SIGNS

- Senses are dulled.

- Holds head in hands.

- Pinched face.

- Clenches teeth.

- Wrings hands.

- Becomes clumsy.

- Face looks vacant or sad (lack of expression).

- Has problems sleeping.

- Feels "tired and wired."

- Feels lethargy or exhaustion.

- Doesn't seem animated.

- Decreases eye contact.

- Gets very agitated.

- Cries or sobs.

EATING, ALCOHOL, AND DRUGS

- Stops eating, noticeable weight loss.

- Eats all day, noticeable weight gain.

- Says food has no taste.

- Drinks to feel better; alcohol problems get worse.

- Uses drugs or caffeine to get some energy or escape the depression.

CHANGES IN DAILY ACTIVITIES

- Sits in a chair and stares into space.

- Can't sit still or focus.

- Gets into bed in the afternoon or stays in bed all day.

- Doesn't want to go out at all—even to see friends.

- Calls in sick to work.

- Misses school or appointments.

- Doesn't connect with partner or children; seems separate.

- Has trouble cooking and doing work around the home.

- Can't finish projects.

SPENDING BEHAVIOR

- Shops to feel better.

- Stops shopping completely, including for needed household items.

- Money is too complicated to handle. Can't balance checkbook or pay bills. Ignores essential money management.

SLEEP SCHEDULE

- Very obvious increase in amount of sleep.

- Can't get to sleep.

- Agitated sleep. Wakes up early and can't get back to sleep.

EXERCISE LEVEL

- Exercise is very difficult due to lethargy.

How to Use This Symptom List

How do you feel after reading all of the symptoms of depression in these twelve categories? Maybe you feel relief to see that your partner is not alone in the way bipolar disorder affects their life. Maybe you feel ashamed for not seeing that the illness has a pattern. Maybe you feel overwhelmed. These feelings are normal. There are many people like you who see the same behavior every day in their own partners and yet don't know it represents the typical symptoms of bipolar disorder.

The goal of creating such a list is to show you that bipolar disorder has specific characteristics. The illness does not behave randomly. Once you have a similar list for each of your partner's major symptom categories, you and your partner can use this list to observe when your partner's behavior starts to change. When you notice a change, you can take out the list and see which major symptom your partner is experiencing. You can then take action to stop the symptoms from progressing any further.

An important fact to remember: If all of the people with bipolar disorder exhibit similar symptoms, this should tell you that even when your partner's behaviors feel very personally directed at you, they actually aren't personal at all. They are simply the symptoms of an illness. The symptoms look and feel emotional and psychological, but in reality they are just symptoms.

When you treat bipolar disorder first, you recognize that the appearance of symptoms means only that your partner must focus on treating bipolar disorder—instead of focusing on what you or your partner may think is wrong with your lives. When you carefully list the specific symptoms associated with each major bipolar disorder symptom category, this will help your partner to see that so many of the feelings and thoughts associated with bipolar disorder are actually symptoms instead of a personal failing or inability to deal with the real world.

If your partner listens to the thoughts and does the things that the disorder tells them to do, the illness takes over and it's hard for your partner to get better. But, if you and your partner can see and understand that there is a pattern to these symptoms, and from the very first minute they start up, you use your treatment plan to stop the illness instead of reacting to the thoughts and actions, you can then stop bipolar disorder from taking over your partner's life and ultimately hijacking your relationship.

EXERCISE: Create Your First Symptom List

It's now your turn to create a specific symptom list under each of your partner's major bipolar disorder symptom categories. It's easiest to start with depression, as you have already read through the example symptoms described above. Using your journal, write "Depression" at the top of a page. Then, using the previous depression lists as an example, write the specific symptoms you see when your partner is depressed.

This is the start of your depression symptoms list. More ideas will come to you as you read this book. You don't have to remember everything at once. This is a process you will use over the next few months to create a comprehensive picture of your partner's symptoms. Don't worry if your final list is quite long. That's normal. Once the basic depression symptoms list is finished, you are ready to do the same with all of the major symptom categories from the list you created in chapter 3. Undoubtedly, you will be adding to these lists for the duration of your relationship, because different situations create different symptoms.

Working together: If you and your partner are working together on this exercise, make separate lists at first. It will be interesting to see what you consider a symptom that your partner might miss. After you have each completed your separate lists for each major symptom category, compare lists with your partner to create a master list. You will receive more instructions in later chapters on how to integrate this list into your treatment plan.

You are not a spy: If you are worried that charting symptoms may feel like being a spy, then it's important that you are clear with your partner about why you want to create this list—this is about working together to prevent the reoccurrence of symptoms. This is not about doing something behind your partner's back. The more you can do this as a team, the better.

Working alone: It may be that you will start this process alone, but don't give up hope. Your partner may join you eventually. The symptom lists are about planning ahead and working together. They are about the prevention of symptoms. Remember that although the process of working together should not be started when your partner is too ill to function, you can start your own list at that time and be ready when your partner is more stable.

Once you have created a specific symptom list under each of your partner's major symptom categories, you will be ready to explore in the next chapter what works to treat the symptoms. You will also explore the reasons that any behaviors you may have used in the past didn't work. Hopefully, creating these symptom lists will help you become more aware that bipolar disorder is simply an illness with specific symptoms. This may eliminate some of the stress and fear you might be feeling regarding the future of your relationship. When you finish working with this chapter, you should have a list of your partner's major bipolar disorder symptom categories, with lists of their specific symptoms under each category. You will use these lists in the next chapter.

REALITY CHECK

If your partner is resistant to new discoveries and change, then you will have to focus on what *you* can do to help your partner treat this illness. Focus on yourself first, and when you are strong enough to know what to expect and how to treat this illness holistically, introduce the idea to your partner. You are in control of how you respond to bipolar disorder. Don't let it control you. The techniques you will learn in this book can help you recognize symptoms before they reach the point where you and your partner can no longer communicate. The goal is for both of you to reach a point in your relationship where you can work together to create a treatment plan.

Learning new tools takes time. Go easy on yourself and praise yourself for what you have accomplished so far. As you become more familiar with your partner's symptoms and learn what helps to keep your partner well, you can both learn to create stability in your relationship.

CHAPTER SIX

The "What Works" List

*It's often difficult to know how to help your partner
when they are ill. The solution is to write down what
works and what doesn't, so that you can read the list as
soon as you see the first signs of bipolar disorder.*

The next part of the treatment plan asks you and your partner to explore what has worked in the past to minimize and ultimately stop the symptoms of bipolar disorder. This helps you recognize that you may already know many ways to help your partner. You will also honestly examine the behaviors you followed in the past that didn't improve the situation. Problems occur because during a crisis it's often hard to remember what works and what doesn't. Often, you just do or say the first thing that comes to your mind. Treating bipolar disorder first with a specific treatment plan for each major symptom category allows you to replace this random way of dealing with bipolar disorder with a more structured and proven plan that works.

The goal of this chapter is for you to create a list of techniques you can use as soon as you see the first signs that your partner is getting sick. This will be called the "What Works" list. Although the ultimate goal of your treatment plan is prevention, the reality is there will be many symptoms that must be treated before prevention can start. It's important that you are very clear about what you want to do to help your partner. It's also important that you understand why your partner may do the things they do.

If you are confused by bipolar disorder behavior, you are not alone. It really is a difficult illness to understand. The good news is that despite the chaos that bipolar disorder creates, there really are some set rules that, if you can remember them even during a crisis, will help you to focus on treating and preventing the symptoms of bipolar disorder instead of once again becoming caught in its trap.

The Facts about This Difficult Illness

- Bipolar disorder thinking is *always* unreasonable and unrealistic. *Always*. There are no exceptions. So if your normally reasonable partner is being unreasonable, you know that you are dealing with bipolar disorder and not with a personality flaw.

- Bipolar disorder doesn't simply go away one day. You must always be ready for it to reappear. It can be very sneaky. It starts small and then becomes a tornado. It's crucial that you catch it when it's small, from the very first symptom, so that you can treat it successfully.

- Like people with any illness where symptoms can be triggered by outside events (such as asthma or diabetes), people with bipolar disorder can learn how to avoid and minimize certain triggers that ignite their symptoms. It just means learning how to live life in a new way. You will learn more about triggers in chapter 7.

- You can never talk to, cajole, or reason with someone who is in a bipolar disorder mood swing. The person you love is temporarily gone and bipolar disorder has moved in. This book will teach you to *respond* to bipolar disorder when your partner is ill instead of trying to talk your partner out of being ill.

- If your partner suddenly decides that medications are no longer needed (because they feel "wonderful" or "cured") and they simply stop taking them without talking to a doctor, this is a sign of poor judgment and an indication that bipolar disorder is in control.

Doing What Works: Recognizing What Doesn't Work

Learning to treat bipolar disorder holistically involves taking an inventory of the behaviors you've used in the past to deal with your partner's symptoms. One of the main reasons that bipolar disorder continues to ruin relationships is that it's human nature to keep trying things that don't work. You are not alone if you have consistently tried to help your partner with few positive results.

Once you start to examine your own behaviors when your partner is ill, you are likely to find that there are many acts you may have done out of kindness that don't work, such as trying to hug your partner when they are irritated or trying to talk your partner out of a manic or depressive episode. You may have tried all of the techniques that work for you with the other people in your life, but they haven't worked for your partner. This is because bipolar disorder often doesn't respond to traditional problem-solving behaviors.

You may find that some of the methods you will learn in this book for treating the disorder don't seem intuitive or easy to remember, but you can learn them. The illness requires you to learn these new behaviors so that you can treat bipolar disorder symptoms specifically by saying and doing the proven behaviors that help your partner get well. Your goal is to educate yourself on the new responses and behaviors that calm and ultimately prevent bipolar disorder symptoms.

As you learn these new techniques, you can write these tools down on your "What Works" list. You will then use the list when your partner gets sick. If you are like most partners, when a crisis hits, you will *not* remember what you are supposed to do, especially if you are in the middle of dealing with the symptoms. In fact, even with a "What Works" list you may automatically go back to your old patterns of responding because they are familiar. This is the main reason for recording your treatment plan on paper: so you and your partner can read it when a bipolar disorder symptom begins.

Creating the "What Works" List

Luckily there is a way to find out what works so that you can continue to help your partner even in the middle of a crisis. The ideas below will give you a framework for discovering new behaviors that do work to help your partner.

Learn What Your Partner Wants and Needs

If you want to practice what works and help your partner find what they can do to help themselves when they are sick, you need to know your partner very well. Though the symptoms of bipolar disorder are similar for everyone with the illness, the most effective way to deal with the symptoms depends on the individual person. Your partner's ideas regarding physical contact, social contact, diet, and exercise, for example, may be very different from your own. When your partner is stable, ask about their needs for each major symptom. For example, a massage may help a lot if your partner is anxious or slightly manic but may be very uncomfortable if your partner is psychotic. Ask when a massage would help. A walk around the block may be a great help if your partner is down and unhappy, but a walk around the block may not be the right treatment if your partner wants physical contact and reassurance. Ask when a walk is a good idea. If your partner is stressed and feeling overwhelmed, you have to ask what you can do specifically to help take the stress away—you may find that something as simple as washing the dishes for them can make a big difference in how they feel. The best way to learn what your partner wants and needs is to ask and then write down what they say on your "What Works" list. Here are some of the questions you can ask your partner:

- When you're depressed and lying on the couch, what's the best way for me to help you get off the couch and do something you would enjoy doing?

- Or, when you're showing signs of being manic, what's the best way for me to help you contact your doctor?

- Or, when you are really angry and I see you hit something or slam a door, what can I do to help you calm down?

Another good example would be to discuss very honestly with your partner how they want you to bring up this new treatment plan when you can tell that they are becoming ill. Do they want you to take over and do what you can to help them, or will that make them feel like a child? Do they want you to get out the "What Works" list and show it to them so you can read it together? Conversations like these are a great tool for learning what works to help your partner get better in the most effective way. All of the information you get from your partner can go on the "What Works" list under each symptom.

Learn to Respond Instead of Reacting

Talking with your partner when they are stable to learn what they want and need is important, but it's not always possible. Many times you will be forced to talk with your partner when they are ill. It can be really difficult to know what to say to help them feel better, while it's very easy to say something that only makes matters worse. Have you ever made any of the following comments to your partner?

- What's your problem? Why are you so unhappy? You have everything a person could ever want and you're still miserable!

- You're so smart. Why don't you just do something with your life?

- I just don't understand why you can't work. Everyone else works. You just have to buckle down and do the job. If you cared, you'd just try harder.

- Why does everything have to be so difficult for you? Can't you just enjoy yourself for once?

- Don't you talk to me that way!

- You bought $100 worth of candles? What do you mean you bought $100 worth of candles?

- Why can't you just calm down?

Don't be too hard on yourself if you have spoken to your partner harshly when they were sick. It's normal for you to make these comments. Bipolar disorder behavior is so unreasonable and frustrating, it frequently causes these kinds of reactions in everyone. The problem is, although these comments make total sense to you, they only make matters worse when your partner is sick. Talking this way may be effective when you are frustrated with someone who is not mentally ill or who is not living up to their potential because of lack of motivation or laziness; but this is not an effective way to communicate with someone in the middle of a mood swing. When you speak this way to someone whose behaviors are a result of the disorder, you are adding to the problem instead of finding a solution.

The key is to learn to *respond* to bipolar disorder instead of *reacting* to what your partner actually says or does. When you react to your partner, you act out of personal frustration at what your partner has said and done. You react according to how your partner's unreasonable behavior makes you feel. A reaction is immediate and doesn't take into account *why* your partner says or does the things that upset you. When you learn that the behaviors are symptoms of a predictable illness, you can teach yourself to respond differently to bipolar disorder. This takes more time and a lot more planning and thought, but it can be learned. When you learn to respond instead of reacting to what your partner says and does, you are likely to see immediate results in your relationship.

Look at the following examples of how you can change the way you talk to your partner when they are ill. Notice how these techniques differ from the ones you may have used in the past, and start to think of the comments you can use in the future to respond to your partner when they show signs of behaviors that indicate the symptoms are starting up.

Here are some examples of how you can use this technique:

- I can see that you're angry. How can I help you?

- Do you need some help with your medications?

- I can see that you're having trouble. I'm going to get out the "What Works" list and do something that will help you.

- It sounds like you are feeling down right now. How can I help you?

- I see the signs that you're starting a manic episode. As we've agreed, I want us to work together to stop this episode before it goes too far.

Use sentences that start with *I can see that you are…* ; *It seems to me that you are sick…* ; or *I know you don't feel well right now. What can we do to treat bipolar disorder so that you can feel better?* Learning how to respond to bipolar disorder symptoms will help ease your frustration with your partner's behavior. It will also result in less defensiveness on their part. This conversational technique is explored in detail in chapter 9.

Help Your Partner Make Wise Relationship Choices

Often, stressful relationships are one of the main problems your partner faces regarding bipolar disorder. If you can be a buffer between your partner and the relationships that cause friction, you can help you partner to become more stable. It helps if you listen, ask questions, and talk with your partner about the effects that stressful relationships have on bipolar disorder symptoms. You can then work together to minimize your partner's contact with these people. You can also encourage your partner to look for help from the people who really can help.

Your personal relationships affect your partner as well. Do you have any stressful relationships that are currently causing your partner stress? Do you constantly talk to your partner about the problems you have with other people? Make sure that you work on fixing these relationships so that their stress does not affect your partner. Bipolar disorder thrives on chaos and there is nothing more chaotic than a troubled relationship. This certainly can be difficult if your problem relationships are with family members. You will learn in the next chapter that bipolar disorder is triggered by outside events, and problem relationships are one of the biggest triggers for the disorder. Sometimes the solution can be as simple as spending more time with the calming people in your life and taking a break from the people who cause stress. This does ask a lot of you, but it's worth it.

Promote Physical Well-Being

Bipolar disorder is very hard on the body. Your partner may experience physical problems because of a downswing or may have a host of problems due to medication side effects. What you may not realize is that you may have stress-related illness yourself when your partner is ill, as can other people in your partner's life, including any children in your family. Many people think that bipolar disorder is strictly a mental illness, but as anyone who has just been through a serious episode can tell you, it wears out the body—yours included. Diet and exercise are two tools you and your partner can use together to control many different bipolar disorder symptoms.

Mania, depression, anger, and especially anxiety are greatly affected by food choices and exercise. From caffeine to junk food, what someone puts into their body can greatly affect their mood. The good news is that a change in diet often can improve symptoms by helping the body find balance. You may wonder how you can help your partner create a healthy lifestyle, especially if they are ill and have no motivation to change anything. You can help by creating meals and an exercise plan for yourself that will help your partner as well. Help your partner learn which foods affect their symptoms. Do they crave certain foods depending on particular symptoms they experience? You really can encourage your partner to move toward stability by creating a consistent diet that supports the body, mind, and spirit.

Your eating and exercise ideas can go on the "What Works" list so that your partner can read what to eat to counter certain symptoms or know when it would be a good idea to exercise. The more you learn about the role played by food and exercise in your partner's overall health, the more you will be able to guide and support your partner. Note that getting on your partner's case for not exercising or for eating junk food is not a good way to start this process. It may be that your partner is too ill to take the initiative. Your goal is to help your partner find something that is fun and offers a lot of rewards, such as a great-tasting natural meal or a walk in the sunshine.

Another physical problem your partner may face is caused by the fact that the medications taken for bipolar disorder may affect their teeth and immune system as well as countering the illness. You may find that your partner becomes sick more easily when bipolar symptoms are active, especially if your partner is deeply depressed. You can help your partner by making an appointment with the dentist and by finding a health care practitioner who treats the whole body as a system, such as a naturopathic doctor.

This illness asks a lot of you, and even though the above can work, it may be that you've moved into an unwanted caretaking role or that it's simply too much for you to make so many changes. Just doing a few of these things can make a difference.

Seek Complementary Treatments

Complementary treatments for bipolar disorder include any treatments that your partner tries that are not a part of the more traditional treatments for bipolar disorder. It may be that your partner has already tried some alternative and supplemental treatments, such as herbal therapy, acupuncture, or massage. (The word supplemental is used here to stress that although these treatments can be beneficial for many people, they are not a substitute for mood-stabilizing medications.) Once again, you can play an important role in your partner's healing by researching these complementary treatments yourself. The following suggestions will give you an idea of the wide variety of complementary and supplemental treatments that may help minimize and prevent bipolar disorder symptoms.

- Clear out the clutter in your home (chaos reduction).

- Aromatherapy (the use of scents to affect mood and emotions).

- Massage.

- Chiropractic treatment.

- Acupuncture to balance the body.

- Herbal teas, such as chamomile for anxiety and peppermint for depression. Note that any herbal therapies must be carefully researched for safety.

- Homeopathic remedies for stress (available in natural food stores or through a specialist).

- Talk therapy that helps you deal with the pressures of having a partner with bipolar disorder.

- Meditation.

- Yoga.

- Join a group of like-minded people to form relationships. This can include groups that share your partner's hobbies. It's always good for your partner to get out of the house and do things unrelated to the disorder. But it's equally important that you take time for yourself.

- Find a naturopathic doctor who can help your partner integrate natural and traditional treatments of bipolar disorder.

Explore options in your area, but don't let your location limit your exploration. There is a wealth of information on the Internet and you may find that once you start asking the people around you for advice, they will know where you can go for more ideas.

A word of caution: It does pay to be careful when you begin to explore alternative treatments. Just because a practice is "all-natural" doesn't mean it's the right treatment for bipolar disorder. For example, practices such as intense massage or stimulating yoga are something your partner should avoid when manic. Esoteric and unproven practices such as astrology or the Tarot can be very confusing for your partner, especially if psychotic symptoms are present. Your goal is to become an observant student of complementary treatments.

Talk with complementary health care practitioners and ask them if they have experience treating bipolar disorder. It's also important that you understand that herbal treatments are not to be taken lightly. If you have questions about herbal treatments and their possible effects, seek the advice and counsel of a licensed naturopath. It's also essential that you make sure any herbs tried do not interact with your partner's medications. This is especially true concerning the popular herbal product Saint-John's-wort, as it has been found to have significant and, at times, dangerous drug-to-drug interactions. Before your partner tries anything new, it's always a good idea to talk with a pharmacist about drug interactions. Don't let these warnings discourage you; just be careful and thorough in what you try. Your goal is to explore what is available, maybe try it yourself, and then discuss the alternatives with your partner.

Help with Medications

The first thing you can do to help your partner with medications is to talk to them realistically about how it feels to have to take pills every day. If your partner has had trouble staying on medications in the past, or if they experience a lot of side effects from medication, your "What Works" list can be the place where you write down your solutions to these problems. For example, if your partner knows that when they start to get manic, they want to stop taking their medications, then the "What Works" list can tell you how to deal with the issue.

The "What Works" list really is about awareness. It can be very easy for your partner to trick you into thinking that they are taking their medications. If, when your partner is stable, you work together to decide what works and what doesn't for helping them stay on their medications, you will have a list of tools to use when you see the signs that your partner is thinking of stopping the medications.

As was discussed in chapter 4, medication side effects are another serious issue. One of the main reasons to have a holistic treatment plan in place is so you and your partner can create a more stable life, which, in turn, may lead to fewer symptoms. Your partner can then discuss changing or lowering their medicine dosage with their doctor once they feel more stable. It's also important that you get help for your partner if you feel the medications are not working properly. It may take a lot of perseverance on your part, but keep trying until your partner has the right medications. Side effects are a major reason that people stop taking their medications. Help your partner if they are too drugged to help themselves.

Finally, Don't Forget Yourself

One of the most effective ways for you to help your partner find what works is to take care of yourself first. When you find what works for yourself, you will have more energy to help your partner find what works for them. Some of the areas that often get brushed aside when your partner is ill are your spirituality, your physical well-being, or working on your own negative thoughts and worries with talk therapy. It makes sense that if you can find some answers for yourself, you may be able to help your partner do the same.

The "What Works" List: An Example

Now that you have some ideas on how you can help your partner by doing what works, take a look at the following example of a "What Works" list for depression. This list also details what doesn't work. Please note that this is a modified list. Yours may be much longer. Although this list focuses on what you can do to help your partner, eventually your partner should add their own ideas on what they can do to help themselves when they are depressed. You will start your own "What Works" list later in this chapter.

SAMPLE LIST: WHAT WORKS FOR DEPRESSION

- I can exercise with my partner.

- I can respond to bipolar disorder by saying, *I see that you're depressed; let's treat the depression instead of arguing.* Or I can ask, *What can I do to help?*

- I can plan something we can do together. Activity beats depression every time.

- I can help my partner set small goals and see that they get done.

- I can learn techniques to stop negative self-talk so that I can help my partner do the same.

- I can encourage regular bedtimes.

- I can create a less chaotic environment.

- I can encourage taking baths using aromatherapy.

- I can learn about complementary treatments for depression including yoga, vigorous exercise, vitamins, supplements, and talk therapy.

- I can watch our diet carefully and educate myself on foods and drinks that help with depression. I can learn what foods and drinks make depression worse.

- I can help more around the house.

- I can remind myself not to take bipolar disorder behavior personally. I can't reason with depression.

- I can help my partner remember to take medications.

SAMPLE LIST: WHAT DOESN'T WORK FOR DEPRESSION

- Reacting to what my partner says by saying *You just need to get motivated!* instead of offering suggestions that help depression.

- Thinking that my partner's behavior is done on purpose.

- Telling my partner what to do.

- Getting frustrated and angry when my partner lies around all day.

- Thinking that medications are the only solution and that my partner should be better already.

- Trying to touch my partner at the wrong time or do something that really doesn't help.

- Always believing what my partner says when sick.

- Using alcohol or drugs to deal with my own life issues.

- Thinking that my partner is better when it's actually mania.

- Trying to talk my partner out of being depressed by telling them they have so much to be grateful for.

- Forcing my partner to do the things that they say are overwhelming.

- Getting into an argument with my partner when they are irritated and want to fight.

- Remaining unaware.

Eventually, your partner will add their own ideas to the "What Works" list. It really helps your partner to have these ideas in writing when they feel too ill to do anything. They can read the list when they feel too sick to help themselves. The list can help jump-start their brain into action. It will also remind them that they get sick the same way every time and if something worked in the past, there is a good chance it will work again.

EXERCISE: Create Your Own "What Works" List

You will now create your first "What Works" list. Here is a short summary of what you have already created. You have the list of your partner's major symptom categories that you created when you were working with chapter 3. You also have the list of specific symptoms under each of these major categories from chapter 5. As you can now see, you are creating a treatment plan for each major bipolar disorder symptom. You will now add a list of what works and what doesn't under each category.

You can start with depression. Take out the symptom lists you have already created for depression and list your own ideas under each of the six categories from this chapter: (1) learn what your partner wants and needs, (2) learn to respond instead of reacting, (3) help your partner make wise relationship choices, (4) promote physical well-being, (5) seek alternative treatments, and (6) help with medications. This will get you started. You can also look over your depression symptom list and ask your partner what they feel does and doesn't work to treat each symptom. This is a positive step, if your partner is willing and able to do this now.

You also will need to learn which of your partner's ideas are reasonable. For example, if your partner says the best thing you can do when they are depressed is to just leave them alone, you know that this is not reasonable. It's also normal that you each may have very different ideas about how to respond to this illness at first. The goal is to work together. Add your ideas to the "What Works" list in any order. The goal is to read this entire "What Works" list every time your partner sees the first signs of depression. You can then choose what needs to be done. You will learn more techniques in later chapters, but for now start with depression and list what you know has worked and what hasn't worked in the past, as well as what you would like to explore in the future now that you have some ideas from this chapter. A "What Works" list should also include a section on medications, doctors, and hospitalization. Once you have created a basic "What Works" list for depression, you are ready to create a "What Works" list for each of your partner's major symptom categories.

You have now completed the first three steps of your holistic treatment plan. The next chapter will cover the final step of the plan: discovering and ultimately preventing the triggers that ignite your partner's bipolar disorder symptoms.

REALITY CHECK

You really can do only so much on your own. If you are trying to do what works while your partner continues to do what doesn't work, there will be problems. It takes two to treat this illness effectively. It's okay to start on your own, especially if your partner is very ill or in the hospital when you start this book. But you will eventually have to work together if you want the plan to be successful.

The "What Works" list can free you from the constant worry of what to do and what not to do when you see the signs that your partner is getting sick. You can take out the list and read what has worked in the past. This will help you think clearly and take action during a crisis.

CHAPTER SEVEN

Bipolar Disorder Triggers

Symptoms are results; triggers are the cause.

You literally could spend your entire relationship helping your partner treat the symptoms of bipolar disorder. You could put out one little fire after another, over and over again, but still wind up back where you started. A holistic treatment plan takes a different approach. It examines the factors that ignite and intensify bipolar disorder symptoms instead of treating only the results of the illness. As you and your partner learn to recognize, minimize, and treat symptoms by doing what works and avoiding what doesn't, you will begin to see that many of your partner's symptoms follow a pattern. They are often a by-product of an event or behavior that your partner experiences. And although these symptoms are what you must deal with on a daily basis, the symptoms are not the real problem. They are only a sign of the problem. The real problem is what triggers the symptoms.

Triggers are situations, events, or behaviors that lead to predictable bipolar disorder symptoms. Once you both learn to discover, reduce, and eliminate these triggers, many of your partner's bipolar disorder symptoms can be prevented or significantly minimized. This is great news, especially for people who have a less-than-optimal response to medications.

Look for the Source

It's understandable if in the past you focused solely on treating mood swing symptoms, instead of looking for their source. A medication-oriented treatment plan is very symptom focused, while holistic treatment looks for the *cause* of the symptoms as they are being treated. The holistic approach looks for the triggers of the symptoms in the belief that stopping the triggers makes more sense than trying to keep up with constant symptom suppression. Please note that this chapter helps you look for outside triggers. It's often the case that the illness alone causes symptoms.

Symptoms Are the Fruit; Triggers Are the Seed

You can look at it this way: Your partner has bipolar disorder. This means that your partner is more susceptible to stress than people without the disorder. Your partner reacts to certain situations and behaviors with bipolar disorder symptoms. During a crisis situation, the symptoms can become so out of control that they appear to be the seed of the problem. This means that all of the focus is on *stopping* the symptoms so that your partner can be stabilized again. This *is* an important step for helping your partner find stability, but there is a more important step that you and your partner can take to prevent the symptoms from going this far in the first place. You can both recognize that your partner's symptoms are simply the fruits of bipolar disorder. The triggers are the actual seeds that cause the symptoms.

When you look at bipolar disorder this way, you can see that symptoms are a signal that you both need to figure out what triggered the symptoms. Then you can work on modifying or stopping the trigger to stop the symptoms from becoming worse or reoccurring. Knowing and treating the symptoms (fruit) of a mood swing is the first step. Learning and stopping the triggers (seeds) is the next. You have already made a list of your partner's major symptom categories and what works and doesn't work to treat the symptoms. The next step is to learn what triggers your partner's bipolar disorder. The key to preventing bipolar disorder symptoms instead of constantly putting out fires is to learn to modify and eventually stop the triggers that make your partner ill. Outside of medications, knowing what triggers your partner's bipolar disorder is the most effective technique of your holistic treatment plan. And the great news is that this technique is free and can be practiced anywhere at any time. This chapter will help you discover your partner's triggers and provide you with the tools you need to stop these triggers from causing more problems in your relationship.

Discover the Triggers: Modify and Stop Bipolar Disorder Symptoms

Before you learn the techniques to help your partner discover, modify, and ultimately stop bipolar disorder triggers, it will help if you understand the big picture of the common symptom triggers your partner may experience. The following list may surprise you in its complexity. As you read it, put a check mark next to each trigger that you think may be a problem for your partner. You will use this information later in the chapter.

Common Triggers

_____ Arguments

_____ Travel or time changes

_____ Work-related stress

_____ Caffeine use

_____ Drug use, including medications

_____ Change in general

_____ Social events

_____ Shopping centers

_____ Driving in traffic

_____ Poor diet, high in refined foods

_____ Alcohol use

_____ Lack of exercise

_____ Unstable family situation

_____ Poor relationship with spouse, family member, friend, or coworker

_____ Lack of balance in life

_____ Poor sleep habits, staying up too late, or sleeping all day

_____ Lack of a schedule

_____ Lack of structure

_____ Too many obligations

_____ Constantly on the move

_____ Constantly doing something

_____ Exposure to television and other forms of media

_____ Hanging out with crazy-making people

_____ Aggression toward self or others

_____ Overly stimulating lifestyle

_____ Lack of spirituality

_____ Overscheduling or overcommitting

_____ Listening to negative internal dialogue

_____ Everyday obligations

_____ Illness or death of a loved one

_____ Stressful world events (and media coverage of them)

Depending on the path your partner's bipolar disorder takes, triggers can lead to depression, anger or irritation, panic attacks, mania, psychosis, suicidal thoughts, and many other symptoms. If you combine this with medication problems, such as having trouble with side effects or refusing or missing medications, the triggers become even more serious. Your partner is also more succeptible to triggers if they ignore the rituals they know are important for maintaining balance in life; rituals such as taking time for themselves, getting adaquate sleep, spending time outdoors, having a hobby, doing yoga and meditation, exercising, carving out nonstressful time to spend with family and friends, quality time with you, religious and spiritual pursuits, reading, or anything else that relaxes and brings pleasure. It may also be very frustrating for you to watch your partner continually return to the situations that have caused bipolar disorder symptoms in the past. The good news is that there is a solution, as you will see later in this chapter.

Why Is Your Partner So Darn Sensitive?

It may be hard for you to understand how such basic occurrences as time changes, job promotions, or arguments could cause your partner to become ill. The fact is that these situations may not be triggers for you because you don't have bipolar disorder. This doesn't mean that you're strong and your partner is weak. It means that your partner has bipolar disorder and shares with every other person with the illness a sensitivity to stress. You may be able to handle the stresses of everyday life, while everyday life makes your partner ill.

It's not as easy for your partner to get back on track after a few late nights as it may be for you. You may be able to raise your voice and have an argument, and then forget about it an hour later; your partner often can't forget it. Your partner's brain chemistry is very different from your brain chemistry, and because of this, situations, events, and certain behaviors affect your partner quite differently than they affect you. People with bipolar disorder often have a very small window in which they can meet demands. Once that window is closed, the triggers create bipolar disorder symptoms.

The Root Trigger

The *root trigger* is a term you will see frequently in this chapter. Trying to find the root trigger of your partner's bipolar disorder may make you feel as if you are up against the age-old question of which came first, the chicken or the egg? One reason for the confusion is that triggers may have many layers. Some triggers cause other triggers, which then lead to symptoms that affect your relationship. Here's an example of how it works: Suppose your partner found out that their hours at work have been cut back (trigger), and this is followed by a poor night's sleep due to worries about the future (trigger). Then, the next day is a really stressful day at work (trigger), and there is bad traffic on the way home (trigger). This may lead your partner to feel such intense irritation and anger that they take it out on you the minute they get home (trigger). This then causes your partner to have thoughts about dying (trigger) that scare them into thinking they can't handle work or life at all. Result: a very serious mood swing that may truly take away their ability to work or have a good relationship with you.

If your partner is not aware that triggers can actually cause them to have bipolar disorder symptoms, they may just treat the symptoms instead of looking for the seed of the problem. The true seed of the problem is called the root trigger.

Just imagine how different things could be if your partner knew, from the minute they heard that employee hours were to be cut back, that this was a potential root trigger for their illness. They could stop right then and decide to treat bipolar disorder first. They could be ready for the symptoms that followed the root trigger and could use the ideas on the "What Works" list to stop the mood swing from going any further than the first thoughts. This means that all of the triggers that follow the root trigger could be stopped as well. Your partner could come home and say, *I just got some bad news at work and I know that's a trigger. We need to work together on this.*

This technique really can change the lives of people with bipolar disorder. Think about it this way: If you and your partner have a list of the triggers for each major bipolar disorder symptom, and you both can learn to modify and, hopefully, prevent these triggers, what changes could this bring to your relationship? It could mean some very positive changes. The following example will walk you through the process of finding the triggers, including your partner's root trigger in each major bipolar disorder symptom category; but before reading the example, here are a few tips to help you discover, modify, and ultimately prevent your partner's triggers.

Trigger Facts

- Triggers can begin very gradually. Little triggers may be set in motion weeks in advance of any symptoms and then trigger a greater problem when they get out of hand. An example would be taking on too much to do at work or in the family, ignoring all of the symptoms that follow, and then getting so sick a few weeks later that a trip to the hospital becomes necessary.

- There are some triggers that are always disastrous—for example, interacting with problem people who you know always push the wrong buttons.

- Some triggers are more immediate and predictable—for example, deciding to discuss a delicate or stressful topic such as finances at the dinner table after a long, tiring day.

- Triggers can change. On some days, a person won't be able to handle any conflict, while on other days the same person may be able to have a very contentious discussion without becoming ill. This may be particularly hard for you to live with, as you will often wonder why something you ordinarily do will suddenly upset your partner.

- The most serious triggers tend to be work- or school-related stresses, death or illness of a loved one, obligations that have a pressured time limit, stressful personal relationships, a move, marriage, a baby, or anything else that is new or causes a big change in a person's life. World events such as a terrorist attack or war also can be strong triggers. In other words, always be aware that any change, whether good or bad, can be a bipolar disorder trigger. Some triggers are so strong it's virtually impossible for your partner to stay well once they take place. When this happens, the goal is to focus on the symptoms, because the trigger is out of your control.

- Trigger lists are not about what someone does wrong; they are simply a way of understanding and getting clear about what specific behaviors and situations provoke stress and bipolar disorder mood swings.

Discovering Your Partner's Mania Triggers

The following sample list will provide you with a guideline for your trigger exploration. At first, the chaotic lifestyle that bipolar disorder creates may make it hard for you to pinpoint the triggers of your partner's symptoms. But with practice and patience, a pattern often emerges. Keep in mind that although the following list relates to mania, most of the triggers listed can lead to other major symptoms as well. It all depends on how your partner personally responds to the trigger. This sampling lists twelve categories of mania triggers. You will be able to use the same categories when you create your partner's trigger lists later in the chapter.

SAMPLE LIST OF MANIA TRIGGERS

- What goes in the body

- Upsetting or stimulating media

- Interpersonal conflict

- Lack of self-awareness and self-control

- Change in sleep pattern

- Work or school obligations

- Opportunities to spend

- Medications

- Certain environments

- Social life

- Changes in stability and routine

- The really *big* triggers

What goes in the body: Food, drink, and drugs can be very strong triggers. If someone has a lot of anxiety, for example, increased caffeine consumption can be a very strong trigger for even more anxiety, and if someone is depressed, alcohol can trigger more serious, even suicidal, feelings. What a person eats also may have an effect on mood. A trigger can be a cause as well as an effect. A person may start using or abusing a substance because their bipolar disorder symptoms are so painful. Substance abuse is seductive because the immediate experience often is relief from painful emotions but, over time, this backfires. Soon the substance use itself changes from something to help with bipolar disorder symptoms to a trigger that causes the very symptoms the person was trying to ease. In other words, a behavior can start for one reason and then turn into something else. Without exception, alcohol and other forms of substance abuse always cause bipolar disorder to worsen. The facts are very clear here. If your partner continues to abuse alcohol or drugs, their chances for stability are greatly limited. One of the main problems with mania is that judgment is often impaired. This means that your partner's choices about what they put into their body will be impaired as well. Examples of mania triggers you should be aware of are shown below:

- Alcohol abuse

- Caffeine

- Recreational drugs

- Stimulating junk food

- Stimulating herbs or other alternative treatments (especially anything that interferes with sleep)

- A poor diet that is undernourishing

Upsetting or stimulating media: Television, movies, the Internet, and video games have become such a ubiquitous part of life that people rarely examine the effect they have on physical and mental health. People with bipolar disorder need to become more aware of how the media affects their mood. For example, your partner may feel that they have to watch the news to keep up on what is happening in the world, but this stimulating and negative news may trigger their symptoms and add to their already negative view of the world if they are depressed; increase paranoia if they are psychotic; or make them feel they have the power to change everything if they are manic. Now that news coverage is available twenty-four hours a day, the media trigger during times of world conflict can be very serious. Try to be aware of the following media triggers for mania:

- Aggressive, violent movies or television programs

- Violent video games

- Overuse of the computer

- Watching coverage of a very stressful event

- Excessively watching television or videos at the expense of other activities

- Pornography

Interpersonal conflict: Conflicts and problematic relationships with others are often a major trigger of bipolar disorder symptoms. Stressful relationships must be mended or avoided if a person with bipolar disorder wants to achieve stability. Recognizing the people who cause your partner trouble as well as helping your partner recognize when the trouble originates with them can be a big step in controlling the relationship issues that trigger bipolar disorder symptoms. Certain situations that can easily trigger mania are shown below:

- Argument with partner

- Argument with a family member or friend

- Stressful situations with others at work or school

- Being asked to do something that is too stressful, such as helping a friend plan a wedding or helping someone start a new business

- Involvement in an abusive relationship

- Saying yes to everyone and doing too much

- Getting involved with unstable or addicted people

- Interacting with people who don't believe that your partner is really sick

Lack of self-awareness and self-control: Your partner will need to learn some self-limiting behaviors to stop bipolar disorder triggers. Often, it's your partner's own choices when they are relatively stable that lead to symptoms. The following examples list the ways that your partner may unwittingly sabotage their own stability and create mania symptoms. This doesn't mean that your partner doesn't want to stay well. It could be that they are not even aware that bipolar disorder controls them in these areas.

- Ignoring the signs that thoughts such as "I deserve to have a good time. I've been sick for so long!" mean that they are ill

- Inability to say no to behaviors or situations that cause mania

- Not having the checks and balances needed to prevent mania disasters

- Being unaware of the small signs that a mood swing is starting

- Thinking that mania is not a problem or that they can control it

- Believing that mania is not as serious as depression

- Stopping visits to their doctor or stopping medications

- Letting the illness take over completely, even when there is a window for getting help at the first sign of the symptoms

- Continuing to self-medicate with drugs, food, and alcohol

Change in sleep pattern: Along with stable relationships, sleep is one of the most important regulators of stability. Regular sleep keeps the body running smoothly, and yet many people with bipolar disorder don't follow a set sleeping ritual. Many people also think that sleep problems are simply a result of bipolar disorder symptoms. In reality, a change in sleep pattern caused by an outside event, such as work obligations or travel to a different time zone, can be the trigger, especially for mania. The following changes in sleep pattern often trigger manic mood swings:

- Staying up all night doing a project for work or school

- Taking a job that requires shift work or interferes with sleep in other ways

- Staying out partying on a work night or staying out late because it's the weekend

- Starting to fall into old sleep behaviors that cause mania

- Justifying staying up late because there is more energy

- Time changes (for example, switching to daylight savings time or traveling across time zones)

- Putting substances in the body that affect sleep (such as caffeine or alcohol)

- Ignoring the lack-of-sleep signals that they are ill, such as feeling wide awake and ready to clean the house at two o'clock in the morning

Work or school obligations: For many people with bipolar disorder, work and school are stressful environments. The stress of having to get something done at a certain time can cause manic symptoms for your partner. Knowing that people with bipolar disorder are much more susceptible to the stresses of work and school will help you both see that you must be aware of the following mania triggers:

- Deadlines

- Taking on too heavy a course load in school

- Troublesome interactions with coworkers or bosses

- A job that is not a good match for your partner's skills

- A job that simply requires too much; too many hours or unrealistic demands

- School deadlines (tests, term papers, and so on)

- The normal everyday routines of work and school

- A new job or school

- Trying to do a job or get a degree that is too difficult

Opportunities to spend: Spending problems are often symptoms of mania, but there are also many spending environments and situations that can trigger the symptoms that lead to spending problems. Spending problems during mania are notorious for creating relationship issues. Be aware that the following triggers can lead to manic spending:

- Holidays

- Working in a spending environment such as a mall

- Overstimulating events

- Getting a new credit card

- Going to certain malls or stores where it's known from past experience that the temptation to spend is great

- Thinking that things are different now that there are medications

- Las Vegas or any other stimulating environment that promotes gambling

Medications: There are a few ways that medication issues can trigger bipolar disorder symptoms. These triggers have to do with the way your partner uses the medications as well as the medications themselves. Some antidepressants are known to cause mania or rapid cycling (National Institute of Mental Health 2003). It's important that your partner be monitored for mania when starting a new medication. Here are some more mania triggers to look for:

- Stopping medications because they feel well

- Stopping medications because of side effects

- Taking non–bipolar disorder medications or supplements that cause mania (e.g., steroids or herbs)

- Taking medications that cause mania symptoms to worsen if the medication itself or the dose is not correct

Certain environments: The environment around your partner can either help or hinder their stability. You may have observed that your partner acts differently in different environments. This is a sign that some environments are triggers for your partner. Look over the following list and ask yourself if any of these items are a trigger for mania:

- Living situation

- Clutter

- A noisy environment where it's difficult to sleep

- An environment that promotes smoking, drinking, and drugs

- Events that are very stimulating, such as concerts, ball games, or casinos

- The work environment

- Family gatherings

Social life: Bipolar disorder greatly affects your partner's social life. From depression to mania, your partner's social behavior can go up and down depending on which symptoms are being experienced. Your goal is to find the social events that actually trigger these behavior changes. When your partner is manic, it may be difficult to tell the difference between the symptoms and the triggers. Symptoms of mania easily can turn into triggers, so it helps if you can become very clear on what acts as a trigger for your partner. Some social mania triggers are:

- Partying

- Hanging out with people who are known to be excessively critical, demeaning, argumentative, or provocative

- Going to stimulating places or events

- Drinking or doing drugs socially

- Having to entertain because of work obligations

- Feeling peer pressure from friends who don't understand why your partner can't go out as much as before

Changes in stability and routine: A stable routine is one of the best ways for you and your partner to have a stable relationship. When this routine is changed, even slightly, it may cause problems for your partner. Stability is one of the most effective treatments for all bipolar disorder symptoms, especially mania. Be aware that the following changes can act as mania triggers:

- Changes to a set schedule

- A large change in the family, such as the birth of a child or a move to a new area

- Travel (especially across time zones)

- Time changes (such as switching to daylight savings time)

- A friend or family member moving away

- A change at work or school, such as a promotion or graduation

- Any change that you go through that may affect your partner

The really big triggers: As mentioned previously, there are some triggers that you can't predict or prevent. It will help if you talk about the possibility of these triggers with your partner before they occur, so that you can discuss how you will handle them if they do appear. Just knowing that a big trigger will almost always make your partner ill will help you to be ready as soon as something happens. For this reason, it's important that you and your partner discuss these triggers before they happen. Here are some really big mania triggers:

- A move to a new place

- Media coverage of terrorist attacks, war, natural disasters, or human suffering

- Serious arguments, especially when accompanied by physical or verbal abuse

- The death or illness of a loved one

- Stressful events, such as a robbery, sexual assault, or car accident

- The loss of a job, or a new job with too many responsibilities

- A large exam or project in school

- The birth of a child

- Marriage

- Divorce, or the end of any relationship

- Any stressful event that changes the life of the person with bipolar disorder

As you can see, triggers that cause mania don't have to be anything out of the ordinary. They are situations, events, and behaviors that normal people often handle with ease; but people with bipolar disorder simply can't deal with them as easily. The key is for you and your partner to explore these personal triggers and write them down under each major bipolar disorder symptom category.

Once again, as when you charted the symptoms of bipolar disorder, this will take some time. Generally, basic triggers can be identified within a week or two, although many people find that it can take up to a year or more to construct a really comprehensive list of triggers. As said previously, many of the triggers for mania can be triggers for other major symptoms as well. For example, stressful events that cause mania in one person may cause depression in another. It all depends on how your partner is affected by the trigger.

EXERCISE: Create Your Own Trigger List

You are now ready to make the first list of your partner's triggers. You can start with mania, as it is the example used in this chapter. You already have a list of your partner's specific mania symptoms along with what works to treat these symptoms. Using the categories from this chapter, list the triggers of your partner's mania. This is something you and your partner can do separately. The ultimate goal is to compare your lists to create a master list.

Then move on to each major symptom category and under each one write down your initial ideas concerning which triggers activate which symptoms in your partner. As you read this chapter and the rest of the book, you will find more ideas. Once you have listed your partner's basic triggers, you will be ready to work on modifying and hopefully preventing the triggers that cause your partner to become ill. Remember, this is not a one-time project. You may find yourself adding triggers to your list for the duration of your relationship.

How to Modify and Stop Bipolar Disorder Triggers

Many bipolar disorder symptoms could be modified or prevented if a person could eliminate all of the triggers of the illness. If only it were that easy. Wouldn't it be great if you could just stop all of the stress-inducing behaviors of yourself, others, and the world to help your partner find stability? Although this is impossible, the truth is that finding, modifying, and preventing many of your partner's triggers is a realistic goal. It won't be easy and it will take teamwork, but you really can help your partner modify or stop many of the triggers that cause bipolar disorder symptoms.

How You Can Help

There are many techniques and behaviors you can use to help your partner find and hopefully stop the triggers of bipolar disorder. Often, when your partner is ill, you are the person who takes care of the home and other responsibilities. This means that you can have a lot of influence in your partner's treatment plan. The next section provides some ideas on how you personally can help your partner modify and ultimately prevent the triggers of bipolar disorder. The eventual goal is for your partner to create a list of their own ideas on what they can do to stop the triggers, as well. All of the ideas below and any ideas you think of while reading can be added to your "What Works" list under each major symptom category.

What goes into the body: As mentioned earlier in this chapter, there are certain substances that bipolar disorder doesn't tolerate very well, including alcohol, recreational drugs, some herbs, excessive junk food, and caffeine. These substances can potentially alter brain chemistry and trigger bipolar disorder symptoms. They should be either taken moderately (depending on the substance) or eliminated because people with bipolar disorder are more sensitive to these substances. Many of these substances can tip the balance between normal behavior and bipolar disorder mood swings.

This problem becomes acute because many people with bipolar disorder use these substances to treat symptoms of bipolar disorder. This is normal. In fact, many people use *all* of these substances and tapering off them can be quite hard. Your partner might start by eliminating something simple, such as caffeine, and go on from there. One way you can help your partner would be to stop using these triggers yourself. It will be difficult, but keep trying no matter how hard it is. Many of the substances your partner uses are very strong mood-altering substances and until the body is cleared from their effects, it may be hard for your partner to stay stabilized.

The two substances that never help and almost always harm are alcohol and any drug or food that interferes with sleep. Sleep disruption is an extremely common factor that provokes symptoms. However, it's also important that you know that a quick withdrawal from smoking or alcohol, for example, can make your partner ill. If your partner needs help with these substances, it's best to seek the help of a psychiatrist or a trained health care professional who understands both bipolar disorder and the effects with-drawal can have on the disorder's symptoms. It's also important that you observe your partner carefully whenever a new medication for bipolar disor-der is started. If you think that a drug is causing more symptoms than it is helping, contact your partner's doctor immediately and ask for help.

Dual diagnosis: A dual diagnosis (when a person has an addiction as well as a diagnosis of bipolar disorder) is very common in people with bipolar disorder. If your partner has a mild addiction because of bipolar disorder, it's possible that treating bipolar disorder first will reduce the need for these substances and help will be more readily accepted. If your partner has a serious addiction, you should know that it has been clearly established that ongoing substance abuse is the single most important factor contributing to a poor outcome for those who have the disorder. If your partner falls in this category, it is imperative that they get help for their addictions. It may sound simplistic put this way, but if you want to have a stable relationship with your partner, any substance abuse that worsens the bipolar disorder has to stop.

Home environment: The home environment plays a large role in bipolar disorder symptoms. Many people with the disorder have trouble controlling their environment. Often they are too depressed to clean and pick up after themselves, or they are too agitated, overwhelmed, and scattered to do even basic maintenance around the house. Have you ever called your partner lazy or uncaring because they don't do their share of the work around the home? It may be that they are not able to do the work you ask them to do because they are ill.

How is the environment in your home? Is it quiet, calm, uncluttered, clean, and safe? Are there peaceful places to go to and peaceful pictures to see? Or is your environment chaotic and messy, filled with books, magazines, and unopened mail? One of the best ways to help your partner find stability is to create a calm living space. If your partner is the messy one, then you can talk with them about what you are trying to do. If household chores are truly too much for your partner, it's well worth the investment to hire someone to come in and clean once a week. It helps if you understand that taking care of a home may be impossible for your partner if they are experiencing serious bipolar disorder symptoms. You may have to do the bulk of the work until your partner is more stable.

Relationships: You may think that you have little effect on your partner's bipolar symptoms, but as the person who spends the most time with your partner, you do have a very large influence on their health. Here is a first step you can take to become a positive influence on your partner: make an agreement with yourself right now that you will no longer argue with your partner. It really does take two to argue. Arguments are very stimulating and trigger many bipolar disorder symptoms, from anxiety and panic attacks to violent behavior and suicidal thoughts. You can be the one to learn new tools to stop the arguments completely. Of course, this will be difficult if your partner is ill and wants to argue, but you have to be the one to stop. In later chapters you will find tips for preventing arguments, but the first step is simply making the decision to stop.

Work or school obligations: It may be hard for you to understand, but many people with bipolar disorder become ill when they are obligated to do something on a schedule. Work and school are all about meeting scheduled deadlines. This is one reason people with bipolar disorder can have so much trouble in these environments. If you can accept that this is a natural part of bipolar disorder and a true trigger of symptoms, you can help your partner stay in work or school by limiting their other obligations.

No, this may not be fair to you and it often makes your partner feel like a burden, but it's a reality. Being obliged to do something on a schedule really can trigger bipolar disorder mood swings, so it's very important that you both decide which obligations are necessary to fulfill, and then get rid of all the others. There is more information on the challenges of work and school in chapter 11.

Social life: Social events often trigger bipolar disorder symptoms. Many people see partying (going out for a few drinks, dancing, listening to music, breathing in cigarette smoke, and staying out later than normal) as fun and joyful. For many people it is. But for people with bipolar disorder, a very stimulating environment can trigger a host of bipolar disorder symptoms from depression and mania to psychosis. You may have no trouble going out with friends on the weekend, but your partner might.

To help your partner, you can also try to take a break from stimulating social events until all mood swings are stabilized. Plan low-key and calming social events. Your partner may rebel against this, but you can explain it will last only for six months or so, in order to see the effects a lower-key social life has on your partner's mood swings. You can then conduct some experiments to see how livelier social events affect your partner. Once you know what is possible (for example, a quiet evening out with friends as opposed to a dinner party with a lot of people) you can then focus on what your partner can do instead of focusing on what is lost.

The big events: If and when any of these serious events happen, such as the death of a loved one or the loss of a job, know that a strong bipolar disorder reaction, even one requiring hospitalization, may be a normal response. You will both have to get out your "What Works" list and work on managing your partner's symptoms when faced with these big triggers. As a partner, you can begin to think of how you will deal with these triggers when they happen, and then work with your partner to limit the effects of the triggers you can't control. Talk about these triggers now. What will you do if a serious event occurs? Add these ideas to your "What Works" list and have it ready in case of a crisis.

Hope for the Future

Understanding triggers, their effects on your partner, and the role you can play in modifying and stopping the triggers can be a very liberating experience. If you feel overwhelmed by all of the triggers you need to modify, start with the easy ones. These could include cutting out or limiting caffeine, nighttime television, staying out late, interacting with stressful people, and going to stressful places or social events. Making small changes now can help you find the confidence and strength to make the really big changes later.

One of the best ways you can create stability is to institute regular meal and sleep times and stick to them. This scheduling helps to regulate the body's clock and gets both of you used to having structure in your lives. If you find yourself saying, "but I can't just make these kinds of changes," this would be a good time to take a hard look at the alternatives. Turning off the TV and switching from coffee to herb tea is a small sacrifice to make for a healthy, loving relationship.

You both will need time to make these changes. It will really help if you are understanding and can work on this together as a team. If you are working on this alone, modify or stop what you can, and help your partner by making the changes in yourself first. If you are the one making the decisions in your relationship due to your partner's illness, make those decisions count.

The Root Trigger: A Final Example

Discovering the root triggers of your partner's mood swings is such an important tool that it will help if you are very clear on how to look for the root trigger. The following example will help you learn to separate the root trigger from all of the resulting triggers and symptoms that usually follow. As you read this account, observe how easy it is to get caught up in treating only the small triggers and the obvious symptoms of a mood swing, instead of recognizing the root trigger as soon as it occurs so that you can go into prevention mode.

David has bipolar disorder I. He maintains his health with medications, but he often has trouble with the symptoms that the medications do not alleviate. He has a good job and two kids. His partner, Megan, works as well. Their lives are usually pretty organized and he gets along well with his family. This is one of the main reasons he has stayed stable for a few years. Recently, he has become irritated and has had a lot of trouble sleeping. Megan has noticed the changes and she knows that David has a lot going on in life and that he just heard that his best friend has cancer. She assumes that his irritation and sleep problems are due to the stress of the news.

Soon David is having trouble at work. He says he feels pressured and unappreciated. He tells this to Megan when he gets home at night, and when she tries to help, he tells her she just doesn't understand what he's going through. He's snappy with his kids and is upset that his son got a bad grade on a math test. Megan yells at him, "Don't be so mean! It's only one test." The next day he breaks an appointment with his therapist and decides he doesn't need all of his medications anymore— although he doesn't tell anyone about his decision.

David's eating becomes erratic and he starts to drink at night to calm down. He tells Megan that he has to get out of the house to release the "pressure" he feels from their relationship. She has absolutely no idea what he's talking about and starts to get really upset. When he gets home from his walk, he goes to the computer and stays online for most of the night.

The next day at work Megan gets a phone call that David just had a fight with a coworker and is now in his office muttering to himself and telling everyone that he has a cure for cancer. Megan comes to get him and on the way home notices that he won't look at her. He's sweating and smells different. He has a wild look in his eyes and starts to tell her about the new plan he has to save his best friend. When she tries to talk to him, he ignores her and keeps talking as though she were not there. Now she is really scared and has no idea what to do. They get home and she finally realizes that she must call his doctor and get help. The doctor tells her to get David to the hospital as soon as possible so that they can adjust his medications.

As the partner of someone with bipolar disorder, there is a good chance that you have been through a similar situation. As you read through the above example, were you able to find the root trigger of David's mania? It was probably easy for you to see that it was hearing that his best friend has cancer, but for Megan, there were so many other little problems that clouded the situation that she wasn't sure what was going on. The example shows that when your partner starts to get sick there will be dozens of little symptoms that may cause you to get caught up in the situation, instead of taking immediate action to prevent the mood swing from going any further. It's hard to find the root of a problem when the symptoms of the problem are so overwhelming in themselves. When you look for the root triggers of your partner's bipolar disorder you have to look for any change in their life that might be difficult for the bipolar disorder brain to process. Think in terms of bipolar disorder and not the personality or strength of your partner.

If only David and Megan had a plan waiting for any potential trigger, they would have known that hearing that David's best friend had cancer meant that they had to use their treatment plan immediately. They would have realized that the minute David heard the news, it was time to get out their symptoms lists, decide which symptoms were starting, look on their "What Works" lists, ask for help, see David's doctor immediately, make sure that medications were taken, and then take time to process the news. If they had done all of these steps, the manic mood swing could have been stopped. It may seem like a miracle, but it's simply the power of using a holistic treatment plan that is already in place, ready to use once a root trigger is activated.

It really is possible to prevent bipolar disorder from going too far if you use your treatment plan from the minute you suspect a root trigger has made an appearance. You and your partner can become experts at what triggers your partner's bipolar disorder, so that you can work on the triggers and ultimately prevent the symptoms before they start to take over your lives.

You have now completed the four steps of your holistic treatment plan. To review, you now have a list of your partner's major symptom categories, with a list of their specific symptoms under each category, a "What Works" list you and your partner can use at the first signs of a mood swing, a list of the triggers of mood swings, and suggestions on how to modify and ultimately prevent these triggers. Chapter 8 will follow one couple as they put their treatment plan into action.

REALITY CHECK

Life is unpredictable and some triggers are not in your control. It always helps to prepare in advance for events that could become major triggers. Discuss today what you will do if there is a death in the family or a lawsuit, or if your partner loses their job. Have a plan ready. Create a "What Works" list for major triggers. Pay special attention to sleep and spending patterns. These are very strong indications of bipolar disorder symptoms and will help lead you to the trigger. If your partner is resistant or too ill to work with you, give them some time. Do what you can and then introduce the ideas to your partner.

Think of yourself as a gardener in a garden full of weeds. Sure, it helps for a few days to cut the tops off the weeds, but if you want long-term weed care, you have to pull those weeds out by the roots and then do whatever it takes to keep them from coming back. It's the same with bipolar disorder. Once you learn what triggers your partner's mood swings, you can help your partner deal with the problem from the root.

CHAPTER EIGHT

A Couple Takes Charge

As you know, it's all very well to read how to do something.
It's a different matter to put what you've read into action.

This chapter will follow a couple, Carlos and Pam, as they create a holistic treatment plan for Pam's bipolar disorder. Before you read their story, here is a review of the procedures you have already learned:

- Medications are an important part of a holistic treatment plan, but they are not a stand-alone solution.

- Decide to treat bipolar disorder first before you move on to the more everyday issues.

- Break bipolar disorder into major symptom categories.

- Write down your partner's specific symptoms under each category.

- Examine what works to treat the symptoms. Write down your ideas and have them ready when bipolar disorder makes an appearance.

- Examine what you have done in the past that doesn't work and decide to change to what does work.

- Determine the triggers that cause bipolar disorder symptoms.

- Modify and stop the triggers.

- Reconnect as a loving couple with hopes and dreams that have little to do with bipolar disorder.

The Car Ride from Hell!

Carlos and Pam are in traffic. Pam is driving, and boy is she mad. "This damn traffic! Did you see that! What in the world is that lady doing!" she yells as she weaves among the cars. She is more aggressive than usual and is using a lot more hand gestures than Carlos thinks is appropriate. Carlos knows she has been irritated for days and that this is the last place she needs to be right now. But he also knows that if he tells her to cool down or drive more carefully she will just explode and really make his life miserable.

In his mind, he has only a few options. He can get stressed and worried and could yell back, "Enough already! Why do you have to get so upset and negative about everything?" Or he can give her the silent treatment. He decides on the silent treatment and they arrive at their destination with both of them angry. This mood is carried over to the rest of the day. Pam becomes even more irritated in the evening and yells at Carlos about the laundry. "Did you put the clothes in the dryer? No? Why not? What's wrong with you? Why can't you do anything right? Do I have to do everything around this place?" Carlos is thinking, "It's only laundry. *What's her problem?* I haven't done anything wrong. I don't have to deal with this! She's such a bitch!" Carlos is really ready to leave the relationship.

What Is Her Problem?

Now that you know that bipolar disorder is more than just mania and depression, you probably guessed that Pam is experiencing irritation symptoms due to bipolar disorder. Pam and Carlos have no idea how to treat bipolar disorder first and bipolar disorder is ruining their relationship. Carlos thinks Pam is just being mean and simply won't control herself. They both feel that blaming each other will somehow take care of the problem. But bipolar disorder doesn't respond to blame, punishment, or even reasoning. Pam and Carlos are doing what many couples do when one partner has bipolar disorder. They are living and reacting in the moment.

Every day brings a new task to face with Pam's changing moods. Pam herself is not sure what will show up and Carlos is worn out from trying to figure out how to help Pam. He really doesn't know who will wake up beside him in the morning. They have never really talked about her bipolar disorder rationally. Neither one of them sees the big picture regarding bipolar disorder, although they both know they need to do something or the relationship will not survive. Luckily, there is hope. The solution is to create a holistic treatment plan that addresses all of Pam's major bipolar disorder symptoms.

Step One: Treat Bipolar Disorder First

Their first goal is to sit down and talk honestly about the role bipolar disorder plays in their relationship. This includes answering the tough questions, such as where their relationship will be in six months or a year if Pam's behavior continues.

Then they must learn to look at the issue holistically so they can create a preventive treatment plan that lets them treat bipolar disorder first with a variety of treatments, instead of relying solely on medications. They can rationally examine their history together and then talk about the hopes and dreams they have for their relationship. Carlos needs to talk honestly with Pam about how her illness affects him so that he can learn to help her find stability instead of punishing her for her symptoms. Pam needs to know that she has to make changes in how she treats bipolar disorder if she wants the relationship to continue.

Carlos: Pam and I have been together for ten years. I met Pam when she was in a hypomanic episode, though I didn't know that at the time. She was so much fun and I loved her personality. After a few months it became clear that she was changing. She stopped going out and spent a lot of time in bed. She talked about how terrible her life was and that she never got anything done. When I would ask her what was wrong, she would reply, "I'm just going through changes!" This was how she explained her constant ups and downs. I really had no idea what to do.

I wanted to help her, but nothing I did was helpful. About three years into our relationship, things got so bad with her depression I was scared for her life. She checked into the hospital and was finally diagnosed with bipolar disorder II and started medications. This was such a terrible time, but the diagnosis was the answer we were looking for. We were so happy to finally realize what was wrong with her. We both believed that things would finally be stable. Nope. It hasn't worked out that way.

The medications definitely help the big swings and Pam hasn't gone back to the hospital, but the medications don't seem to take care of the everyday problems she has with the illness. She has trouble with side effects and often says she wants to find ways to treat bipolar more naturally, but nothing ever happens. I feel that bipolar disorder is our whole relationship now. It wakes up with us every single morning and I'm tired of it. Pam's work is not going well, and she's constantly irritated and unhappy, and most of it is directed toward me. We fight a lot, and I usually just leave the room when she gets so unreasonable and mean. I don't know who she is anymore. I don't want to be around her.

Pam: I really feel that bipolar disorder is too much to deal with right now. I thought that the medications would give me my life back and instead it seems like they just dull things a bit and I'm still left with these ups and downs. I know they help the big mood swings. I no longer obsess about killing myself and I haven't had a serious hypomanic episode since I started the meds. But I still have to do so much work on myself. I read self-help books and I see a therapist to deal with my emotions, but I'm still just all over the place. I really don't want to take things out on Carlos so much, but once things get started, it's like I can't control myself. I just feel so terrible inside. I feel like such a failure and I know I'm a bad partner, but I can't deal with this illness, my work, and a relationship. It's just too much.

A Normal Problem

The situation Carlos and Pam describe is very normal. Carlos doesn't know how to respond to Pam; instead he overreacts to everything she does because he is *flooded*. Flooding takes place when someone has dealt with a stressful situation so many times that even a little part of the issue can make the person feel burdened under the full weight of the problem. Pam is so caught up in her bipolar disorder symptoms she is unable to sustain a loving relationship with Carlos. However, when bipolar disorder is raging, it really is not a relationship issue. It's a bipolar disorder issue and must be treated that way. Both Carlos and Pam felt a lot of relief when they took the first step and agreed to treat bipolar disorder first.

How They Created a Plan

Pam: Carlos and I sat down and got out our journals and started to think about what we needed to do to treat this illness. I don't think we had ever really discussed a plan before. I think we both thought that was up to the doctors. But as we talked, we both realized that the doctors helped with my medications and then referred me to therapists or self-help groups. The rest was up to us. I guess we just thought it would take care of itself.

The first thing we did was to write for five minutes about how we felt about bipolar disorder. We then read this to each other. I was shocked to see how Carlos is affected by my mood swings. He wrote that he feels that bipolar disorder rules our lives and that he has no say in our relationship because we are always dealing with my illness. This was scary and sad for me. I hadn't thought about how this affected Carlos.

Carlos: When I started to write about bipolar disorder, I was so angry I couldn't believe it. This damn illness has taken so much from us. Pam just can't seem to get stable and I'm so tired. I want to have some fun for once. I want to do normal things and see people and go places. Writing this made me see that we have to do something or I can't stay in this relationship anymore. I knew this already, but this made it certain. I'm ready to do something—anything, to find some stability for both of us.

Creating Goals

Pam and Carlos then used their journals to write down their goals as to how they would approach their new treatment plan. Pam wrote that she was willing to do everything she needed to do to see some positive changes in the next six months and that she wanted to find a way to spend more quality time with Carlos. When Carlos finally saw that Pam was willing to do something about her illness instead of just living with it, that really made Carlos feel better. They both wrote that they wanted a better sexual relationship and agreed to get some help with their financial problems. Carlos wrote that his main goal was to learn how to help Pam instead of getting angry at her when she was sick. When they were finished, they found that they were not as far apart as they had thought they were. They both wanted the same thing—a happy and stable relationship—and if it meant changing their lives in order to help find Pam stability, it was worth it.

Carlos: I'm not much of a writer and, at first, I felt silly writing things down in a journal. But then I found that making the lists of our goals was really helpful. Seeing them on paper does make a difference. I can go back to them to remind myself to stay focused.

Step Two: Break Bipolar Disorder into Major Symptom Categories

The next step was to break Pam's bipolar disorder into her major symptom categories. Like most couples, Carlos and Pam thought that bipolar disorder was basically just two moods: mania and depression. They assumed that all of the other behaviors were just part of Pam's personality and that she needed therapy and a little more self-discipline to get matters under control. When they first started to list Pam's symptoms, their lists were short.

Pam's Original List

- Depression

- Hypomania

Carlos's Original List

- Depression

- Mania

- Irritation

If you think about it, their lists are pretty funny. Pam's symptoms have completely affected their lives in every possible way, and yet they can only see the small picture of how the illness affects her behavior. They know that she is also unhappy and restless with life, easily irritated, sexually unresponsive, often mean, and frequently unfocused and unproductive when it comes to her goals, *and* she feels that people talk about her at work.

That they focused on what they thought bipolar disorder was supposed to mean was normal, but in order to really treat bipolar disorder holistically, they needed to discover the many facets of Pam's mood swings. After thinking about their years together and all of their ups and downs, Carlos and Pam were able to create a more definitive major symptoms list—one that looks at the whole picture of Pam's bipolar disorder.

Pam's Major Symptom Categories

- **Depression:** Pam often puts herself and others down, and she sees her life as a constant struggle against some unseen force that wants her to fail. She is often bored and wonders what her purpose is on earth. She can be very negative toward herself and others. She is very cold and nonresponsive when she's down and rarely wants sex.

- **Hypomania:** Pam's mania starts with a feeling of euphoria, but it's usually short-lived. Instead of feeling that the world is a welcoming place, she becomes agitated and restless. She does too much and rarely finishes what she starts. She has trouble sleeping and gets frustrated very easily.

- **Psychosis and paranoia:** Pam sometimes feels people talk negatively about her work performance and she often worries that she has no real friends. She often feels that someone is following her, especially if she's in a crowded store.

- **Irritation:** Pam becomes irritated when she is depressed and irritated when she is hypomanic. She is constantly negative and complaining and can't see that this has affected her relationship with Carlos in a very serious way.

- **Feeling overwhelmed:** Pam reaches a point where her work and all of her responsibilities weigh so heavily that she just crawls into bed and doesn't want to get up for any reason. When she feels better, there is then a mess to clean up, as few things get done when she is in bed.

- **Attention and focus problems:** Pam can't concentrate very well when she is ill. She is full of ideas but has trouble finishing them. On some days she feels as if her brain stops and starts and can't focus on one project. This inability to focus affects her job and the craft projects she used to enjoy.

Seeing the List for the First Time

Carlos: Looking at bipolar disorder this way just blew my mind, and I mean that. I had no idea that all of this could be caused by the illness. I feel terrible for blaming Pam for so long. I assumed so much. Why didn't the doctors talk to us about this? I can see that there are many things we can do to help Pam with these symptoms. When we broke matters down like this, it didn't seem so overwhelming to me. For the first time in years I had some hope that we really could deal with this illness in our lives. I thought that bipolar disorder was just mania and depression with a few other symptoms thrown in. It never entered my mind that something like irritation could be a bipolar disorder symptom.

This list helped Pam and Carlos finally see that in Pam's bipolar disorder there is a lot more than mania and depression. When they had a list of her major symptom categories, they were ready to create their treatment plans for each problem. They decided to address Pam's irritation with their first treatment plan, as it was the symptom that caused the most trouble at the time.

> *Carlos:* We decided to focus on irritation first, because it seems to be Pam's main problem these days. Everything bothers her, especially me. I feel like a punching bag sometimes. I used to feel that Pam needed some serious anger management classes, but now that I know that irritation is a part of bipolar disorder, I'm more willing to see that she needs bipolar disorder management and not anger management. I also know that I have to learn new tools for dealing with her mood swings. What we have done in the past simply doesn't work.

Step Three: List Pam's Irritation Symptoms

Pam and Carlos used their journals to write down all the symptoms they could remember associated with Pam's irritation. (They knew that eventually they would do this for all of Pam's major symptom categories.) They began to see that these symptoms were signals alerting them that something was wrong. They agreed that they would pay more attention to the first and seemingly minor symptoms and learn what to do to stop the progression of Pam's irritation. Her symptom list included the twelve symptom categories from chapter 5. Pam and Carlos worked together on this list. Carlos's input was very important, as he often saw the signs of irritation much earlier than Pam did.

Pam's Irritation Symptoms

- Pinches lips together and pouts.

- Looks at people as if they're stupid.

- Easily frustrated.

- Emits sighs of anger.

- Thinks, "Carlos is so stupid."

- Thinks, "Get out of my way."

- Says, "You never do anything, Carlos, and I'm sick of it!"

- Wants to kick, punch, or break things.

- Drives aggressively and dangerously.

- Engages in negative talk about self and others.

- Has mean and uncomfortable thoughts.

- Is restless and unhappy in her body; says, "Sometimes it feels like I'm being stuck with pins and needles."

- Feels as if her brain is in a blender.

- Thoughts will not stop.

- Body is tense and wants to lash out.

- Says, "People are crowding me."

- Thinks, "I feel guilty when I have these terrible thoughts about Carlos."

- Says, "When someone touches me it makes me angry; even Carlos's touch makes me want to push him away."

- Sleeps badly; too restless to sleep well.

- Dreams very vivid and wild dreams.

- Says, "I get very angry at people at work and feel they are stupid and incompetent."

- Says, "I'm disgusted with myself over the way I behave."

Symptoms Are Signs

As seen from Pam's list, there are plenty of signs that she is irritated. Now that Carlos and Pam have a list of Pam's symptoms, they can identify the irritation symptoms from the beginning and do something about them before they escalate. This symptom list became a tool Pam and Carlos used to focus on treating bipolar disorder first, instead of acting out the behaviors.

Pam now understands that the thought "Carlos is so stupid!" is always an indication that she needs to treat her bipolar disorder first, instead of getting on Carlos's case for the things she thinks he is doing wrong. She knows that she doesn't think Carlos is stupid when she is well, and her goal is to stop acting on these unrealistic and damaging bipolar thoughts. She is learning that there are some very specific clues that signal to her when the irritation symptoms are starting up, and if she can recognize them immediately, she can then start to treat bipolar disorder instead of allowing it to control her life.

An Illness, Not a Personality Flaw

The symptom list helped Carlos and Pam talk about Pam's bipolar disorder more realistically. When they looked over the list, Pam agreed that irritation was no longer acceptable in their relationship. She agreed that she was ready to learn what works to treat the symptoms. She knew that she had to be ready with a plan the minute she felt the first signs that she was getting sick. Carlos learned to recognize Pam's body language and breathing. He agreed that reacting to her anger didn't work and that he needed to learn how to respond to her when she was ill. The list helped them see that Pam has an illness with typical and predictable symptoms. It's not something she does on purpose.

> *Carlos:* This was very new for me. I was so used to reacting to her irritation with anger that I wasn't sure how to deal with all of these symptoms. I made a list in my journal and Pam made one in hers. We then realized we wanted a notebook we could both use when she got sick, so we created a separate notebook for our treatment plan. We took the lists from our journals and made a master list in our notebook. We both just stared at the list when we saw how long it was. It just kills me that Pam has gone through this for all of these years and we had no idea what it was. I really could see the pattern once we combined our lists. It showed me that the irritation was always the same.

It did have a pattern. I could see that she said and did the same things every single time. How did we let this go on for so many years?

Step Four: Create a "What Works" List

Carlos truly wanted to learn to help Pam and he realized that he also needed a plan for helping her with the symptoms. They both got out their journals and made a list of what seemed to have helped her irritation in the past. They were surprised to discover that they had done many things that had worked in the past. The problem was that they hadn't seen the connection between what worked and what didn't. Many of the behaviors that hadn't worked were being repeated, as well. Finally, to get started, they created a list that included the old behaviors they would try to keep, the behaviors they would try to stop, and the new behaviors they hoped to add to their lives to treat and ultimately prevent the anger and irritation caused by bipolar disorder.

What Works for Pam's Irritation

- Regular pattern of sleep

- Regular, calming meals

- At the first signs of irritation, stop eating stimulating (spicy) foods and drinking caffeinated drinks

- Nurturing behaviors such as back rubs, baths with lavender oil, and spending time together

- Intimate time together to solidify their relationship

- Exercise

- Calming herb tea like chamomile

- Saying no to overwork

- Discussing issues instead of arguing; set up specific times to discuss upsetting topics in a calm way

- Carlos helping more with housework and the bill paying when Pam is feeling overwhelmed

- Recognizing that what Pam says when she is irritated is a sign that she needs help

This list helped Pam and Carlos see that they already knew plenty of ways to help Pam treat her irritation. Further suggestions on what works include the following:

- Recognizing when bipolar disorder symptoms are starting; this takes the focus off Pam and puts it on treating bipolar disorder

- Reducing irritation by talking with each other every day about moods

- Holistic herbal remedies for stress and irritation from a local natural food store

- Quality time together without television, radio, or videos

- Deciding that arguing is not an option

- Carlos not allowing Pam to mistreat him when she is irritated

- Carlos learning to respond effectively to Pam's irritation instead of reacting to it

- Both partners determining whether Pam's irritation is caused by mania or depression; both partners resolving to treat those symptoms, as well

- Asking for help from each other, as well as from friends and family

- Yoga and yoga breathing

- Meditation

- Professional massage and bodywork; healing arts such as tai chi and qigong

- Learning to say no to excessive demands

These are just a few of the tools that Pam and Carlos can use together to help Pam stay well. The next step for Pam and Carlos is to focus on what doesn't work. Pam is learning that it is essential for her to be clear with Carlos about what she needs. She has to understand that he really can't read her mind. Writing down what doesn't work reminds them what not to do, especially when they are stressed and might fall back into old patterns.

What Doesn't Work for Pam's Irritation

- Carlos getting angry at Pam when she gets irritated

- Carlos leaving when things get tough

- Pam blaming others for her irritation

- Carlos trying to reason Pam out of her anger (saying things like "Come on, Pam! It can't be that bad! Why do you have to be so negative?")

- Carlos trying to touch and hug Pam when she is irritated

- Carlos ignoring Pam's body language

- Blaming outside events for internal problems

- Going to overstimulating social events

- Driving in traffic (Pam should let Carlos drive)

- Staying out late

- Ignoring the early signs of a mood swing

- Consuming caffeine in coffee, black tea, and colas

- Taking on too much at work

- Gossiping about coworkers

Notice that the list of what doesn't work includes many of Pam's triggers. She and Carlos will use this list as a guide when they make their trigger list later in this chapter, but for now this list is a great way for Pam to let Carlos know what she doesn't want him to do when she is ill. The list also helps her to see that she plays a large role in her own moods, especially when she makes choices that make her symptoms worse.

Pam: Of course I knew that caffeine makes things worse. The odd thing was that when I started to get irritated, caffeine was the first thing I wanted. That and junk food. It just seemed to make me feel better, at least in the moment. Why is it that when I felt bad I would do the things that made me feel worse? Why did it seem that they made me feel better? I think it may be that I was so unaware of where all of these feelings were coming from that I just masked them with all of these unhelpful behaviors. No one had ever talked to me about prevention. Bipolar disorder feels so in the moment. I just treated it that way. I think the big change came when I realized that this irritation was simply not acceptable anymore. I made a goal to stop letting it control me. I decided that no matter what I was feeling inside or what my brain was saying, I wouldn't take it out on another person or an object.

Carlos: One thing we learned from the "What Works" list is that I have to learn new ways to talk to Pam when I notice she is irritated. In the past I just reacted. I've learned to remind myself that these are symptoms, not personal attacks. When I read her lists, I realized that she didn't want me to try to touch her or change her when she was sick. Instead, she wants my understanding and help.

Learning New Tools

Pam and Carlos both acknowledged that they knew a lot of their behavior wasn't working, but they didn't know how to stop the old patterns. They needed new tools to turn their negative behaviors into positive, healing behaviors. One effective tool for Carlos to use is creating agreed-upon responses to say when it's very obvious that Pam is irritated. Chapter 9 addresses this technique in more detail. Carlos now uses the following responses when he sees that Pam is irritated:

- I see that you're irritated. How can I help you?

- We agreed that anger is not an option anymore. I can see that you're having trouble. I'm going to get out the list of things that work and do something that will help you.

Pam also can create some set phrases to help her tell Carlos she needs help. These phrases may be hard for her if her irritation is very strong, but if she catches the symptoms early enough, she can use them. These can include the following:

- I'm so angry right now, I don't know how to ask for your help.

- As you can see, I'm a bit irritated. Can you get out our "What Works" list and go over it with me?

- I'm sorry I'm so snappy.

Another very effective way that Pam can tell Carlos she needs help is for her to simply say, "I'm sick today." Sometimes this is all that bipolar disorder will allow her to say, but Carlos can learn that when Pam says this, it's a sign she needs his help and compassion. He can then get out the "What Works" list and help her deal with the anger.

Step Five: Finding the Triggers

Pam and Carlos now have a better understanding of bipolar disorder and the role it plays in their lives. They have a list of her symptoms for irritation and they have a good idea of what works and what doesn't to help her deal with the symptoms. They are communicating better and are ready to look for the triggers to Pam's mood swings. Until now, their focus has been on dealing with Pam's symptoms in the moment. When a couple first starts a new treatment plan, this is important, but eventually Carlos and Pam must examine why Pam is not stable.

It's too easy to say, "Well, she's not stable because she has bipolar disorder," but the reality is that she is not stable because she is not *managing* bipolar disorder properly.

Pam and Carlos started to think about what causes Pam to go up and down. They learned about common triggers, as discussed in chapter 7, and realized that most of Pam's mood swings were reactions to some external event that Pam had experienced. They noticed that Pam got irritated when she had too much to do. They realized that her irritation was a reaction to events, not something out of the blue. The next step was for them to get out their journals and separately write down all of the ideas they had about what triggered Pam's irritation.

Pam's List of Her Irritation Triggers

- Traffic.

- Too much television, especially late at night.

- Poor eating habits.

- Not able to sleep as much as I would like.

- Carlos is so laid-back and uncaring. He doesn't participate in life.

- My life makes me angry.

- My work is not going the way I would like it to go; in fact, it never has.

- I can't seem to get a handle on my life and this is irritating.

- I don't have very good relationships in my life. I seem to cause problems with people, and I'm often told that I'm negative.

- My work dictates my daily routines.

- Money problems.

- I'm afraid that if I don't overwork, I'll lose my job.

- My depression usually comes with irritation.

Carlos's List of Pam's Irritation Triggers

- Pam's workload is the main trigger for her irritation.

- The lack of a good diet and exercise. She drinks diet cola all day.

- She's impatient and doesn't listen.

- I seem to be a trigger, although I'm just trying to keep out of her way.

- Depression and other mood swings can make her angry.

- Bipolar disorder, in general, must be hard to live with and maybe that makes her irritated.

- Her medications seem to irritate her, although she won't listen to me when I say this.

- She refuses to call her doctor when I suggest that might help.

- She won't accept my help; no matter what I do, it makes her more irritated.

- She's really down on herself and very impatient with herself.

- On some nights she stays up way too late and then feels tired and irritated the next day.

- I walk away when she's in a bad mood because she's impossible to deal with and this makes her even more irritated.

- I see that I could do more around the house to help her.

- I'm not very compassionate when she's ill.

After looking at these trigger lists, Pam commented that some of the items on her list seemed like symptoms. This is true. Triggers can be confusing. If you are uncertain what's a symptom and what's a trigger, that's normal. The reason for this confusion is that what begins as a trigger can become a symptom and what starts as a symptom can become a trigger.

For example, consider sleep. Deliberately sleeping only three hours in one night can trigger a mood swing, but one of the symptoms of mania is that a person may not be able to sleep more than three hours a night. The main thing to understand is that although basic triggers and symptoms often are interchangeable, root triggers almost always come from external sources. Pam and Carlos's ultimate goal is to find the root triggers of Pam's bipolar disorder symptoms.

Why Pam Has Difficulty Finding Her Root Triggers

Pam is overworked and frustrated with her life. Much of the time she feels unappreciated and worthless. She has no idea where her thoughts come from and certainly has no concept of how to deal with the stream of negativity she hears in her head all day long. It seems that whenever she tries to deal with her negative thoughts through therapy or positive thinking, they return just as soon as she gets stressed again. It's a never-ending cycle.

To Pam, her thoughts were the problem. She felt they triggered her unacceptable behaviors, such as fighting with Carlos and having trouble with people at work. She thought that if she could only get her thoughts under control, she would become more loving and kinder to the people around her. When she finally understood that her thoughts were often symptoms caused by the root triggers of her irritation, she began to hope that by stopping the triggers, she could stop the thoughts, which would then make it possible to lead a more stable and happier life.

Finding the Root Triggers

In the past, Carlos and Pam were both too angry to really examine the causes of Pam's irritation. The trigger list helped them to focus on the most obvious triggers, such as caffeine and sleep deprivation issues. They felt that working on these issues would defuse some of the problems, so they could focus more on helping each other, instead of being angry with each other. They then began to think more deeply about their general lifestyle. They realized that being angry at each other just set in place a vicious bipolar disorder cycle, one with no end in sight.

Carlos started to recognize that he triggered some of Pam's irritation by walking away whenever he saw the first signs of a mood swing. Pam realized that becoming irritated over slow people or people she thought were incompetent had nothing to do with the people involved but everything to do with the mood she was in when she had to interact with them. They both realized that although they needed to deal with small triggers like traffic and laundry, their main goal was to find the root triggers. They reminded themselves that, as they had agreed on, the issue is not about Carlos blaming Pam for being sick; neither is it about Pam blaming Carlos for walking away when she needs help. Instead, it's about learning a new way to prevent these mood swings.

Their trigger list became more and more thoughtful as they worked in their journals. When they compared their lists, they came up with a root trigger list to put into their treatment plan notebook. They chose the following root triggers and decided to create a plan to make the changes Pam needed to help her prevent her irritation from taking over their lives.

Pam's Root Triggers

- Work schedule and obligations

- Too much caffeine

- Poor diet and lack of exercise

- Medication problems

- Lack of a supportive health care team; not making use of the health care team available to her

- Lack of a stable sleep schedule

- No relaxing time with Carlos

- Housework and bills

- Overstimulation from shopping, social events, and the news media

- The bipolar disorder itself. Her depression and hypomania typically show up with irritation

This is a simple root trigger list that can be tackled item by item. They both agreed on the list. The next step was for them to decide how they could work *together* to stop the triggers.

Step Six: Stopping the Triggers

Pam first looked at her diet and especially her coffee and diet cola consumption, as this was an easy place to start. She agreed to switch to decaf coffee and start decreasing the number of diet colas she drank, with the goal of quitting caffeine completely in the future. Pam and Carlos then made the simple agreement that they would eat dinner together at the same time every night. They both decided to learn more about what foods affected Pam's moods. Pam agreed to set up regular appointments with her doctor to discuss and explore her current medications and their side effects. She made a list of the topics she wanted to discuss with her doctor the next time they met. She also decided to use breathing techniques to help her manage her irritation once it started.

They looked over their home and decided that hiring someone to come in and clean once a week was the realistic solution to their arguments over chores. They talked about what each of them would do if Pam were too ill to do her share of work around the house. Carlos agreed to take over paying the bills until Pam was more stable. Pam gave away all of the magazines lying around the house and made a deal with herself to pick up her clutter on a daily basis (and to ask for help when this was overwhelming).

They decided that a more regimented sleep schedule was needed, and Carlos said he would help them get to bed at the same time every night and would learn more about natural sleep aids, such as chamomile tea and relaxation techniques. They also decided to take a half hour before bedtime each night to lie together and talk about the good things that had happened during the day. They could then meditate or just be together with love until they fell asleep.

As to their social life, Carlos agreed to be patient with Pam and allow her to become more stable so that they could do more things socially together. They decided to set aside time each week to have a bipolar-free evening, a time when they did something fun and romantic that would be good for their relationship. (You will find tips on what you can do for fun as a couple in chapter 15.) They also agreed that Carlos needed social time to himself.

Carlos agreed to learn new techniques to respond to Pam when she is ill instead of just reacting to her. He knew he had to be the one to defuse the situation once a mood swing starts. He decided to look for a therapist who could help him with the issues he faces because of Pam's bipolar disorder. (The techniques that Carlos learned to use to respond to Pam are covered in detail in chapter 9.)

Carlos also learned that it's essential for him to remember that once symptoms are raging, Pam will have a hard time asking for help. Carlos has to have his responses written down and memorized for those times when she is ill. He knows he can't wait for her to ask for help. The minute she becomes irritated with him, he's learning to get out the "What Works" list and respond with a suggestion that works, instead of letting her irritation get to him.

The biggest issue Pam must deal with is her obligation to work. She and Carlos had a serious discussion about this, and Pam admitted that her work schedule was making her ill. She recognized that, since starting her job, she has never been stable. She decided to make some changes at work to create some stability so that she will be able to make more serious decisions about her work in the future.

You may find that your partner is in a similar situation regarding work. Going to work provides both a stimulating and aggressive environment for many people with bipolar disorder. Chapter 11 will cover this topic in more detail, but Pam and Carlos had to have a realistic discussion on how Pam could reduce her stress level at work so that she could reduce her bipolar disorder symptoms and enjoy more quality time with Carlos. After carefully examining Pam's list of triggers, they agreed that work obligations were her main root trigger. Note that it took them quite a bit of writing and talking before they found the main trigger of Pam's irritation. That length of time was entirely normal.

Finally, they both realized that Pam must also focus on her other major bipolar disorder symptoms (especially depression) in the same way that they focused on her irritation. Depression can cause a lot of irritation; so until the depression is addressed, some of her problems with irritation will remain. After some time, they created a treatment plan for depression and the other bipolar disorder symptoms that created problems for Pam, and now they have a holistic plan in place for each of Pam's major symptoms.

Pam and Carlos's Lives Today

Carlos: Our lives are much different now. It has taken a long time, but we have learned to prevent the irritation outbursts. Pam made some big changes at her work. These changes were hard on us financially but meant everything to me relationship-wise. I now see that I didn't help with Pam's irritation at all. I didn't help around the house and I was often distant when she started to get sick. Now, instead of thinking, "Oh God! Here she goes again!" I have learned to recognize the first signs and I get out my list of symptoms and immediately see that she's sick. I just go up to her and say, "I can see that you're irritated. How can I help?" Or I say, "I can see that you're angry, and I know that you don't want to take it out on me. Let's work together."

I now know I can go to our list of what works and get ideas on how to help her. I can also see what I did in the past that didn't work. This has changed our lives. It took about six months for us to get into a routine. Pam was also depressed when we started our plan, but we followed the same procedures we used to manage her irritation and we created a plan for depression. We now have plans for hypomania, depression, anger, and paranoia. All of her symptoms have really gotten better and we are both learning to recognize the very first signs that something is starting, so that we can get out our "What Works" list. At first I thought this would really limit our lives, but it hasn't been that way at all. We can actually do more things together now that Pam is more aware of what makes her sick, and I'm more aware of what I can do to help.

Pam: I really had no idea that my irritation was a part of bipolar disorder. It was so hard for me to see clearly when I was in a rage. I'm so glad I didn't hurt someone with the car or yell at the wrong person. I was out of control and Carlos had no idea how to help me. The first time we listed all of my triggers I couldn't believe how I was increasing my irritation by doing the things that cause bipolar disorder to get worse. I never saw the connection between stress and my moods. It all felt so disconnected to me. Now I immediately recognize the first signs of irritation. I know that Carlos and I both have to go into prevention mode and I have to really examine what I'm doing with my life.

I made some big changes after we discussed my triggers. I stopped drinking diet cola. I did it cold turkey. That wasn't easy. I started to work out at a gym and discovered that swimming was calming. I made some big changes at work. I cut back on my hours and stopped volunteering for every new project that came my way. I started to focus on what I could do. It changed things for me financially, but, luckily, I work for a good company and they were willing to let me cut back. If they hadn't been understanding, I would have quit. That's how bad it was before we started working on the bipolar disorder symptoms. I also noticed that my irritation was a sign of depression as well, and we've created a plan for my depression. I started to see my doctor more often, so that we can discuss my medications, and I asked for a therapist who understands bipolar disorder.

My therapist helped me see how self-centered I had become. She was kind about this, and even though it was hard to hear what she was saying, she was right. Everything really was about me. My mood swings took so much time, no wonder Carlos felt left out and unhappy. I'm not sure where I was in all of this either. I lost myself somehow and let bipolar disorder take over everything.

I now know that I'll have to treat bipolar disorder first for the rest of my life. It's not fun and I'm not happy to have this illness, but I want to stay well. I've also reconnected with Carlos. Our relationship is no longer about my illness. It's about us. We now have the pleasures and problems of an ordinary couple, instead of having to deal with bipolar disorder all day long. He has learned so many new techniques that really help. I can't believe what loving support he gives me. I wish we had known these techniques earlier, but I'm so glad we have them now. I don't want to make this sound too simple; we've had some trouble adjusting along the way, but we stuck with it and I know it saved our relationship.

Like Carlos and Pam, you can use your new treatment plan to make the changes you want to make in your relationship. The following chapters will help you add more ideas to your "What Works" list and will address in greater detail many of the tools you learned in the first chapters.

REALITY CHECK

Pride is a problem with bipolar disorder. Even though your partner knows their behavior is unreasonable and out of control, something happens inside that will not let them say the words "I need help." Just as you both decided to treat bipolar disorder first, you can decide to leave pride outside when it comes to helping your partner find stability. You can let your partner know you understand that bipolar disorder often will not let them ask for help or say they're sorry.

One way to look at it is that *bipolar disorder is always wrong,* not the person with the illness. The illness is the problem, and when you accept this fact, you can both be more compassionate toward each other. People who don't have the illness have no idea how terrible it is to live with, and those with the illness usually have no idea how terrible it can be to live with someone who has bipolar disorder. It's so much easier to focus on bipolar disorder when someone is ill than to start the blame-and-shame game that only adds stress to an already stressed relationship.

The next time you find yourself in a bipolar disorder crisis, turn to this chapter and reread how Pam and Carlos approached the problem to remind yourself that change takes time, but it is possible. Start with the first steps of creating a holistic treatment plan and keep going. You can do it.

CHAPTER NINE

The Bipolar Conversation

Have you ever had a conversation with your partner in which it feels like your partner is talking about something completely different from and unrelated to what you're talking about?

When your partner is ill, normal conversations often become difficult or even impossible. They become conversations where you are talking normally, thinking that your ideas and feelings are being heard, but your partner is ill and not in control of what they are saying. Simple conversations suddenly turn into arguments and your partner may start to get angry, start to cry, or say something completely unreasonable such as "You never listen to me!" or "You just don't understand." You probably sit there stunned and wonder once again what you have done wrong. Bipolar disorder symptoms then might compel your partner to make a scene or leave, and you have no idea what is going on and eventually think, "I just can't take this anymore!" This is the bipolar conversation.

Stable relationships are based on good communication. Bipolar disorder often takes away a person's ability to reason, which means the person with the illness often says and does things that are neither a part of their real behavior nor an honest reflection of their true and deeper feelings. Naturally, this interrupts your normal ability to communicate with your partner and causes problems in your relationship. Just because you love someone, it doesn't mean that you innately know how to deal with these behavior changes, and the usual result is a huge misunderstanding that puts the relationship under terrible stress. Another problem is that the conversations seem real to both partners, which is what makes bipolar disorder so dangerous. It's almost as though a third person has been sitting in on the conversation like some twisted bipolar Cyrano de Bergerac. Your partner gets further into the mood swing, and you just can't understand why the person you love is acting so oddly.

The good news is that there is hope. You can learn to recognize and then prevent these bipolar conversations so that you can treat the symptoms of bipolar disorder before they get out of hand and cause serious damage to your relationship. This technique can become a powerful tool on your "What Works" list.

Bipolar Conversations Are a Sign

These bipolar conversations happen no matter what mood swing is starting and are an excellent way for you both to see the symptoms when they first start, instead of waiting for them to get so out of hand that the behaviors can no longer be controlled. Knowing the early signs of bipolar disorder by noticing what your partner says when they are first ill, and observing how you respond, are the first steps to take to prevent major bipolar disorder symptoms and the problems they create in relationships.

EXAMPLE: THE BIPOLAR CONVERSATION

Paul, who has bipolar disorder, and his partner, Suzanne, are sitting outside a coffee shop on a nice sunny day. It's pretty outside and lively. There are a lot of people and dogs out in the sunshine, as well as a market next door. Suzanne just wants to drink some coffee and enjoy her day, but Paul can't seem to let go of his worries. Read the following conversation and see whether you can recognize when bipolar disorder is talking.

Paul: I just want to work on my new software idea. I don't feel I have enough time to do my own projects. I do my work for four hours in the morning and then the day is gone, and I don't get things done.

Suzanne: Paul! What are you talking about? You have a lot of time to do your projects. You just don't do them. You just talk about them all of the time. I don't understand you. You only have to work four hours a day right now. What do you mean you have no time?

Paul: It just feels like the day slips away from me, and I don't get any further with my software project.

Suzanne: I've given you tons of ideas on how to market your projects. I really believe you can make this work. God! I'm so tired of listening to you talk about your lack of time. Just do the damn thing and I'll help you market it. You just need to finish something so you can feel good about yourself.

Paul: Why do you always have to put me down? You never listen to what I say. You're treating me like I'm a failure! I know I never finish my projects. I just don't like to do the marketing stuff. I feel like this will never work out for me! Why can't you support me in what I do?

Suzanne: Paul! I'm not putting you down. I want to support you! I'm just giving you some ideas on how to deal with your time issues and all your worries about the project. I will help you with the marketing. I told you that! Why do you always have to twist things around? You know I support you!

Paul: I know that, Suzanne. I just can't figure out where all the time goes.

Suzanne: *(getting mad)* Where all the time goes? You have a work contract that lets you work only four hours a day! You have tons of free time! You are free from noon until midnight. What do you want? How much time do you need? What's going on with you?

From this point on, the conversation just travels in a circle. Paul says he just can't seem to find the time to do things, and Suzanne gets more and more frustrated and angry to see such a talented person talk such rubbish. Here is how they describe the situation.

Paul:　　When I'm depressed, I really do feel like I don't have enough time to get things done. It doesn't matter how much time I have; it's just never enough. I tend to obsess about this over and over and can't really do anything about it. It feels so real and I just get caught up in the thoughts that my brain is sending to me. I can't focus on reality. This is my reality. When the feelings hit me, I have no objective thoughts about them.

Suzanne:　　He just constantly talks about time. I hear him and I think, "Is he crazy?" He's got a lot more time than I do. Why can't he just sit down and do the work he keeps saying he needs to do? He talks about this time thing more than he works on it. It's driving me crazy. I give him suggestions and even list the ways I can help him, but he just keeps saying I don't understand and comes up with excuses for why he can't get his project done. I can feel I'm overreacting to what he says. But I really never thought that this was a sign that he was depressed. I think this is because his symptoms can be quite mild, at first. He's not saying that life sucks and he wants to kill himself; instead he talks about how he doesn't want to work and how he has no free time, and since these are real concerns for most people, it's easy to get caught up in what he says.

Paul and Suzanne's bipolar conversation illustrates how difficult it is to have a healthy relationship when one partner is controlled by bipolar disorder. These conversations can go on in the same way for years. So don't feel guilty if you didn't notice them in your own relationship. The first step is for you to recognize when your partner is starting one of these conversations. Eventually, both of you can learn to recognize bipolar conversations and recognize that they indicate that your partner is having a mood swing. This is why the symptom lists you created in chapter 5 are so important. You can use these lists to write down what your partner says when they start to get sick so that you can recognize the symptoms before they turn into the bipolar conversation. Paul and Suzanne will definitely add Paul's saying that he "never has enough time to do things" to their symptom list.

Walk in Your Partner's Shoes

One way for you to understand how these conversations happen is for you to walk in your partner's mood-swing shoes for a while. What do you think is going on inside your partner's head when these conversations start? Is it possible that they really believe what they are saying and can't help their behavior? If you had bipolar disorder, do you think you would talk in the same way?

What do you experience when bipolar disorder is speaking through your partner? Do you become frustrated, scared, angry, or worried? Is your partner frustrated, scared, or worried? Who is in control when these conversations start? You may be surprised to find that neither one of you is in control; bipolar disorder is in control.

What Is Real?

When your partner is being swept away by intense emotions, they truly believe what they are thinking and saying. The thoughts feel real. Their mind tells them they are real. In some cases, they know something is wrong, but they just can't control what they say and do. The bipolar disorder is so completely in control it's as if your partner has become a puppet, and bipolar disorder controls the strings. You may feel that your partner talks this way to make you angry and to cause trouble. Maybe you see your partner as weak. Or you may feel that your partner just needs to think before they talk. But it's not that easy when bipolar disorder makes an appearance. This is a situation where you, as the partner, have to take over and respond with compassion and effective tools to stop the symptoms before they go too far. This is where you can truly make a difference.

Do you remember the last time you knew something was wrong with your partner's thinking, but you attributed it to some failing in your partner? Maybe you thought, "Why can't they just see that they are obsessing about this?" Or, "Why can't they just stop being so darn unhappy and just get on with their life?" It's quite normal for you to react to what your partner says and does in this manner, but it's not helpful. Our society teaches us to stick up for ourselves. We are told, "Tell people what you think!" "Take care of yourself so people don't walk all over you!" The problem with this advice is that the person who is in the middle of bipolar disorder doesn't respond to the normal conventions of society. A new response must be learned and the first step is to recognize when the bipolar conversation begins.

The Leading Comment

Bipolar conversations usually start with a *leading comment*. These comments are often very upsetting to you and cause you to get drawn into and emotionally involved in a bipolar conversation before you even have time to evaluate whether your partner is ill. You hear these comments and react to them, which is only natural, as they are often unreasonable comments that would frustrate anyone. Your goal is to write all of these leading comments on your partner's symptom list so that you will recognize these comments as a part of your partner's major symptoms and not as indicative of what your partner really feels. Here are some examples:

LEADING COMMENTS

- No one ever calls me.

- Work's terrible, and I don't want to go back tomorrow.

- You never want to do anything with me.

- I have no desire to do anything. Just leave me alone!

- Why do you always want to ruin my fun?

- I have plenty of money and it's none of your business what I buy. Don't you want me to enjoy something for once?

- People are looking at me strangely.

- I don't feel I can go on with my life.

- I need to go to Vegas. I've worked really hard and I deserve it.

- Sleep is such a waste of time!

When you analyze these comments, you may notice that your partner can be very all-or-nothing in their thinking. When your partner is ill, they often can't see all the aspects of a situation and may draw conclusions too quickly and make snap decisions about other people and life in general. The use of words such as *never, always, should, can't,* and *none* is a good indicator that the whole picture is not seen. Your partner may make comments quite different from those listed above, but the feelings are the same. "Nothing" is right, "no one" is helpful, and you are just not good enough as a partner in many ways. Or, on the other, manic, end, "everything" is "great," "wonderful," and "fantastic," and you're just trying to ruin your partner's fun. If you take the bait and react to these comments at face value, the result will be a bipolar conversation.

Don't Be Tricked!

It's so easy to get tangled up in these very serious leading comments. Your goal is to learn to recognize them as comments originating from bipolar disorder so that you can respond to the disorder instead of reacting to the words your partner is saying. You need to say, *Hey! Wait a minute! Hold it! This is bipolar disorder talking and I don't have conversations with bipolar disorder. I have conversations with my partner.* You can then address the real issue. Leading comments are a signal that your partner is ill and you have to treat the bipolar disorder first.

How to Respond to Leading Comments

There is a big difference between reacting to what your partner says and responding to bipolar disorder when your partner is ill. Your goal is to immediately recognize the signs that your partner is not speaking from who they are but instead speaking the language of bipolar disorder. You want to learn how to defuse the bipolar disorder symptoms by being ready with set responses that address the symptoms of the illness instead of what the illness causes your partner to say.

The following examples will show you how a person in a mood swing talks, show you how you might *react* to what is said, and then give you tips on how you can *respond* instead of reacting. As you read through these examples, take notes in the margins when something sounds familiar. You will use these ideas later, in your journal.

PARANOID DEPRESSIVE EPISODE

I have no friends. No one ever calls or e-mails me. It feels like people look at me strangely and follow me when I go out. You never want to do anything fun anyway, and I just sit here in this apartment with the four walls closing in on me. I need some space! It's so dark here at night!

It's normal for you to react to what your partner is saying. It's frightening to hear them talk this way and you probably don't know how to help. You might say:

Reaction: *But you have a lot of friends. I saw you answering e-mails today, and a friend called last night. What's wrong with you? We went to a movie last weekend and we ate out at a nice place just a few days ago. If you want to get out of this apartment, then go take a walk. Nothing is closing in on you. You were fine in the apartment just a few days ago. What do you mean people are looking at you? No one's looking at you!*

A better way to help your partner is to respond to the bipolar disorder language and not to what is actually being said. You can say:

Response: *I know this feels very real to you right now. When you worry about friends, this is a sign that you're ill. I know those kinds of worries are on your paranoia and depression symptom lists. I think we need to focus on bipolar disorder right now. What can we do together to stop these thoughts? I can tell you that I'm your friend and we can work on this together. We can turn on some lights or go take a walk together. Let's get out the "What Works" list. I know that you have these thoughts when you're down and too much is going on. I'm here to help you.*

Here are some more examples on the difference between reacting and responding to what your partner says.

MANIC EPISODE

Why do you always want to ruin my fun? I've been down for so long and now I'm finally happy, and you just want me to sit here and do nothing! I want to get out and live life and just be a part of the world. Why would you want to make me unhappy?

Reaction: *I'm not trying to ruin your fun! I just don't know why you want to do so much all of the sudden. Did you even sleep last night? And when was the last time you ate something good for you? I haven't seen you do your work for days. Don't you have projects that are due? I'm worried that you're just flaking out and* *not taking care of yourself. I know you were down for a long time, but this isn't a good reaction. You're going to make yourself sick if you don't slow down. What on earth were you doing on the computer until three in the morning? You've never done this before. I just don't understand you! What's wrong with you?*

Response: *The last time you were manic you talked just like this. We decided to work together on this problem and now is the time to deal with the bipolar disorder. I see the signs that you're manic. Can you see them even just a little? These manic episodes have been devastating to our relationship in the past and now is our chance to stop this one before it gets out of hand. I'm going to get out our "What Works" list of things to do when you're manic, and I want us to work on this together. I want you to call your doctor or I can do it for you. I want this time to be different because I love you and I want our relationship to work.*

DEPRESSIVE EPISODE

I don't think I love you anymore. I don't think I can give love to anyone anymore. I just need to be alone and get away from all this.

Reaction: *You don't love me anymore? What's wrong? What have I done? I don't understand. We have a good relationship. Why are you doing this to us? Why do you want to ruin our life together? What about our children?*

Response: *It must be terrible for you to have these feelings. It scares me to hear you say such things, but I remember that you said them the last time you went to the hospital. When you got your medications stabilized and got out, you never said these things again, until now. This tells me you're depressed. We've been happy together and I think you know that deep inside yourself. So instead of reacting to what you are saying, I'm going to get started on our plan to help you when you're down. I love you and I know you love me. We're going to work on this together.*

ANGER AND IRRITATION EPISODE

Get the hell out of my way. Why do you have to always crowd me and get on my case? You're driving me crazy! (Slams hand on the countertop.)

Reaction: *Don't you talk to me that way! What do you mean I'm crowding you? This is my damn kitchen too. If you don't like it here then just get out! You are driving me freaking crazy!*

Response: (Take a very deep breath.) *We made a deal when we started working with the techniques in the book that your anger and irritation are not* *acceptable. Right now I'm telling you that this is not acceptable and we need to work on what's causing this. You're not normally like this and I'm not willing to live with it. I'm going to do the things on the "What Works" list we talked about when you were well, and we're going to take care of this anger together. If you can't do that right now, it's fine. I know how strong the bipolar disorder is. You can go cool off somewhere or I can leave, but I won't allow this anger in our relationship. What can I do right now to help you?*

Try It: It Works

It is often astonishing to see how well this method works. It takes a lot of patience, thought, and work on your part. It requires that you *respond* to your partner as soon as you notice the signs of the mood swing. You have to be ready for the leading comment. Yes, at first, this is a lot to ask of you. You will have to learn to control your natural emotions. But as you learn these skills, you will begin to see the signs of bipolar disorder before you even get into one of these conversations. It gets much easier over time. Often your partner will feel incredible relief that you're able to see through what the bipolar disorder is saying. Your partner may not be able to stop the behavior immediately or even be able to thank you for your help, but they are hearing you and they will be able to say thank you later. This technique saves relationships, but it takes practice and teamwork. When combined with the techniques you learned in the preceding chapters, this procedure can help you stop the major symptoms that are harming your relationship.

It's also important to know that a leading comment doesn't have to take verbal form; it can be a leading action, as well. Some of your partner's leading actions may include crying, sighing, holding their head in their hands, wringing their hands, being short of breath, making exasperated sounds, giving big hugs to everyone, or muttering under their breath. You can learn to respond to these nonverbal clues just as you do to verbal leading comments.

Responding Instead of Reacting Takes Time

You may be tired of hearing this, but learning how to use all of these techniques take time. At first, even when you learn to recognize the signs of these bipolar conversations, you will still get caught up in them. Just remind yourself that this is a process. You are only human, and bipolar disorder is strong. Just keep trying and learning and it will become easier each time you use the techniques. Once your partner learns this technique as well, you may see an improvement in your relationship you didn't believe was possible. Using this technique also requires insight on the part of the person with bipolar disorder and it may be very difficult at first. But the more aware your partner becomes of the signs they are becoming ill, the more insight they will have, which means they will able to ask for help before they lose their ability to reason.

EXERCISE: Practice Your Responses

Now it's your turn to practice what you will say to a leading comment or action. Using your journal, write your response to the following examples of what your partner might say or do:

- *I can tell that no one likes me at work. I feel people looking at me and I know the boss is just waiting to fire me.*

- *I'm just not sure how I feel anymore. Everything seems so pointless and I'm just not happy with my life.* (Starts to cry.)

- *I really don't need sleep like I used to. I have so much energy. It feels great to finally be happy and get things done after being depressed for so long.*

- *You never want to have any fun! Why can't we take a vacation and do something exciting for once?*

- (Pinches lips, expels breath out in anger, and glares at you.)

Think of the times you've heard your partner make similar comments or seen them take similar actions. Now that you have an idea of what leading comments or actions are like, write all of your partner's leading comments and actions you can remember on the symptom lists, under your treatment plan for each major symptom category. Over time, you may observe that many of these comments don't change. Every time your partner becomes ill with a particular symptom, they will say the same things. This is always a sign that bipolar disorder is talking and not your partner.

Crying is almost always a sign that something is wrong. Note when your partner cries and put it on the symptoms list. Crying is just a nonverbal leading comment, and you need to have a response ready when the crying starts.

Paul and Suzanne Stop Their Bipolar Conversation

Earlier in this chapter, you saw how Suzanne *reacted* to Paul's downswing when he kept telling her he had no free time. The following conversation shows how Suzanne now uses new techniques to *respond* to Paul when he is ill, instead of reacting to his unreasonable but understandable bipolar conversation. Suzanne has taught herself to recognize the signs that Paul is depressed. She now knows that the minute he starts sounding unreasonable and obsesses about his lack of time, he is starting a downswing and that they need to focus on stopping the mood swing and what caused it, instead of focusing on the content of what Paul is actually saying. She knows that she regularly needs to look at Paul's depression symptoms list and their "What Works" list so that she will be familiar with what he says and does when he is depressed.

Paul has also taught himself to respond to Suzanne when she says she thinks he's starting a mood swing. He realizes that he has to trust Suzanne's judgment when he is ill. You will notice in the following example that Suzanne still gets caught up a bit when Paul first raises the topic, but this is normal. It takes a lot of practice to unlearn old behaviors. Notice the difference in Suzanne as you read the following conversation.

> *Paul:*   I just want to work on my new software idea. I don't feel that I have enough time to do my projects. I do my work for four hours in the morning and then the day is gone, and I don't get anything else done.

> *Suzanne:*   Paul! What are you talking about? You have a lot of time to do your projects! You just don't do them. (*She stops talking and suddenly realizes that they have had this conversation before. She looks at Paul and can see that he does look a little sad.*) Wait a minute. We've been through this before. This is how you always talk when you're starting to feel down. Are you okay?

> *Paul:*   It just feels that the time slips away from me, and I don't get any further with my own projects.

> *Suzanne:*   I know you feel this way. You know, you don't talk like this when you're well. You usually love your free time and

you get a lot done. I think that this is bipolar disorder talking. Have you been feeling worried or down?

Paul: Yeah, I guess so. I just don't wake up with any desire to go on with the day. I guess you're right. I don't feel all that great.

Suzanne: Something is going on to make you feel this way and it sure isn't a lack of time. Can you see that you have a lot of free time?

Paul: If I think about it rationally, I can see that I have plenty of time. It just feels so real when I have these thoughts.

Suzanne: I know. Let's get out the symptom list for depression. I think you'll see that you say these things every time you're sick. What can you do from the "What Works" list?

Paul: (Reads over the "What Works" list and actually feels some hope for the first time that day.) I certainly can go outside first thing in the morning and take a walk and get some daylight. I can check my meds too. I can look at my diet and sleep patterns. I can also say no to the thoughts that tell me I don't have enough time. I can respond to them instead of just listening to them as if they're real. It makes me mad that I can't remember to do this when I have the first thoughts.

Suzanne: Well, I guess we both have to learn how to be ready for this. What can I do for you right now?

Paul: A hug would help! Thanks, Suzanne. I really do feel better. I'm so glad you were here to listen to me. I get so tired of this illness, but it helps a lot to know you understand.

Here is how they describe their current situation.

Suzanne: I used to react to what Paul was saying instead of responding. I've learned to see the first signs that he's going down, and I'm now ready to deal with the illness, instead of what he's actually saying. I think that I just have to learn the signs really well and not let the conversation go on for even ten minutes. I have to remember that he's sick and that I need to focus on fixing the bipolar disorder instead of reacting to what he says and trying to fix his problems. Lecturing him just makes him sicker and causes more of these pointless conversations. We both get upset when I react to him in a negative, bossy way.

I can see such a difference in our relationship now that I know what to look for. I'm a lot less frustrated. Having this space also allows us time to look for Paul's triggers. We realized that when his work went from eight hours to four hours a day he lost a lot of the structure that he needs.

Paul: Until I learned to look for the signs that I was down, I just felt so out of control with my moods. I'd be fine for months and then one morning I'd wake up and life just wasn't fun anymore. Then the thoughts about work and my lack of free time would start up. Now, the minute I have one of these distressing thoughts about the lack of time, I know that I have to look at my bipolar disorder and see how I am with that. I know that these time worries aren't real, and going on and on about them is a sign that I need help.

Suzanne and I are more of a team now instead of my being a "bad boy" she has to scold all the time. I really need her help when I get sick, and this has taught us how to help each other. It's such a relief. I don't want to make it sound like this is a super-easy thing to do. It isn't. But it's a lot better than having the same problems over and over again. I agree that it helps to figure out why I get so down in the first place. Talking about triggers has helped us focus more on what we need to do, instead of constantly going around in circles when I start to get sick.

When you and your partner learn to recognize and stop these bipolar conversations, you will have more time to look into the triggers of the symptoms that are causing the conversation in the first place. After reading the dialogue above, you may think, *My partner is never this reasonable. My partner won't listen to me when I try to talk rationally.* This may be because the bipolar disorder has gone too far, and your partner is no longer reasonable enough to accept your help. You can prevent this by noticing the symptoms very early. The leading comment can be very subtle at first. Learn what it sounds like and have a plan ready.

How to Prevent the Bipolar Conversation

Over the next few months, observe how bipolar disorder seeps into your conversations. Both of you can pay attention to this. Look back on former problem conversations and think about the signals that told you bipolar disorder was speaking, not your partner. What did the conversations sound like? Were there certain phrases used? Was there specific body language? Did the conversations happen in particular situations, such as at family get-togethers or concerts? Did the conversations involve typical household problems or children? Did they come up around money?

Here are some steps you can take to recognize and ultimately stop these conversations before they go too far.

1. Make a pact with yourself and eventually with your partner that, once you've learned the techniques presented in this chapter, at least one of you will try to stop the bipolar conversation before it gets out of hand. You have to set aside pride and the need to win or to be right if you want to stop bipolar disorder from taking over your relationship. You have to let go of your ego and be willing to say, *Wait, let's just stop this right now and look at the real issues. It sounds to me like you're sick and that this is a bipolar conversation.* Or, your partner can learn to say, *I'm sorry I'm so depressed and unhappy. I think it's bipolar talking and I'm willing to stop this right now and get some help for myself.* Write down your ideas in your journal about what your partner might say when they need help. This can be a signal to you that you have to take over and get out the treatment plans.

2. You really do have to allow love to be a part of this. Love can be stronger than bipolar disorder, and if you work on this problem from a place of love instead of who's right and who's wrong, you will have a greater chance to succeed. This isn't about punishment or winning. It's about learning how to live with this illness and learning how to have conversations that promote your relationship instead of constantly tearing it apart.

3. You must recognize that this is a permanent commitment. This means that from now on, for the duration of your relationship, you will look for the signs that your conversations may not be real conversations. Whenever you are talking to your partner and things just don't feel right and you can feel an argument coming on, or you are confused by what your partner is saying, or you can tell that matters are just too good to be true, as they can be when your partner is manic, you have to stop, think, and evaluate the situation. Eventually, you will learn the difference between a real conversation and a bipolar conversation. This may seem like a huge commitment, but it's no different than what most healthy couples try to do. Once you learn the skills, the changed behavior will become natural.

4. Remember that it takes two to do this work. It really has to be a partnership. Each of you has a unique role. And your roles will change. On some days, especially during stressful situations, one of you will be full of pride and anger and won't be able to say, *Let's just stop this now and look at the real issues.* On some days, these conversations will go on for hours until one of you finally sees that there is illness involved and not just the two of you. But if you both consistently listen for these conversations and learn how to stop them, you will have more time to discuss the real issues in your lives. Think about how you and your partner can add this tool to your treatment plan.

5. If you're working on this alone, you can still use these techniques to stop your part of the conversation. When your partner is better, you can explain what you are trying to do and help them learn the techniques, as well.

6. You can also involve family members with this new tool and teach them how they can help your partner. Who do you feel needs to learn this technique and how do you want to teach it to them? Remember, this is a tool that children and friends can also use.

You now have the tools you need to recognize and hopefully stop the bipolar conversation from taking over your relationship. As you become better at recognizing these conversations, you can then focus on the triggers that start them in the first place. This is one of the best ways to prevent bipolar disorder symptoms.

REALITY CHECK

What if your partner won't listen to you when you try this technique? What if your partner is so ill that they think you are the one with the problem? What if they say, *Did you see that! I just saw someone looking in on us through the window. I think we need to call the police,* but you know that there's no one outside? If your partner has reached the point where reason is no longer possible, then it's time to see a health care professional or go to the hospital. Psychotic comments are always an indication that something is very wrong, and help is needed immediately. If you find yourself in one of these conversations and it's obvious your partner is psychotic and very manic and can't see that they are ill, then it's time for you to ask for help.

You are probably familiar with the situation where your partner is saying things that are just not right, and you get that terrible sinking feeling in your stomach. Listen to those feelings and take action. This is not the time for a conversation. If your partner is completely unreasonable and is frightening you, don't try to contradict what they are saying. Respond calmly and make sure that you are safe. If your partner is suicidal, get immediate help. You simply cannot handle such issues by yourself.

Recognize the bipolar conversation as another strong tool to add to your holistic treatment plan. When combined with the ideas presented in the preceding chapters, this new technique can put you well on your way to learning how to prevent bipolar disorder mood swings. In many ways the bipolar conversation is a gift because it allows you to see from the very beginning of a mood swing that your partner is ill and needs your help.

CHAPTER TEN

Your Emotional Response to Bipolar Disorder

Bipolar disorder raises a lot of unfriendly emotions. You are not alone if you alternately feel anger, fear, guilt, hopelessness, and many other emotions that cause discomfort.

When you fell in love with your partner, you probably didn't expect that bipolar disorder would play such a large role in your relationship. Maintaining a loving relationship has enough problems as it is, without having to deal with bipolar disorder and its troubles as well. It's normal that you might feel cheated, angry, sad, or worried. You didn't ask for this. This is not your illness, and yet you must live with it every day. The emotions this reality causes can be intense.

For someone in your situation, intense feelings are completely normal, but they may feel out of control to you. Bipolar disorder—especially when it's untreated—can be like an uninvited, unwelcome guest. It can affect your ability to travel with your partner. Sex often becomes extremely complicated. You may lose your social life, or you may become stressed and depressed yourself. This can lead to a lot of emotions you may not want to feel, but the fact of the matter is this: they are often part of being a partner of a person with bipolar disorder.

The sooner you observe, think about, and finally accept the many emotions you may have to endure because of your partner's illness, the sooner you will be ready to make the changes needed to create more stability within yourself. You may even become more objective about the role bipolar disorder plays in your relationship. Greater objectivity will help you when you and your partner begin using your holistic treatment plan.

This chapter discusses many of the emotions you may feel as the partner of someone with bipolar disorder. Your goal in this chapter is to discover what you really feel about the illness and then to figure out what you can do to help yourself establish emotional stability. You may not want to do all of the journal work in this chapter at first. That's okay. Do it anyway. You don't have to want to do it, but you may find that writing about your emotions makes you feel better about your life, especially when you realize that all of your emotions are normal reactions to bipolar disorder. Writing can help you find solutions to these unfriendly emotions. Give it a try.

Fear

I need to know that she's okay. I'm so scared that she's sick again. I'm scared she'll kill herself. I'm scared she won't make it if I'm not there for her at every minute. I'm scared that I'll do or say something that will make her sick and send her over the edge. How can I describe what it was like when she was psychotic and I thought she would jump out of the car on the way to the hospital? I feel like she can't be left alone. How can I have my life when she's like this? Will this go on forever?

Words are often inadequate to describe the fear you feel when your partner has active bipolar disorder symptoms. How can you explain to anyone what it feels like when the person you love literally changes overnight and starts to hear and see things that you can't hear or see? How can you explain what it's like when you realize your partner is missing, and you haven't a clue where they are?

The ultimate fear arrives when your partner says they want to die or when your partner actually attempts suicide. Those words *I want to die* feel like a bucket of ice water pouring onto your head. Sometimes it gets so scary when your partner is sick that you can taste fear in your mouth. Have you felt this kind of fear? How did you handle it when you felt it? How did it affect you physically? Did it change the way you look at the world? You now know that when your partner talks about suicide, it's a symptom of bipolar disorder, and if you treat bipolar disorder first, you can learn to recognize the first signs of a depressive episode before it goes too far. You also know that manic behavior, which may include some frightening decisions by your partner, is normal when they are experiencing a manic mood swing, and you know that you now have some tools to prevent manic disasters.

Now, using your journal, write down your ideas on what you can do to prevent the bipolar disorder symptoms that cause you to feel so much fear. How has what you learned in the previous chapters changed the way you feel about the frightening side of bipolar disorder? It makes sense that if your fear is a result of untreated bipolar disorder, then a treatment plan that may help your partner get better will make it unnecessary for you to live with such fear. Fear doesn't have to be a part of your relationship.

Lack of Attraction

I keep picturing my husband in the hospital. He had a really dry mouth and smelled funny. He made odd comments about other people and seemed more attracted to fellow patients than to me. He slumped and walked with a shuffle like a 100-year-old man. Now that he's home and doing better, I just can't get this image out of my head. I don't know what to do. I don't want to touch him. Does this mean my feelings have changed? How do I know if I still love him? I'm scared my loving feelings for him will never come back.

When someone is often sick, it's hard to keep your attraction alive. If they are depressed and no longer take care of themselves or if they gain a lot of weight due to medications, it's natural that your feelings may change as much as your partner has changed. You're not a saint, and it's normal if you're not attracted to your partner when they're sick. No one expects that of you, except your partner. This is where matters become complicated. Your partner needs your affection because they have been ill. You don't feel attracted to your partner *because* they have been ill. The good news is that this situation doesn't have to be permanent.

What you have to do is help your partner get better so that your attraction can return. If you were attracted to your partner before, you can be attracted to your partner again. In your journal, write about this topic as honestly you can. Are you attracted to your partner when they're sick? Does it matter to you? How do your feelings change when your partner is ill? The two important things for you to discover are these: what feelings are temporary and a result of your partner's illness, and what feelings regarding your attraction to your partner are the real you?

For example, if you met your partner while they were in a manic episode, it's natural that you would feel upset and cheated when the depression began and there was no more manic sex. Give yourself six months to try the new treatment plan. As your partner gets better, your feelings may return to what they were before. If they don't, then you will know that your feelings are not just stress reactions to your partner's illness. You may have to face the fact that you truly are no longer attracted to your partner and make your decision from there.

Anger

This simply isn't fair. I can't do anything I planned to do. Everything is about this damn illness. I'm sick and tired of how it controls our lives and how sick she is. Can't I get a break? What am I supposed to do? I take care of everything. I make all of the money and clean the house while she is just sick all of the time. I hate this illness. I hate it and sometimes I hate her for putting me through this.

It's easy to be angry at your partner when they're sick. They may seem pathetic, lazy, or weak. Your partner may do things that would make anyone angry. Rest assured that you're not alone if you want to beat up bipolar disorder over what it's done to your life or what it's done to the person you love. Bipolar disorder is not a nice illness. Using your journal, finish this sentence: *I'm angry because…* Write as much as you can on this topic and really let bipolar disorder have it. Once again, try to do this even if you don't feel like it. Often expressive writing can help you discover your true feelings.

The next step is to use your anger as a catalyst. Use it to make changes in yourself and your relationship. If you're angry about what this illness has done to your relationship, then change what you can. Create a treatment plan that works. Take action and do something for yourself. You may have lost a lot because of this illness, but what are you going to do about it? Anger is fairly ineffective unless you view it as a sign that something has to change. What is your anger telling you? What do you need to change and how are you going to do it?

Feeling Pressured

Why does everyone expect me to know how to take care of my partner when he's sick? It's like there is some kind of conspiracy against me. I'm not a doctor. But they send this sick person home with me. They don't give me any suggestions I can use. I have to deal with medications and sometimes I even have to make sure he stays alive. How on earth am I supposed to do all this and why do the doctors and all of my family expect me to do it? Could they do it? I don't think so.

No one asked you when you first got together whether you wanted to take care of your partner twenty-four hours a day when they are sick. No one asked if you were willing to give up your life to help them keep theirs. And yet when the illness struck, it was just expected that you would do all the caregiving work. When your partner is sick, they need security. But how can you help them feel secure when you have doubts? It's as though you have to be a superperson in order to protect your ill partner. This puts you in a tough situation. You may feel that you must be extremely careful in whatever you say and do or your partner will have to return to the hospital. How does this make you feel? Is it fair? Is it something you can handle? It's not fair to assume that you can become a full-time caretaker overnight when your partner is diagnosed with bipolar disorder, but this is probably your reality in the moment.

There is much more on this subject in chapter 13, but for now, think honestly about the pressure you're under when your partner is sick so that you can become clear about your feelings. Write about this by finishing the sentence: *It's not fair that I have to…* Let it all hang out. You will not show this to anyone, so be as honest as you can.

Guilt

My girlfriend is having such a hard time. How can I have such selfish feelings? Her body is so different now that she's taking so many medications. How can I be so superficial? She's depressed and she needs my love, but I just want to wait until she gets better before we have sex. How can I do this to her? It's not her fault she's sick. I know that, but my feelings are so different since she got out of the hospital. I know it will just kill her if I tell her these are my feelings. What kind of person am I? Now that she needs me I want to run away.

Naturally, there is a lot of guilt when you feel all the emotions that having an ill partner brings up in you. You may feel that you have no right to feel what you feel, and then the guilt can tear you apart. Your partner is needy and vulnerable and you wonder how you can think only of yourself in a time like this. If you think about leaving the relationship, this can bring up even more uncomfortable emotions; but rest assured, your thoughts are normal here, as well.

If you feel guilty for having mean thoughts about your partner, not wanting to have sex, or wanting to leave the relationship, this simply means that you're human. The answer is to give yourself some time. Now that you have the new treatment plan presented in this book, you'll be able to get a clearer picture of how much your partner can be expected to change and how much you can live with—if matters don't change significantly. This doesn't mean you have to leave, only that you are having the feelings. When you have these feelings, this lets you know that leaving is always a possibility, but it may also mean that you can stay and see whether your relationship improves, now that you have a new treatment plan.

You don't have to feel guilty about wanting to be in a healthy relationship. You have needs and dreams, and bipolar disorder is affecting this; you have a right to be upset. You don't have to keep it all inside. You can talk to a friend, family member, or support group. You can see a therapist. You can learn to turn to other people with your intense feelings so that you needn't feel so guilty. Finish this sentence in your journal: *I feel guilty because...*

If you have a lot of guilty feelings, it may be that some of your feelings are actually regret for what could have been, if only your partner were well. You may have lost a lot because of your partner's illness. What you experience because of this loss may feel like guilt, but could it be regret as well?

Frustration

My partner has maxed out the credit cards again. We've talked about this over and over and yet she still does it. I don't want to treat her like a child, but when she acts like one what can I do? I'm sick of this and don't want to deal with it anymore.

When your partner is depressed they're going to act like a depressed person. Why do you expect something different from them? When they're manic and it's not treated, they are very likely to spend money like a manic person. You should expect this behavior as well. This is an illness with specific symptoms as you now know. When you create a treatment plan that helps your partner take charge of their major symptoms, you may see a significant change in their behavior. Getting frustrated is totally normal, but it will not help you or your partner. Feel the frustration and then use that energy to create a plan for their recovery. Action is the best way to deal with frustration. It's okay and normal that you feel it, but something has to change if you want it to go away. Using your journal, finish this sentence: *It frustrates me so much when my partner...*

Feeling Trapped

I know that if I make the changes I want to make, it might cause my partner to go to the hospital or try to kill himself. I'm so overwhelmed with this pressure, but I've got to be very careful in what I do because it might affect him in a bad way. I feel so responsible for him and yet I'm dying in this relationship. It's all about him and I don't know what to do. I just couldn't handle it if he killed himself because of me. What if I want out? I feel like I'm in jail. Should I stay with him just because he's sick? What do I get out of this?

At some point you will have to face the big questions when it comes to bipolar disorder and its effect on your relationship. As stated in previous chapters, this illness is often treatable. If you and your partner create a treatment plan that helps them find stability, maybe you will not feel so trapped in the relationship. If you feel that you are in a prison because of this illness, then you might require professional help to find the answers you need. Chapter 13 covers this caretaking issue in greater detail, but if this subject brings up big emotions for you, it's something you have to address. The feelings will not simply go away if you push them to the back of your thoughts and just keep filling your days with distractions. The emotions will return and you will have to deal with them eventually. You need to find answers to the questions that all caretakers face. You then have to decide what you're willing to do for yourself. If you feel trapped, ask yourself how you can use this book to help you feel less a prisoner and more a part of a loving relationship, or to help you make the decision to leave.

Answer the following questions in your journal: *Can I live with this for six more months? A year? Five years? What has to change in order for me to stay in this relationship?* Once you are clear about your answers to these questions, you will at least know what you really feel. It will be up to you how you act on these feelings.

Sadness

My partner's illness just makes me want to cry. It's like watching someone thrown into the air over and over again like a rag doll. She tries so hard. She really does, but this illness always wins. We had so many hopes when we first met. We had plans for our lives and nothing has worked out the way we wanted it to. She's too sick to travel and we feel we can't have kids because she couldn't be there for them. I've lost so much of myself as well. I feel hopeless and can't see a way out.

It's time to get clear with yourself and the reality of your relationship. A person with bipolar disorder can go only so far. Healing can happen, but there may always be limitations. This can be a very sad realization for both of you. What if your partner continues to have trouble for the rest of your relationship? This may be a truth that you have to face. If you're feeling terribly sad, it's also important that you pay attention to your own mental health. Are you depressed? Do you need professional help? Your partner may be more ill than you are, but this doesn't mean you don't need help as well. Look over your partner's symptoms for depression. Do you share any of these symptoms? If so, it may be time for you to get some professional help for your sadness. Using your journal, finish this sentence: *I'm sad because...*

Feeling Hopeless

This has been going on for five years now. My partner is constantly sick. Sometimes it's physical; sometimes it's mental. I can't see how anything can change. She doesn't respond well to medications and tends to stop them once things get slightly better. I can't control her and I don't even want to try anymore. Is this what I'm supposed to do in my life? Am I supposed to take care of a person who doesn't even seem to want me around most of the time? I see no future for us.

It may be true that there is no future for your relationship if your partner remains ill. But what if your partner gets a lot better because of your new treatment plan? If this is the case, then there is realistic hope and you may be able to find happiness again. Once again, this all depends on what you need in your life. Maybe this has gone on for too long and you need out. It may help you to talk with a therapist about your feelings. A person can take only so much. How much more can you take? Using your journal, finish this sentence: *If I leave my partner, ...*

Fears Associated with Hospitalization

My partner stayed in the hospital in a manic/psychotic episode for six weeks. He came home and I was so happy. I had missed him so much. He then went into a suicidal depression and I had to take him back to the hospital. I was scared out of my mind. There are no words for what I went through and no one, and I mean no one, understood. I woke up scared and went to bed scared. I couldn't work and couldn't seem to get a handle on my own emotions. I was like an animal. I just went through the motions of my life, but I wasn't there. I lost myself for a while and this is very upsetting. I wasn't the one who was sick. Why did this happen?

There are few things more stressful than putting your partner into the hospital because of bipolar disorder. There is so much uncertainty and fear. There are many questions that the staff doesn't have time to answer. There are worries about the future of your relationship and how well your partner will be when released from the hospital. There are financial worries and family worries and often you are the main person to shoulder this burden. Other family members and friends may not have any idea of how frightening this time is for you. They may not understand bipolar disorder and often can't empathize with you in what you are going through. This is all very common. You're not alone in this.

There are some important facts to remember when this happens. Your partner is in the hospital to get better. Your partner is safer in the hospital than at home with you. Use this time wisely. Use the emotions you are feeling to get started on a treatment plan you can use when your partner returns home. You do have some options. Accept that you are going to be very frightened at first and then try to get on with your day by doing the things you have to do. Don't let a hospital stay stop you from living.

Loneliness

When my partner's ill, I'm alone in this relationship. We can't go to the movies or see friends. She doesn't want to make love or spend time together. She's been in the hospital two times this year. I miss her. She wasn't like this when we first met. She was so much fun and we talked for hours. I feel like our old life has died. How can an illness affect her personality like this? Where is she? I miss her so much. Will she ever come back?

Loneliness is one of the hardest emotions to face when your partner is ill. It can combine with sadness to make you feel depressed. It may seem impossible to find hope when the person you love is so ill. But once again, you have a new treatment plan that you can try. You just have to keep going and moving forward and make the changes suggested in this book. You also may have to look for more friendship from friends and family. If you are used to being with your partner all of the time and are then very lonely when they withdraw from you, it is up to you to find support elsewhere. Using your journal, finish this sentence: *I feel so lonely when...*

Change Is Possible

You may wonder how you're supposed to deal with all of these emotions, especially when you have obligations at work and to other friends and family members. One solution is to become future-oriented. This means you realize that the future can be different from the present. These emotions always feel as if they will last forever, but, in reality, you will most likely feel very different emotions in the future. What frequently happens is that your partner does change and become better, and yet you are still left with the feelings the episode brought up in you. And it may not be so easy for you to just let those feelings go and get on with life. The following suggestions can help you calm many of the emotions you may feel because of bipolar disorder.

Talk with a Professional

Talk with a therapist about your feelings and then decide what you can and can't live with. Be honest with yourself. When you look for a therapist, try to find someone who is familiar with the issues you must face as the partner of someone with a serious mental illness.

Be Clear with Yourself about How You Feel

Even when your partner makes you feel that your life is very chaotic and randomized, it helps if you are always clear with yourself about what you're feeling. It's so easy to get caught up in your emotions and just go with them, instead of examining them and doing something to change your situation.

Just as you learned to respond to your partner instead of reacting to them, you can learn to respond to yourself in the same way. When you come home and your partner is once again on the couch, what do you feel? When you see the credit card bill and realize that your partner went on a manic spending spree once again, what do you feel? Many, many people do. Now, using the treatment plan you have learned in this book, what are you going to do to make things different for the future? You can use your feelings as a gauge and a catalyst for what needs to change. You can say to yourself, *I'm very angry with my partner right now.* Or, *I'm so scared my partner will die,* and then use your new treatment plan to make changes.

You can hope that your partner will use the new treatment plan and you can do everything possible to help them use the plan, but in the end, you are in control only of what you do. A lot of uncomfortable emotions come up when bipolar disorder is in control. But what happens if you and your partner take control? What if you get the illness stabilized? Many, many people do. Naturally, the intensity of the emotions will lessen and, hopefully, go away. You can spend a lot of time focusing on how you feel without seeing many results, but when you are aware of how you feel and then change what is causing you to feel this way, you can see results quickly. This often means changing yourself, so be willing to do whatever it takes.

Let the Feelings Come and Go

Be willing to allow your feelings to come and go. You don't have to be scared all of the time. You don't have to be turned off or frustrated all of the time. Try not to see everything in black and white. Be willing to see that there are some good times as well as some bad ones. Do you doubt your love for your partner when they're sick? This is normal. Why should you have to stay in love with someone who is not the person you originally fell in love with? That is asking too much of yourself. You don't have to be perfect. In any relationship, love ebbs and flows. It's only natural it would fluctuate more often when one partner has bipolar disorder.

Emotions Are Not Wrong—They Just Are

The truth is that you're going to feel what you feel whether you think it's wrong, disloyal, or even mean. Your feelings are not controlled by your intellect and you can't tell them what they should do. Listen to your feelings and learn about them, so you can take the actions that are right for you.

Don't Numb Your Emotions

Try not to use drinking, drugs, or food to deal with your emotions. This is a simple statement to read, but it's a harder thing to put into practice. Just as your partner may have a dual diagnosis, you can also develop a dependence on an external substance to deal with your emotions. If you think carefully about the results of this dependence, you can see that numbing out now will only lead to problems in the future.

When to Talk with Your Partner

You may want to talk with your partner about all of these emotions, especially after you write about them in your journal. But please be careful. You don't want to burden your partner with all of these feelings at once. Hopefully, you will be able to work together on this in the future, but there are some things that your partner really doesn't need to know if they are currently ill.

Learn to use your judgment in this situation. Turn to others, including a therapist, if you feel the need to talk about your feelings. When you do talk with your partner about these emotions, you may be surprised to find that their emotions are quite different from your own. Theirs may include self-pity, shame, or embarrassment. It's also important that you both learn which of your partner's emotions are symptoms of bipolar disorder and which emotions are a response to having the illness. This is something you can do together in the future. For now, focus on your life and be honest, at least to yourself, about how you really feel.

REALITY CHECK

Some emotions are too strong to ignore or to change with the techniques presented in a book. If you're afraid for your personal safety, if your partner is in the hospital often, if you are truly no longer attracted to your partner, or if your partner threatens suicide every time you try to make a change, then it's up to you to decide to take the next step. No one is meant to save someone's life on a daily basis. That's asking too much. If you are in this situation, you need to get some help. You may have a tough decision to make regarding your relationship if your emotions (and your partner's) are too intense for you to handle. It may be that for your own emotional well-being you do need to make some space between yourself and your partner.

Give yourself time to let the new treatment plan start to work. Examine your emotions now and compare them with how you feel in six months. There is hope.

CHAPTER ELEVEN

Work and Money

Most people with bipolar disorder
have trouble with work and money.

Strictly speaking, work and money problems are not symptoms of bipolar disorder, but they are so common among those with the disorder that they might as well be called symptoms. Many people with this illness can't handle the stress of daily work until they are stabilized. As you learned in previous chapters, bipolar disorder symptoms are often triggered by outside events. Work can be a very powerful trigger for people with the disorder. It's natural that your partner might have problems staying in one job for a long time or staying well enough to work at all. Naturally, this can also lead to some serious money problems.

Often the pressure from friends, family, and society cause your partner to feel so guilty over their work and money problems that the guilt may trigger even more symptoms. Not only does this affect your partner's self-esteem, it affects your relationship financially in many ways, as well.

Has your partner had trouble with work in the past? How do you feel when you think about your financial situation? Has bipolar disorder created a mess in your financial life? Then you are not alone. Unmanaged bipolar disorder almost always creates work and financial problems in relationships. From depression to mania and everything in between, your partner's behavior in regard to work and finances can be completely controlled by bipolar disorder symptoms if a system of checks and balances has not been put into place.

Although this chapter specifically addresses work that is rewarded with money, people with bipolar disorder are equally stressed by any situation that requires time-scheduled work, such as attending school, volunteering, or parenting. Anything with strict time obligations may cause your partner to experience major symptoms of bipolar disorder. The good news is that once you have your treatment plan in place, your partner's sensitivity to time pressures can change, and they may be able to do more. This chapter will first discuss the effects of bipolar disorder on your partner's work history, past, present, and future. It will then examine money issues and your current financial situation.

Work

As you learned in the preceding chapters, bipolar disorder is an illness triggered by stressful events. Whether the stress results from a good or bad experience makes no difference: stress is the problem. Can you think of a more stimulating or stressful place than an ordinary work environment? If you can understand that it's the time-scheduled obligations that can cause problems for your partner, you can then understand why it's hard for so many people with this illness to work.

It's not about talent or desire. It's not about intelligence or living up to some potential. It's about bipolar disorder. The obligation of having to be somewhere at a certain time combined with deadlines and expectations for eight hours a day can make your partner ill. You are probably not like this, so this may be hard for you (or others) to understand. This is the reality, however, and you don't really have to understand it—you just have to accept it.

The United States has become work-obsessed. The work ethic has seeped into every part of our lives and our first question when we meet someone new is usually *What do you do?* The work we do is how we define ourselves. He's a writer, teacher, mechanic, lawyer, or gardener. She's a manager, salesperson, doctor, actor, dentist, or chef. We rarely define ourselves by our qualities. So what happens when your partner can't do what they are supposed to do to get ahead? In other words, what judgments and pressures are put on your partner if they can't work?

Perhaps you or another family member have judged or pressured your partner to do something that obviously makes them ill simply because people in our society are supposed to work. It's fairly certain that those with bipolar disorder already judge themselves harshly if they can't work, so this extra pressure can be overwhelming for your partner. Although this is not true for all people with bipolar disorder, it might be that your partner is someone who can't work in the way you and society want them to work. Once you can recognize and accept your partner's limitations regarding paid employment, you may be able to work together to find something fulfilling your partner can do.

EXERCISE: Construct a Work History

Your first goal for this chapter is to get a clear picture of your partner's work history. This work history will help you become realistic about your partner's ability to work and bring money into the relationship in the future. Although it's best if you do this work with your partner as a discovery process, you can certainly get started on your own. Using your journal, take the following steps to create the work history.

Step One: Make a chronological list of your partner's work. Write down the dates of all of your partner's jobs, with brief descriptions. Do this for every year since your partner's first paying job. If possible, interview your partner to discover all of this information. Also, if your partner had a lot of schooling after high school, write this down as well. School behavior often mimics work behavior. If your partner had to leave work to be hospitalized, make a note of this. When a job ended, write down the reason for leaving. Don't worry—this is not a resume. It is just information.

Step Two: Look for patterns. Has your partner changed jobs often? Maybe your partner hasn't been able to work much at all. You may discover that your partner was fine regarding work, until the bipolar disorder symptoms became more obvious. Think of the big picture. Does your partner have a steady and stable work history or a chaotic and unreliable one? Does your partner have work problems because of one type of mood swing in particular? Is their work ability affected by the seasons?

Step Three: Determine how much money your partner made each year. If you are unsure of this, write to the Social Security Administration for a report about your partner's taxed income. Or, estimate what was made in cash.

Step Four: Discover your role. How have you reacted to your partner's work history in the past? Were you accepting if there were limitations, or did you feel frustrated and cheated? Were your expectations realistic? This is where you must be honest with yourself about what you expected from your partner regarding work and earning money from that work.

Step Five: Set realistic work goals for the future. Once you have compiled your partner's work history, you can create a realistic picture of what your partner may do in the future. The new treatment plan in this book can help your partner find stability, which means that they may be able to work a lot more regularly if that has been a problem in the past. However, if work is an overstimulating and stressful place for your partner, it may be that way in the future as well. If your partner has never been able to meet the obligations of a stressful working environment in the past, the chances are good that they may not be able to meet such obligations in the future—no matter how much you want your partner to be normal and work like a "regular" person.

How to Use This Information

Now that you have a clear picture of your partner's work history, you can work together to make a plan for the future. When your partner is stable, sit down and talk with them realistically about work. If your partner has not worked for a while or may not work in the future, what are you both going to do about the situation? What plans have you made for the future? Are you willing to support someone who can't work? Talk about this together and try hard to remember that your partner may feel very sad, guilty, and worried about their work issues.

If you both can accept that bipolar disorder is the reason they have work problems, it may help your partner to accept their possible limitations. It will really help your partner if you try to understand what it must feel like to have the intellectual ability to work and yet have an illness that keeps them from working in a traditional setting. Talk to your partner about these feelings.

Look for Alternatives

The next step is to discuss the possible changes that the new treatment plan may bring. If your partner can find more stability, will this create more work options? Talk together about alternative work choices that your partner can do that may not trigger mood swings. Then, you can discuss how your partner might contribute to your relationship even if they can't work. Is it possible that being a great parent or partner is the job they were meant to do? It may be that you both will have to think outside the box in order for your partner to find a fulfilling role in life. Society places a lot of worth on work. Your partner may have to find their worth elsewhere.

Once you have a clear picture of what your partner can do in the immediate future, you will then be ready to discuss money matters realistically and calmly because you will know what is possible for your partner. It makes sense that when there are work problems, there may be money problems. The next section will help you to become clear about your present financial situation and will discuss what you need to do to feel secure financially in the future.

Money

The "M" word: For many people, talking about money and getting a very clear picture of their financial situation is like picking up a poisonous snake. They will do anything to avoid it. Unfortunately, this topic can't be avoided if your partner is to find stability. You may be deeply in debt because of your partner's bipolar disorder, or you might have to support your partner because they can't stay well enough to work. It could be that *your* spending problems have affected the relationship. Maybe this is a fearful topic you would rather sweep under the rug. Many couples with no illness in the relationship still must struggle with money issues. Your situation is more complicated because your partner has an illness that often affects your financial situation whether due to manic spending sprees, a serious depression, hospitalizations, or an inability to work. Your partner may have totally wrecked your finances while ill. The good news is that with your holistic treatment plan, you may be able to prevent this from happening again.

Now that you're thinking about money, you're ready to get clear on your current financial situation. This next section may be difficult, but it's necessary. You're going to find out exactly where you are financially and then you will create a plan to help you become more financially stable in the future. If your finances are really in a mess, it may be tempting to skip this section, but please don't. This is the way to clear a path for your partner's healing.

EXERCISE: Take a Financial History

Just as reconstructing your partner's work history helped you create a realistic picture of your partner's work future, a financial history can help you honestly examine the financial realities you may face in the future. Using your journal, take the following steps to construct a clear picture of your financial history.

Step One: Know your financial status to the penny. You may be afraid of this step. Many people are. Writing down your financial status is not going to make anything worse. But it can help you achieve your goal of financial stability in the future. First, list all of your debts and expenses. These include monthly house payments or rent, car payments, loans, and credit card payments. Now, write down how much money you have to pay these debts, including any salaries that come in each month. This will give you some idea of where you are financially. If it's very stressful to think about this, that is okay. You are about to do something about it.

Step Two: Know your rights. Make sure you note whose name is on which papers. Is the house or car in your name? How about the credit cards and bank accounts? Investments or retirement funds? There will be information later in this chapter about protecting yourself from your partner's bipolar disorder spending, so first get clear on what you owe and own and what your partner owes and owns. If you're married, it's important that you are familiar with the laws in your area regarding debt.

Step Three: Get a realistic picture of the money that will come in the future. You now have your partner's work history. Realistically, what financial role do you think your partner will be able to play in the next six months to a year while you work on your new treatment plan? What is your current salary? Together, how much money will you make per month in the next six months to a year? Write down this figure. Can you survive on this amount?

Hopefully, doing this work will give you a clear picture of your current finances and where they might be in the future. The next step is to deal with the specific money issues you and your partner face because of bipolar disorder.

Manic Spending Sprees

Mania really does alter the way your partner thinks. Judgment goes out the window and decisions made in the moment have absolutely nothing to do with your partner's intelligence or with past discussions about the risks of overspending. When a person is manic, spending just feels right. Just as a depressed person feels worthless and hopeless, a manic person feels the *need* to spend money. These desires are not intellectual or rational. For your partner, it feels like a basic need, like needing air to breathe. If you can understand this, you will see that staying upset about your partner's manic spending is not effective. Once mania goes too far, your partner does what the illness tells them to do. Spending money is a symptom of bipolar disorder, not a character flaw. *The only way to prevent this spending is to prevent the manic mood swing from going too far by using your holistic treatment plan, which includes using and staying on medications.*

This goes for mania and hypomania equally. Both forms of mania can cause terrible spending sprees. You have to learn how your partner manifests their spending problems. Is it by buying musical instruments, custom furniture, electronic equipment, designer clothing, gourmet food, or expensive items for other people? Or is it by giving away money to help those who are in need, or by gambling? Does your partner overspend on classes or expensive seminars when manic? Naturally, you will be more aware of the big expenditures, but by then it is already too late. Although this has been discussed in earlier chapters, it's essential that you know the early signs that your partner is becoming manic or hypomanic if you want to prevent the mania from turning into a manic spending spree.

You both need to be very clear on your partner's exact thoughts and statements about money and spending from the very first stirrings of manic feelings. You must write these symptoms on your mania symptom list and then use the "What Works" list to stop the mania before it goes too far. *This is the only way to prevent manic spending.*

If your partner, who has been depressed for months, suddenly gets happy and wants to take you to Las Vegas, your first, natural response might be to think that your partner is finally well. But, in fact, the greater likelihood is that depression has just been replaced with mania. You have to recognize these signs so that you don't get sucked in and go on a spending spree as well. The fact is that mania and spending go together. Don't be naïve and think that your partner can control this on their own. It can't be done. You must have a treatment system in place to prevent manic spending. If you're aware of the smaller symptoms from your partner's mania symptom list, you can be prepared for the spending that will surely follow if action is not taken immediately to prevent the manic mood from progressing.

When Mania Goes Too Far

Ideally, you will use your treatment system to prevent mania from getting out of hand, but there are times when this is not possible. A preventive system will not work if your partner is already manic. It's important that you recognize and understand the point at which mania is no longer treatable at home. If matters go this far, it's time to get help from a professional so that your partner can receive psychiatric care. Remember, it's very normal for a person with mania to refuse medications. It really will be up to you to get help for your partner.

There are also some steps you will need to take to protect yourself when mania goes too far. You can certainly try to take away the credit and debit cards. You have the right to do what it takes to protect your personal finances. Your partner may get angry while sick and then be very grateful when they are better. If your partner already has had a severe spending spree, you need to face it head-on. Return what you can immediately. Explain your situation to managers and business owners. Educate your banker and the credit card companies. Explain that you need help. You may be surprised at how kind some people can be.

Remember, in the stress of the moment when your partner is this ill, you are likely to feel overwhelmed by the money crisis. Just keep fixing things step by step. And then work on your treatment plan so that a manic spending spree never happens again.

Depression and Money

Although money issues are usually a more serious problem with mania, they can also be a problem with depression. The issues can be quite different; for example, instead of spending money, your partner may never leave the house, which means that no money (except what you earn) is coming in. Your partner may ignore bills and may even be unable to count money when very sick. In some cases, people suffering from depression will spend money in a desperate attempt to feel better. If your partner has a dual diagnosis, they may spend money on alcohol, drugs, or food when depressed. Once again, all of these behaviors have to be examined and noted on your partner's symptom list so that you can work together to prevent money crises from developing in the future. Just as you will use the first signs of mania to help your partner stop the symptoms before they lead to manic spending, you will need to work with your partner to prevent depression from going so far that it affects your finances.

Money Solutions

You may be wondering what you can do with all of this information. The first step is to record all of your partner's spending thoughts and actions on your major symptom category lists. Manic spending can be prevented if you work together to create a plan that documents what happens when your partner is ill, so that you can have a system in place to prevent the spending from happening again. Depressive spending can be stopped if the depression is treated first. As odd as it sounds, the spending can feel really good to your partner. This is why it has to be prevented. The following section will give you some ideas to add to your "What Works" list.

Create Checks and Balances

From plastic to cash: If your partner spends using credit or debit cards, then it may be necessary to have your partner go on a cash-only system where everything that is spent is written down, and then that list is shown to someone else, most likely to you. Once again, this has nothing to do with spying. For this to work, your partner must be willing to cooperate to stop excessive spending. This system may seem to go against everything that society teaches us about money today. We live in a plastic culture, but plastic can be dangerous when a person has bipolar disorder.

Observe your partner: Just as you will learn the specific statements your partner uses when they start to get manic, you must observe their sleep, eating, and work patterns as well. Look for odd items around the house that your partner would not normally buy, such as new dishes in the kitchen, posters on the wall, magazines, specialty foods, tools, or any other small items that may cost a lot of money but are not easy to notice. Don't be blind and allow spending to get out of hand. Eventually, you and your partner will work together so that your partner can notice the early warning signs themselves and learn how to stop the behavior even before you have to get involved. Yes, this is possible.

The money check-in: Many partners of people with bipolar disorder ignore the money situation until it's too late and then they get very angry with their partners. When you find out how much a purchase cost, you may say, "You bought a $5,000 chair? You must have been out of your mind! What were you thinking?" In reality, however, you have to ask yourself what you were thinking. You saw the chair and you know that your partner has bipolar disorder. Why was the problem not taken care of sooner? Many times, all of the clues are out in the open that a manic spending spree is starting, but you may be in a hopeful mode of denial or be too busy to see them.

It's also possible that you didn't know how to look for the clues. One solution might be to institute a "money check-in" on a daily basis, where you both sit down and talk about money at the same time every day until you create a system that will help your partner prevent spending problems in the future. You will then need to check in at least once a week for the duration of your relationship. Mania is sneaky and if you don't do these check-ins regularly, you will be caught again.

Using a day-planner, pick a time each evening when you can talk about that day's spending with your partner. Agree that both of you will write down what you spend each day and then show each other your list of expenditures every night. No judgment is allowed here, just constructive talk.

After you get used to this and your partner is more stable around money, choose a time to meet once a week to talk about the week's spending. You will continue to do this for the rest of your relationship. These money check-ins are the times you can talk about financial goals and really see the progress your partner is making with their new treatment plan. It also provides a structure to contain out-of-control behavior.

The "before you buy" checklist: Create a checklist that you both must use before you make any large purchase. You can also set up a rule that all major purchases must be put off and discussed for at least two days. You may feel that you don't need this kind of check and balance, but do it to demonstrate to your partner that you are not out to "get" them, as you are also willing to examine your own spending and discuss it with them. If your partner feels the need to buy something immediately, you can both be alerted to look out for mania. Another way to spot mania is to know that the desire to spend feels more like an intense need to have the object than just wanting it. It's a good idea for your partner to write the following questions on a card to keep in their wallet and to look at when they are thinking of buying something:

- Have I bought something like this in the past when I was manic?

- Am I being impulsive? Can I wait to buy this instead of buying it right now?

- Will this damage my life in the future?

- Does this cost more money than I have? Am I buying on credit?

- Am I being reasonable?

- Will my partner be upset?

- Why do I want this?

- Why can't this purchase wait?

- Am I having any of the thoughts I listed on my mania symptoms list?

Protect yourself: If your partner has a history of money problems, it's important that you immediately protect yourself financially from bipolar disorder spending. If you have children, they must be protected as well. Bipolar disorder has absolutely no conscience. Because of this, you must protect your credit, bank accounts, and investments.

Keep everything having to do with your finances 100 percent separate, so that you and your partner can be safe. If your partner doesn't understand why you need to do this, explain as best you can, and then do it anyway. You must be clear about your situation before you can work on solutions. Once again, remember to be very kind and calm about this issue with your partner. Make it a team effort if you can. You don't want to cause more stress and pain for your partner, but you do need to let them know that you are now going to take care of yourself, as well as help them with their new treatment plan. This is so important that it bears repeating. If your partner has trouble with manic spending, keep your money separate. Have separate credit cards, bank accounts, and investments. If you have never done this in the past, now is the time to change.

You must protect your own finances, even if it feels uncomfortable and hurts your partner's feelings. It may be that your partner wants to protect their normal self from their manic self, as well. The best way to deal with this issue is to involve your partner and make this decision together. What do you need to do to start protecting yourself today? This may include putting money into a retirement plan or a separate savings account or canceling any joint accounts that you think may be unsafe for your financial future. After you have your list, choose one thing you can realistically start working on immediately.

Most money problems have potential solutions, even the big problems caused by bipolar disorder overspending. There will be times when your partner is able to work with you on these solutions; at other times you will have to take care of these problems yourself. If your partner is willing to help you get your financial life stable and functioning and then help you create a plan for a stable financial future, that's great. If not, you must move ahead on your own. You must have your own retirement fund separate from your partner. If you have children, they must be taken care of separately. Don't feel guilty about this. All partners are responsible for their own financial futures. Think of your future and what you need to live the life you want to live financially. What changes do you need to make?

Your Partner Has Feelings, Too

Aggressively arguing about the problem right after a spending spree will only hurt your partner and make them feel like a punished child. This is why a plan must be in place to prevent spending sprees from happening in the first place. Remember, you can't punish your partner for having the symptoms of an illness, but you can help them prevent the symptoms by becoming more aware. Having separate checking accounts is a very good idea for any couple where one partner has bipolar disorder, but wait to discuss this issue if your partner is just ending a serious mood swing or a stay in the hospital.

A relationship that treats bipolar disorder first must be honest, and when your partner is stable, they have to see that they need to protect themselves and you from their bipolar disorder spending problem. Sometimes, there is no way you can avoid hurting your partner's pride. Your partner may also feel very frightened that you are making financial changes. Talk about this. Hopefully, by creating the treatment plan discussed in the first seven chapters, your partner will see that this has to be done to protect both of your futures. It helps if you honestly reassure your partner that you must do this for financial reasons and that it's not personal. It's just about money. Understand that this will be hard for your partner. It hurts and you may need to have a lot of compassion for what they are going through.

Hopefully you are now clearer on where your partner stands regarding work and money. The next section will help you talk to and work with your partner about the issues you both face.

Tips to Help Your Partner

If your partner can't work right now or has had trouble working in the past, there are many things you can do to help your partner find a way to become productive and fulfilled in life. If your partner has a history of financial problems, you now have some ideas on how to help the situation. Here are some tips to get you started on helping your partner find stability around work and money. Anytime you have a new idea of your own, write it in your journal and, if appropriate, add it to your "What Works" list for each mood swing.

Forget the guilt trips: You may be adding to your partner's guilt about their work situation and not know it. Once you answer the questions in this chapter you will have some idea of what your partner can or can't do and you can take it from there. It won't work if you try to force your partner to find employment and make some money. If work makes your partner sick, help them find alternatives. Be honest with each other about the work and money issues so that the pressure and the guilt are turned off and planning for the future is turned on.

Face the truth: Disability is a reality for some people with bipolar disorder. It's very possible that the treatment plan you established in the early chapters of this book will help your partner go back to work or teach them how to find a less stressful job. That has happened for many. But it's also a reality that the normal fast-paced work environment (an office with other people) may never work for your partner.

Redefine success: Work problems in the present don't always predict work problems in the future. It may be that your partner just needs to find work that doesn't make them ill. If you were overly concerned in the past with how much money your partner could make or how powerful their job could be, you may have to change. Success can be measured in many other ways than financial rewards and work accomplishments.

Foster self-esteem outside of work: Help your partner learn to measure their self-worth by what kind of person they are, not as a function of what they do. Can you do this yourself? Can you help your partner become a success in whatever they do outside of work? One way to start this is to focus on what your partner does well and let them know you appreciate it.

Is work worth it? It may be that your partner will remain ill until a certain project is finished. If your partner can accept this and keep working, it may be possible to succeed with the obligation. Your partner will then have to decide if the work is worth getting sick. How much bipolar disorder can they live with? What is the trade-off for work and money? What are the realities of their work? Some people can handle the mood swings that a particular project brings on, so long as they know the swings will end once the project ends. For other people, the stress may be too much.

Look for work alternatives: Your partner may need to find alternative, less-stimulating work. Talk honestly with each other about your financial future. What are the realities if your partner needs to find less-stimulating work?

Be very clear on how you feel about money issues: How do you feel if you will be the sole income earner in the relationship? This must be discussed—not to make your partner feel guilty, but to take care of yourself. Are there things you need from your partner in order to continue with your current financial arrangement? Do you feel your partner does what they can to stay well, or do you feel as if you are being used to support someone who doesn't want to work?

Talk honestly with each other: Work and money can be taboo topics. Don't let this happen. It's easy to live in a dream world even when the bills are not getting paid. Know where you are with money and be very realistic with each other about the future. Talk about how your new treatment plan may open new doors to financial stability.

Change your priorities: Many people talk about putting friends and family before work, but few practice it. Can you and your partner accept the idea that work may not come first for some people with bipolar disorder and that this may be a gift instead of a curse? Ultimately, all decisions about work or other lifestyle choices are arbitrary. One of the biggest traps is believing that you "must" stick with certain jobs. This is not a matter of "musts," it's a matter of making decisions that make sense in the long run.

Understand the role of pressure: Pressure is a big trigger for many people with bipolar disorder. A job with little to no pressure may be better for your partner than a creative job filled with deadlines and obligations. This has nothing to do with your partner's abilities or intelligence. It has to do with the way their brain functions. Pressure changes your partner's brain and the sooner you accept this and learn to help your partner avoid or deal with pressure, the more stable your partner can become, and the more stable your relationship will be.

Take responsibility: You have eyes and you can see what your partner is buying. Now that you know the symptoms of this illness, you will have to take responsibility if you allow your partner to float into another episode and then get upset with them when the work and money problems become acute. In the same way, your partner has a responsibility to use the treatment plan to stay stable, but if the illness takes over, it really is up to you to take charge. Can you live with this responsibility?

Make lemonade: If your partner has serious work and financial limitations, help them turn their limitations into opportunities. Once you both shift your focus away from work and making money, there is a chance to grow in many other areas, including self-awareness, becoming a better partner or friend, taking a class, taking care of children, or joining groups. It really can make a difference when you change your perspective.

At first, the suggestions in this chapter may seem a bit overwhelming. But when you realize that most couples have issues about work and money, it's only natural that couples in which one partner has bipolar disorder may have some really *big* issues regarding work and money. Give yourself plenty of time to start work on the ideas in this chapter. Start with constructing your partner's work and financial histories and go on from there, step by baby step. Change really can take place. You just have to be patient and hopeful even through the tough times.

REALITY CHECK

If your partner remains unstable and continues to live with untreated bipolar disorder, their work and money problems will continue. These problems will not disappear just because time passes. As optimistic as this chapter sounds, the reality may be that you are in a financial situation that can't be fixed using the techniques described in this chapter.

You may choose to get out of the situation entirely in order to protect yourself financially. You may also have to take steps to protect your children's financial future. If you're approaching retirement age yourself and you feel that your future is insecure as long as your partner is out of work or spending heavily, do what it takes to protect yourself. The choices are up to you.

It's prudent to be realistic but optimistic about your partner's future concerning work and money. Your financial affairs really can change once you and your partner learn how to prevent mood swings. This takes work and constant vigilance, but you can do it.

CHAPTER TWELVE

S-E-X

There is nothing romantic about bipolar disorder.

If your relationship has sexual problems because of bipolar disorder, you're not alone. Issues may include your partner's lack of sexuality when depressed, excessive sexuality when manic, a general lack of affection toward you when they're too ill to have a fulfilling and intimate relationship, and the side effects of medications. You may also have problems that include feeling obligated to have sex with your partner when they are ill or having to deal with the physical changes that some medications can cause. Many couples without illness issues also have sexual problems, so it's no wonder that the sexual problems caused by bipolar disorder can seem overwhelming.

Although it may seem impossible at this time, as you learned in the early chapters of this book, many bipolar disorder symptoms can be modified with a holistic treatment plan. This includes sexual symptoms as well. Your goal is to help your partner get well enough so that your natural and passionate sexual feelings can return. This takes time, but it is possible.

Treat Bipolar Disorder First

By now, you are probably used to reading that you and your partner must treat bipolar disorder first if you want to have a stable relationship. Nowhere is this more important than in the area of sexual relations. You can get counseling, try Tantric yoga practices, read books, and watch erotic movies for years without results if the underlying reason for your sexual problems is caused by bipolar disorder mood swings and/or medications. In other words, if bipolar disorder is the cause of your sexual problems, then you must stabilize the bipolar disorder if you want a fulfilling sexual relationship. The good news is that with a new treatment plan, your sexual life has a good chance to improve dramatically.

The following section will cover many of the sexual problems you may be facing in your relationship because of bipolar disorder. Each problem is a normal one, and you're not alone if you have all of them. The solution is to find ways to treat bipolar disorder so that the problems can improve when the mood swings are stabilized.

Medications

My antidepressant doesn't affect my sex drive. In fact, it makes me want to have sex even more because I'm feeling better. The problem is that I can't have an orgasm. I want to feel well, but if it means that I can't have a good sexual relationship with my partner that only makes me more depressed.

Many bipolar disorder medications can cause your partner to have sexual functioning problems. The best way to determine if this is the case is to recall how your partner was before taking the medications. Trouble reaching orgasm and low sexual drive are two common side effects of medications, and there are medical solutions for these problems. Your partner should talk to their doctor about different medications, and both women and men should get their testosterone levels checked to make sure they are normal.

Some people may have to wait it out and be sure they are sufficiently stable to warrant changing medications. Whatever you and your partner decide to do, remember that the situation doesn't have to be permanent. It may take time for your partner to stabilize with your new treatment plan, but once this takes place, you will be able to discuss medications with your partner's doctor. Let the doctor know that your relationship needs to be sexually active.

It may be hard for you not to take medications side effects personally, but it's important for you to understand that these side effects are not a reflection of how your partner feels about you. Talk to your partner about your feelings. If the medications are affecting your partner's sexual behavior, let your partner know that you want to find other ways to be intimate until the problem is solved.

Depression

All thoughts about sex literally leave my mind when I'm depressed. I have no desire to read a book or go to a movie, much less do all of the preparations that are needed to have sex. It just seems like so many steps to go through and I get overwhelmed and feel pressured. It's hard enough just to make it through the day. I know my partner wants and needs sex from me, but how do I find the energy?

Depression and sex are often polar opposites. If you can remember this, it will help you understand why your partner may not want sex when ill. Depression causes a profound feeling of dissatisfaction with everything in life, including the body and its functions. This has nothing to do with you. It has nothing to do with how good you are in bed or how attractive you are. It has everything to do with depression. When your partner is depressed, having sex can seem impossible.

It makes sense that if you create a holistic treatment plan for depression and help your partner to end the symptoms of depression, your sex life can get much better. It's normal if you worry about your own sexual attractiveness. You can work on these feelings by remembering that bipolar disorder has specific symptoms and one of these symptoms is depression, which often causes a lack of sexual desire. Your partner's behavior when depressed is about the illness and not about you.

It often happens that when their sex drive is practically nonexistent because of depression, your partner may just need a little encouragement to start feeling sexual again. If you set time apart from your ordinary tasks for nurturing intimacy, and you slowly start touching each other, you may be able to stoke the fire that is just burning low.

Mania

When my partner was first in the hospital he was very, very manic and psychotic. He was hypersexual and made a lot of sexual comments to the staff and anyone else who was in the room. It was very embarrassing at first. It was so unlike him. He never talked this way in public in all of the years we've been together. I was mortified. I wish the staff had talked to me about this more and helped me to understand what was going on. Finally, I decided I had to deal with this in a different way. One day, after he had yelled, "Nice ass!" to every single woman who walked by his room, I just started laughing. It really was funny. Some of the women were skinny, some were very large. One woman was about seventy-five years old! I laughed a lot. Right then I realized that this wasn't him making these comments, it was bipolar disorder talking. And I just had to believe that this behavior would stop once the medicines started working. It did stop and it has never come back. We can laugh a lot about it now. For me, it's the only way to deal with this part of bipolar disorder.

You may enjoy having sex with your partner while they're manic. Mania can cause wild and uninhibited sexual behavior. The problem is that this uninhibited sexuality frequently means that your partner may feel very sexual toward someone other than yourself. This can be a huge problem for relationships, and the only way to deal with it is to prevent the manic swings from going too far.

Just as people who are depressed are not interested in having sex, people who are manic often think constantly of nothing but sex. It's one of the symptoms of mania. To someone experiencing a manic episode, people look good enough to eat. Period. If you can accept this, you will be able to let go of past behavior. What happened in the past is past. This doesn't mean that your partner's promiscuous behavior should continue into the future. But it does mean you can accept past bipolar disorder behavior as symptoms of the illness and move on to create a future where unacceptable sexual behavior caused by bipolar disorder is prevented.

If your partner refuses to take medicine and continues to be manic, you have a big decision to make. Mania is a serious mood swing that can't always be treated at home. It's quite different from depression. If you want a happy, healthy, and monogamous relationship with your partner, and your partner has a history of serious manic episodes, you will have to insist that your partner stay on their medications. This means that you must have a section of your treatment plan devoted to medications. Mania and inappropriate sexual behavior often go together. The truth of the matter is that if your partner is often manic and refuses help, there will be sexual issues for you to deal with.

Sexually transmitted diseases: If your partner is having manic sex outside of your relationship, there is a good chance it's unprotected sex. You must face this reality and protect yourself if you are in this situation. Don't be naïve when it comes to your own sexual health. The costs are too high.

Psychosis

When my partner came home from the hospital after a very serious psychotic episode he wanted to have sex. I was still unsure that he was well. I felt I didn't know who he was. This whole bipolar thing was so new to me. I felt uncomfortable and scared. And he wanted sex. His hair was a lot longer than when he went in the hospital, and I swear his body was completely different. It was all soft and rounded. I knew he was still the same person I loved—somewhere inside of him. But I still saw him as that incoherent person he was in the hospital. It was as though I had to have sex with a helpless person.

Psychosis is often terrifying. It's completely understandable that when your partner has had a psychotic episode and then wants to have sex, you may be scared and hesitant. Who is that person in there? Is your partner really better? Will your partner say those scary things or make those scary faces again? Will they accuse you of having had an affair if you show an interest in having sex? The first time these kinds of things happen you may feel as if your sex life will be affected forever.

In reality, life often returns to normal as though the episode had never even happened. There is an adjustment period for both of you after a serious episode, but life really can get back to normal. Medications and your treatment plan can then prevent serious psychotic episodes.

Lack of Attraction

These days my partner isn't the person I fell in love with. I don't know how I'm supposed to have sex with someone who has changed so much. I was attracted to her for certain reasons and now those reasons seem to be gone. Will they come back? I have no idea. It's like getting into bed with someone you love and desire and then waking up in the morning with a completely different person.

What if you are the one who has sexual problems in the relationship? What if your partner still wants to have sex with you, but you are no longer interested? It's hard to keep your attraction alive for someone who is often sick. If your partner is depressed and no longer takes care of personal hygiene, or gains a lot of weight due to medications, or can't reach orgasm due to medications, you may find that your sex drive simply disappears. What do you want to do about this?

Is it easier just to keep quiet about your feelings and not make waves? Or do you think of looking elsewhere for sex? The price you pay may not be obvious now, but how will you feel in five or ten years when you realize that you lost the best years of your sexual life and didn't do anything about it? Your sexual feelings matter whether your partner is sick or not. It's up to you to find a balance between what you need and what your partner can give. Once again, your new treatment plan can make a big difference in how you feel about your partner, so it may be that time will take care of the problem.

Once you feel more compassion for what your partner goes through and you start to play a role in their healing, you may feel more like starting up a sexual partnership again. Or, it might be that the two of you met when your partner was manic, and the sex was wonderful. It's difficult for most couples to recreate this kind of manic sex and it may become an unrealistic dream that you both want to come true again. The problem is that the sexual behaviors that accompany mania also come with other manic symptoms. The trade-off is not worth the great sex. If this describes your situation, you and your partner will have to find a way to reconnect in a more stable way.

When It's Over

I've decided to leave my partner. I'm not sure how to do this or how she will handle it, but I can't go on like this anymore. I have a life too. I didn't choose to live with this illness and since it's not being taken care of I have to leave. We haven't had sex in a long time. She pushes me away when I try to touch her. My whole life revolves around her mood swings. I want a life for myself.

There are some relationships that can't be repaired. If sex is important to you and you haven't had sex for years and feel that your partner will not want sex in the future, you may have to make the decision to leave. There is only so much work you can do on a relationship. Worries about bipolar disorder may have made you stay in your relationship longer than you normally would, and this may mean that leaving will be very hard for you. When it comes to your life, you really do have choices. Sometimes love and sexual interest simply die. This happens even when both partners are well. It may be hard for you to understand why your sexual interest in your partner is gone. What matters is that you be honest with yourself about how you feel, what you want, and what you need to do.

Forgiveness

My partner told me he had sex with someone else. We were in his hospital room and he told me in front of all of the staff and my mother. I went out into the hall and crumpled into a heap and felt like screaming. I was so humiliated. How could he do this to me and then tell me with all of those people around? He was psychotic when he told me and I thought that maybe he was making it up, but he wasn't. Though this was a truly terrible experience, I finally got some perspective. Six months before he went to the hospital, he had a one-night stand when he became manic on a business trip. He didn't even know what bipolar disorder was at the time. He kept it to himself because he didn't want to hurt me. It finally all came out when he got too sick to control what he was saying. He was so full of pain. He had never even thought of cheating before and then it happened to him and he had no idea why. Now we know and I can let it go. It never happened again and I don't feel it was him at all. It was bipolar disorder and he suffered so much because of this. Why should I make him suffer any more?

Maybe your partner had sex with another person while manic and you feel you can no longer trust them. Maybe it was more than a one-time fling, and for you that is not about bipolar disorder, but about something personal. What is important is that you must get a clear idea of why your partner had sex outside of your relationship. Was it due to bipolar disorder? Did it happen before or after your partner began medications?

It may seem impossible to forgive your partner, but if you want to rekindle a fulfilling sexual relationship, you must forgive. Anger, blame, and punishment are not good bedfellows. A transgression may happen only once, but human beings have an amazing capacity to punish the person responsible for that event for the rest of their lives. Don't allow this to be your model. Forgive your partner when the wrongful behavior is directly related to or caused by bipolar disorder. Your lives together can be different now that you have a holistic treatment plan.

When you let go of the past and focus on the present, you have the opportunity to create a better sex life in the future. If your partner made mistakes when they were untreated, but they are now taking medications and are willing to work with you on a new treatment plan, then accept the present reality. Let go and move forward.

On the other hand, living with someone who has sex outside of a committed relationship may not be something you want in your life. Talk to your partner about this. Tell your partner how you feel about this and ask your partner how they feel. You may find that your partner's sense of guilt is enormous. A treatment plan that prevents mania from reoccurring can be the solution to this problem.

Walking the Tightrope

I love my partner. I really do. But I no longer feel that we can have a sexual relationship. I've thought about putting an ad in the personals just to find someone in a similar position, so that I could at least have some physical contact. We haven't had sex for so long. This has gone on for a few years now. I really don't want to leave my partner. We have children and a life together. But his sex drive is zero and I'm too young to live without sex. How do I deal with this when I don't want to hurt him, but I'm only human?

How do you get what you need without hurting your partner? This is quite a tightrope you have to walk. You are only human and you want to have sex, but you know that your partner can't or won't have sex right now. Your partner even may feel so guilty about being sick they just give up and tell you to have sex with someone else.

As discussed in chapter 10, this issue can bring up a lot of emotions. This is when you need some outside help with your feelings. You don't want to make quick decisions that will hurt your future, so this is the time to think carefully and give the situation some time. Your new treatment plan may make so much difference that your sex life will get back on track and the problem will take care of itself. But until then, get some help. Talk to a trained therapist who has some experience in dealing with your particular problem. Help your partner get better and then wait and see if your sex life gets better.

Don't let your sexual frustration build until it explodes and you either have an affair or leave your partner because of unresolved sexual problems. Don't let these feelings sneak up on you to the point that you suddenly announce to your partner one day that you can't take it anymore. Take care of the problem now. The following paragraph suggests how it might be possible for you to talk with your partner about this issue.

I love you and I want to have a fun and interesting sexual relationship with you. It's important to me to have this sexual connection in our relationship. I'm hoping that the new treatment plan we will create together will help you get well enough so that we can connect again sexually. How do you feel about this? You can be honest. I need to know what you're thinking. Then we can work together on the treatment plan honestly.

Once you have a good idea of how your partner feels about this issue, you can make a reasonable decision.

Tips for Improving Your Sex Life

The following suggestions are tools you can use to help improve your sex life. The ideas outlined below can be added to your "What Works" list.

Know the common sexual symptoms of bipolar disorder: As stated at the beginning of this chapter, sexual issues are common symptoms of bipolar disorder. They may feel incredibly personal and upsetting, but they are symptoms that can be treated—if you treat bipolar disorder first. Here are some of the very common symptoms your partner may have depending on what mood swing they are experiencing.

- Feels no sexual desire

- Feels that sex is too much work, and can't understand why sex is so important to you

- Has stopped caring about their physical appearance

- Responds to your advances with statements like "Can't you just leave me alone?"

- Doesn't want to be touched or turns away or becomes startled when you try to touch them

- Doesn't want kissing or touching; has trouble with you being in their "personal" space

- Stays in bed all day, but not for sex

- Changes completely from who they once were sexually and you have no idea why

- Changes suddenly into a sexual maniac who wants you to try new and kinky things in bed

- Talks dirty or seems constantly turned on

- Touches you more often and touches other people more often

- Wants sex all of the time and is never tired (At first you love this, and then it starts to worry or scare you.)

- Looks at other people sexually or makes sexual comments

- Does something very sexually inappropriate, but doesn't seem worried or ashamed about it at all

- Starts to disregard you and your feelings

- Has sex with someone else and doesn't seem to care that you know

If a list can be compiled of very specific sexual behaviors that accompany bipolar disorder, doesn't it make sense that when your partner engages in these behaviors it's not because they want to hurt you? Your partner does these things because of bipolar disorder. This is hard to understand and it may seem impossible for you to deal with because sex is so personal, but the point is that excessive sexual thoughts and actions during a manic episode are symptoms, like not being able to sleep, talking too fast, or spending money wastefully. When your partner wears a bathrobe and stays in bed all day because of depression, it has nothing to do with you. It has to do with the symptoms of an illness.

The solution is to treat the symptoms specifically and then prevent bipolar disorder from going too far. This is done through medications and your treatment plan. What's important is for you to be aware of the sexual symptoms of bipolar disorder so that you don't take the behavior personally.

Talk with your partner: If the topic of sex is taboo, your problems can't be solved. Think of what you want to say and what you need, and sit and talk with your partner and make long-term plans for improving your sex life. Talk about your goals for six months and a year from now. Yes, you can have sexual goals in your relationship. The point is to communicate and compromise. Ask your partner the following questions and let the conversation go from there. How do you feel about our sex life? Do you think the medications are affecting you sexually? I know there are times you don't want to have sex, but I do. What can we do about this? What can we do to be together intimately that doesn't involve sex? What do you need right now, and how long do you think you'll feel this way?

If you have trouble saying what you mean and feel, then write out the questions and let your partner read them. There are many ways to start a discussion. As with any talk you have with your partner, make sure they don't feel attacked and let them know that you come from a position of love.

Ask for help: There is help for sexual problems. One way to get help is to visit a health care professional who understands bipolar disorder and sexuality. Or you can see a sex therapist and explain your situation. Learn alternative ways to be intimate. Look for medications that don't have side effects that affect your partner's sex drive. Once again, remember that you have to treat bipolar disorder first, even when you search outside your relationship for help. It may be that the people you turn to for help will want to deal only with emotional issues. It's important that you make it clear that your problems are not necessarily emotional but instead are related to very clear bipolar disorder symptoms.

Take advantage of the good times: Have fun when your partner is well. If you have a good sex life when your partner is well, focus on that and remind your partner of the good times when they do get ill. Make the good times your goal. It's so easy to forget the joyful times when a person is in the middle of a mood swing. It's easy to focus on all that is wrong in a relationship. It helps if you can maintain a balance. Create intimate times that reinforce your relationship. See chapter 15 for more details on this topic.

Couples can and do recover from the sexual problems caused by bipolar disorder. If you are clear on what you both want and need and understand which problems are caused by the illness, it makes sense that if you can learn to modify and stop the bipolar disorder itself, your sexual situation has a great chance to improve.

REALITY CHECK

It's not okay to have long-term sexual problems because of bipolar disorder. You have desires and needs. If you deny yourself these desires, you're cheating yourself and you may regret it later. Take care of the problem now. Use the tools you have learned in this book to create a treatment plan that will help you get your sex life back on track. It doesn't help your partner get well if you force yourself to live without sex when you want sex. You have rights in your relationship. What do you need to do to help your partner get well so that you can have a joyous sex life? As long as your partner is ill, it may be hard for you to have a fulfilling sexual relationship. Can you live with this reality if your partner can't or doesn't get well? Be honest with yourself.

If after six months of trying the new treatment plan, your partner still doesn't want sex and you don't think they will want it in the future, then think about what you need to do for yourself. This means that you may have to ask yourself if the problem is related to bipolar disorder or if it's a lack of sexual compatibility in your relationship. Illness often masks the real problems in your relationship. The only way to know for sure is to examine how it was before your partner got sick. If your partner has always been ill, you will have to wait and see what sex is like when your partner has been stabilized after using the treatment plan.

When you treat bipolar disorder first, there is a good chance that your sexual relationship can improve. It may take some time and it will be work, but change is possible.

CHAPTER THIRTEEN

What about You?

*It's difficult to have a loving and intimate relationship
when one partner is a caretaker and the other is a patient.*

Do you sometimes feel that you have a child instead of a partner? You may
sometimes wonder why you are in the relationship at all if it only means
taking care of someone who is ill. Maybe bipolar disorder cast you in a role
you have no desire to play, but you see no way out because there is no one
else to play the role and the person with the illness needs help. You may be
asking yourself, *What about me and what I want from life?* Well, what about
you?

What do you want and need? Now that you and your partner have the
tools needed to treat bipolar disorder first, it's time for you to become clear
about the role you want to play in your relationship. You may feel that bipolar disorder has taken your choice from you. When your partner is ill, you
may feel you *have* to play the role of caretaker. You *have* to hold things
together. Well, the truth is *No, you don't.* Everything you do is a choice.
Whether it's going to the hospital every day, helping your partner remember
to take their medications, or putting up with constant mood swings, there
is a choice. It may not be an easy choice or even what you consider a moral
choice, but you do have the power of choice. If you choose to stay in a

relationship with someone who is often sick, it's important that you at least know who you are and why you do what you do.

In Sickness and in Health

A great many of the people who are married to a partner with bipolar disorder say that, if they had known ahead of time what they would be getting into, they would not have married that person. This lets you know you are not alone in the sometimes tremendous struggle you face when it comes to living with someone who has bipolar disorder. As you read in the first chapter, so much is expected of you when your partner gets sick, but your partner probably is the one who gets all of the attention. Your fear, pain, worry, and frustration are rarely treated. You are not the sick person. You are simply supposed to take care of the sick person.

You may wonder if this is what it means to be in a relationship. Well, is it? Maybe that is what it means to be in a doctor-patient relationship, but not a normal romantic relationship. "In sickness and in health" can be hard to take when there is no health. You often have to be a financial planner, a confidant, a therapist, a nurse, a parent, a provider, and a lover all at one time. This is a lot to ask of you and very few can do it all. So don't despair if it's wearing you out. It wears everyone out.

Answer this question honestly: *What is my role in this relationship right now and how do I feel about it?* Did you say caretaker, babysitter, nurse, helper, friend, confidant, or therapist? All of these are important roles when someone is ill, but if the roles are unbalanced or the illness goes on too long, there will be problems. Most people in loving relationships are willing to do almost anything for their partner during a crisis, but most life crises are time limited. There is often a rude awakening when one begins to really see the long-term nature of bipolar disorder. An illness like cancer may speed you into action, but you probably assume it will end, either with death or with recovery. What does it mean to you to know that bipolar disorder is lifelong? Yes, the illness can be managed very successfully, but it will not go away. This means you will have to find a way to balance the many roles you will be asked to play to help your partner stay stable.

Balance is definitely possible. To find it, you must address your caretaking role. Some people can handle the caretaking role and others can't.

The solution is to find a balance you can live with. Read over the following caretaking descriptions and decide where you fit in.

The Supercaretaker

I'm used to doing everything anyway. It was easy for me to take over when my partner got sick. I make sure he takes his meds and gets up in the morning. I'm patient when he's sick, and I understand that I have to do almost everything around the house. But I must admit I'm getting a little resentful. I also feel like these thoughts are unkind. I want to help him, but can't he help himself when he's depressed? I feel like his doctor, friend, and therapist, but I certainly don't feel like we're a romantic couple anymore. How did this happen? I realize that I'm more like a mother now than a lover.

Many of you choose to be the caretaker in your relationships. In our culture this role is often expected of women, although there are many men who play the role easily as well. It may be that you want to feel needed and admired. Or maybe your mother or father played a similar role when you were growing up. The problem with playing the caretaker for too long, however, is that you lose who you are. You have to ask yourself if you are willing to be like Mother Teresa for the duration of your relationship or if there is something more you need.

Romantic relationships are different from other relationships. It may be okay to be the caretaker of a chronically sick child or an aging parent, but constant caretaking can cause trouble in a romantic relationship. The main problem for people who live with a person whose illness is not yet successfully managed is that there are so many crisis situations that it becomes natural to simply react and deal with what comes day to day and never really have the time to ask, *What am I doing with my life?* If you identify with the supercaretaker, answer the following questions in your journal: *Do I really have to do all of this, or is this something that just happened and I'm going along with it? Am I being a martyr? Am I taking care of myself? What do I need and what does our relationship need in order to be happy, healthy, and stable?*

The remainder of this chapter will help you to clarify your answers to these questions. You might also want to consider that although you may be comfortable with the caretaking role, it may not be the best thing for your partner. It may prevent them from making the changes they need to make in order to get well. Once you start your new treatment plan, your partner should start becoming more self-sufficient and you will no longer need to be the supercaretaker. You will have to be ready to change roles.

The Anticaretaker

Maybe you don't identify with the supercaretaker role. On the opposite end of the spectrum are the people who have no desire at all to be a caretaker in a relationship. These people are often judged as cold or unhelpful, but, in reality, they may have simply been forced to play a role they can't and don't want to play.

I've been suicidal a few times in the past few years. I reached for my partner and every single time he brushed me away like you would dirt from your shirt. I love him but can't need him. He becomes so angry when I'm sick. He can't give pity or empathy to anyone who's ill. He sees it as a weakness.

Does this describe you? Are you in a dilemma because you love your partner but don't want the responsibility of taking care of them? Maybe you just don't like to deal with illness and you certainly don't want to be the one your partner needs when sick. Or, you may be a bit harsh on your partner when they're ill. This puts a strain on your relationship and your desire to leave may grow stronger. And then you feel guilty.

Although you're not willing to play the caretaking role, it may be you will have to play it anyway. When the mood swings are active, you are constantly faced with bipolar disorder whether you want to be or not. The good news is that your new treatment plan can give you the tools you need to find more compassion for your partner and can also help you see where your partner truly needs your help. If these are big issues for you, you have a lot of thinking to do about your future.

You may not want to write about this subject in your journal, but it will help you to at least get clear on what you are willing to do in the future. Ask yourself what role you are willing to play in the new treatment plan. Write a list of what you are willing to do and be absolutely clear with yourself.

The reality is that there will be times when your partner will need caretaking, and if you are clear on what you can and can't do, your partner can learn when to ask you for help and when to go to others. You may also have to cultivate compassion for what your partner needs and make changes to your own behavior if you want to stay in the relationship. The "What Works" list can help you find ways to help your partner effectively without playing the caretaking role. Here are some examples of how you might talk with your partner about this dilemma:

I know I get really angry when you have mood swings. I'm working on this and I'm willing to help you now. It will help me if you write down what you need on the "What Works" list. Just let me know exactly what I can do to help when you get sick. I promise I'll read the list and do what I can when you need help.

Please try to understand that helping you when you're sick doesn't come easily for me. It brings up a lot of feelings that I don't like. I'll try to do what I can because I love you, but it will help me a lot if we can work together to find outside help so that I don't feel under so much pressure when you have mood swings.

Everyone gets tired eventually, even the supercaretaker. For many people, being a caretaker 24/7 goes on for too long, until the caretaker finally collapses. This collapse can take the form of physical exhaustion, depression, or just being fed up. Often, by this time any love the caretaker used to feel has evaporated and the relationship is held together out of guilt or a sense of obligation. One outcome may be that the caretaker quits and just leaves. Sometimes this is entirely understandable. Even if you thrive on caretaking and feel that it was a role you were meant to play, you too can take only so much before you burn out. And if you are the type who runs from the caretaking role, you too will have to beware of this collapse.

You Have Options

As you have learned from this book, there are options even for those of you who have no desire to deal with bipolar disorder on a daily basis. Yes, if you are in a relationship with someone who has bipolar disorder, there will be times when you absolutely must be a caretaker. Your goal is to see that this is a temporary accommodation and not a permanent role that you have to fill for the remainder of your relationship. If you're a supercaretaker, start taking care of yourself more and your partner less, so that they can learn to take care of themselves by using the new treatment plan.

If you're not sure how to break out of your current role, find a therapist or a self-help group that specializes in helping caretakers find a balance. Your partner's doctor may be able to help you find a support group. This will help you deal with the resentments being a caretaker may bring up in you. Getting your emotions out in the open and learning that they are the same feelings that other people in your position feel can help you move forward to find new solutions. The emotions you're experiencing are more normal than you think. The following section will give you some ideas on how to create a balance between being a partner and a caretaker.

Know yourself: You can't be all things to everyone. You don't want to lose yourself. Use the questions in this chapter to get a clear picture of the role you now play, and ask yourself whether this is truly what you want and whether it is the best thing for your partner.

Help your partner find independence: If your partner is overly dependent on you to stay well, they may have a hard time finding stability on their own. You have to help your partner learn to take care of themselves with your love and help. Don't allow bipolar disorder to define your relationship. Caretaking is not a foundation for a relationship and doesn't create a loving and stable future.

Establish clear and firm limits: An alternative to the all-or-nothing approach of getting burned out is to rethink your role in terms of establishing limits. At the heart of this may be the necessity to adopt a view that says, *I do care and I will help, but I'm not devoting my whole life to rescuing.*

"Rescuing" really means believing that you have to be responsible for fixing your partner. An antirescue perspective says, *I'm not responsible. I care, and I'll help, but ultimately I don't assume full responsibility for fixing everything.* This involves a humble acknowledgment of your limitations as a human being. It's okay for you to be human and have limits—even when it seems that your partner desperately needs you.

Focus on prevention: Looking to and planning for the future can make all of the difference in your relationship. Whenever you start to take care of your partner, ask yourself if this will help them or yourself in the future. Try to structure your treatment plan so that your partner is the one to make the changes instead of you having to do everything. You now have new tools that can help your partner modify and prevent mood swings. This will naturally diminish your caretaking role.

Create an equal relationship: It will help a great deal if you can create a relationship where you're equal partners. This must take into consideration what your partner can actually do. If you're doing 90 percent of the work, yours is not a balanced relationship. Set limits. Decide what you will do if your partner can't or won't change. Also, be aware that you may be so used to the caretaking role that you aren't even aware of your own behaviors. Have you taken your partner out of the equation because they can't work or because they're often sick? Does your partner feel worthless or helpless? Have you contributed to this? Have you even talked with your partner about this? It's normal if this happens, but it needs to be corrected so that your relationship can become more equal.

It's not permanent: The caretaker role doesn't have to be permanent. In fact, it needs to end at some point. It's okay for a crisis or even for a year, but after that it creates an unequal balance in a relationship. It affects romance, sex, and the relationship as a whole. You have a new treatment plan now and you can do what it takes to get yourself back on track. Your goal is to learn how to leave the caretaking role while still being an important part of your partner's treatment plan.

Caretaking and sexuality: There is nothing sexy about the patient-caretaker relationship. If your sex life is nonexistent when you're taking care of your partner, it may be that you will have to leave the caretaking to someone else, so that you can reestablish yourself as your partner's lover, not their caretaker.

You may feel that the above suggestions look great on paper but will be hard to do because you have so many responsibilities already. One way to help yourself with this process is to ask others for help.

Asking for Help

The secrecy and shame surrounding bipolar disorder can place a heavy burden on your relationship. It's very important that you and your partner learn to look outside of your relationship for help to avoid overloading each other so much that the relationship either becomes abnormally unbalanced or doesn't survive. It's true that when your partner is ill, it's very difficult to find balance. Even if you have many responsibilities in your life, such as paying the bills and taking care of children or perhaps an ill parent, the burden still falls on you when your partner is sick. So what can you do about this situation?

Often, especially when the focus is on keeping your partner alive, you may think that you have to do it all yourself because you have no one available to help. It's probably true that no one readily helps you with these issues. But the reality is that you can't do it all. You need attention and support to keep things going smoothly when your partner is ill. In other words, you have to ask for help. It's amazing what asking for help can do for your peace of mind.

It Is Human Not to Know What to Do

Your friends and family probably have no idea what you need when you're in crisis. It may seem to you that they should know. They should know when you're in pain and that you need them when your partner is sick. Unfortunately, people are not mind readers. In fact, many people are not intuitive at all. When your partner is ill, you may feel abandoned by your friends and family and wonder why they are not there for you when you need them.

The truth is that, despite very good intentions, most people who don't live with this illness will never be able to fully appreciate what you're going through. Often, this is the chief reason you become the major caretaker in your partner's life. This situation can change when you accept that it's not natural for most people to know what to do about illness. You will have to learn whom to turn to when you need help, and you will have to teach them what you need.

Open up to your friends and family: Ask your friends and family to read this book so they can understand what you go through. Be honest and ask for help: "I can't handle the bills this month. Can we sit down and go through them together? I need help with the kids when my partner is in the hospital. Can you help me? I can't do the housework right now. I'm overwhelmed with everything." You have to swallow your pride and tell people the truth. It's the only way to get help. It's also important to remember that though you may think your family is the natural place to turn for help in a crisis, it may be that they're not equipped emotionally to help you. They may be able to offer love, but not the help you need.

Choose the right people: *When my partner almost died after a suicide attempt, most of the people in my life just left me alone. I couldn't believe it. I was alone most nights when he was in the hospital. His family lived in another country and our friends just seemed to disappear when I needed them. Then I got a call from a person I hardly knew. She asked me out to dinner and talked to me about my partner and the hospital and everything. I couldn't believe this. It helped me so much. While everyone else acted as though things were normal and got on with their* *lives, this friend realized that nothing was normal for me. My life was a mess. I found out later that she spent half a year in the hospital when she lost her eye due to complications with diabetes. She understood! I learned from her that you have to ask the right people for help during a crisis. My family and friends love me. I know that. But they didn't know how to help me when I really needed them.*

Learn to turn to people who can actually help. It may be that you want assurance and help from your partner's doctor, but there is a good chance that you may not even get to meet your partner's doctor when they're in the hospital. The nurses are there, and they are often a great help, but they're busy and have seen this so many times they may forget it is the first time for you.

You may want to turn to the people who love you, but these are not always the best people to turn to for practical help and understanding. Use what they can offer and then find others who can give you what you need. Think of the people in your life who are good listeners. Who in your life offers good advice and an open mind? You don't have to be close to these people at all. You just have to be open to asking them out for coffee and asking for their help and support. You may be surprised at the new friendships you create by simply being honest about your feelings and needs.

Your partner's family can play many roles as well. Some may be able to help; others may not. Who called or sent you an e-mail? These are the people to turn to, even if you don't know them very well. Ask them for help so that you can work together as a team. Tell them what you need. Send a group e-mail to your friends. Let them know you need support and tell them exactly what you need. This will help to spread the burdens of your needs so that you don't overwhelm one person.

Look in unexpected places: It may be that your partner's illness has kept you from moving out on your own to find friends. It's a good idea to create bipolar disorder–free relationships. Find friends and people who are all about you and not about your partner. Talk with them about yourself and your life and let the bipolar disorder rest for awhile. Another good idea would be to help others who are in need and could use the compassion you have learned because you're a partner of someone with bipolar disorder. Use what you have learned to help others and take the focus off yourself.

Find a support group: Support groups can be a good source of help when you are not sure what to do. Unfortunately, they can also be a place where people vent and tell their horror stories with no solutions. Choose your support group very carefully. If you can find one that is moderated by a professional, this may provide the structure you need to move forward with the changes you want to make in your relationship. Don't limit yourself to bipolar disorder support groups for family members. Find one for caretakers as well. If you don't find the kind of support group you need, then create one of your own. Become vocal with what you need and create it for yourself. You can ask your partner's health care team for suggestions or call a local mental health organization.

Protect your own mental health: Depression in partners of people with bipolar disorder is common, just as it's common for those who care for people with chronic, severe illnesses, such as Alzheimer's disease. The paradox is that, because of the stigma often attached to mental illnesses, you as a caretaker of a person with bipolar disorder may not receive the support and compassion that someone who takes care of a person with a more obvious illness may receive. It's natural that you might feel depressed because of your situation. Much of this results from the helplessness you feel when you must play so many roles and be so many things in a relationship.

When people have cancer, they often keep their ability to reason even when their body is going through crises. When you have to help a partner who is no longer reasonable and may even be dangerous, it's natural that this would create depressive feelings. Know yourself and what you are capable of handling and then get help with the rest. How is your mental health these days?

It may be that there is so much focus on your partner that you're not taking care of your own mental health. What do you need to do to make sure that you're healthy? Write your ideas in your journal under the heading *What I need to do for myself right now.* If taking care of your partner's affairs really does become too much for you to handle, then you have every right to take a break. Tell your partner's family that they will have to take over for a while. If your partner still needs more of a structured living environment to get well, talk with their doctor about your options. Any change you decide to make does not have to be permanent and doesn't have to be something terrible, but you do have to stay well yourself.

Don't overwhelm others: When you're in a crisis, it helps if you can spread your needs around so that you don't overwhelm one or two people. Be aware of their feelings and observe their body language. You may be in crisis, but other people are not. Remember that the people who are helping you are coming from a different place than you do. For those who are more practical, ask for help with your caretaking issues and making changes. For those who are more emotionally open, ask for hugs and love. But don't ask for too much from too few. Some people may just want to be your friend and not your emergency confidant, while others can easily play the role of helping you through a crisis. The reality is that when you're in a severe crisis, you do need too much from others. You're desperate for answers and for help, and this can scare away many people. Try to remain calm in your neediness.

When your partner gets better: The first chapters of this book taught you to create a plan that prevents major bipolar disorder symptoms. They taught you that bipolar disorder can be a treatable illness and that you play a large role in your partner's health. This means that your roles may begin to change. This also means that your partner may start to get well. Your partner may become much more independent and you will have to learn to let go. Some people may have to learn to help more and judge less. Whatever role you currently play, simply be willing to look at it and change it if it's not healthy. You want to be happy and healthy yourself. Finding a role that you can play easily will help you achieve that balance. Relationships change all of the time and to survive the changes each partner has to be willing to play new roles. Will you be ready to play a different role when your partner starts to improve and stabilize, as many do?

So, What about You?

What have you learned about yourself from this chapter? You may have discovered new aspects to the role you now play, and you may have decided that you want to play a different role in the future. You may have learned that you don't have to be the caretaker all of the time when there is a preventive treatment plan in your partner's life. You now know you need to surround yourself with people who can help. You need support and love. You need to let your partner take more control over their own treatment. You have to let everyone know what you need, but you also have to make sure you understand that many people have no desire to play the role you want them to play. It's a balancing act that may be quite difficult at first. If you use the information presented in this chapter, you can create your own caretaking treatment plan, one in which you write out the specific things you are willing to do to help your partner, what you're not willing to do, and whom you will ask for help. When you find the right balance between taking care of yourself and asking others to do the rest, you will find it easier to realistically help your partner, without losing a part of yourself every time they get sick.

REALITY CHECK

You may find that the suggestions above simply don't work in your situation. Maybe your partner will continue to get sick and you will still be asked to play the caretaking role. Please understand that deciding to leave the relationship, especially if your partner's illness is affecting your children, is an honorable and self-preserving choice. Hope, encouragement, and new treatment tools can take you only so far. If your partner refuses to use the ideas in this book, and you know that you will have to continually take care of your partner when they're ill, you have the choice to leave. You may feel selfish or ashamed even if this decision is the only decision left for you to make. Feel these emotions and be honest with yourself about what you need. Get help with your decision and make sure you are taken care of so that the transition can be a healthy one.

Try not to turn into a caretaker or stop being a friend and lover just because your partner is ill. Once you and your partner create a treatment plan and learn how to manage bipolar disorder, you will not have to play the caretaker role anymore. You can be a partner, a friend, and a lover again, once the illness is managed properly.

CHAPTER FOURTEEN

The Hard Truths about Bipolar Disorder

There are many things about bipolar disorder that you may not like, but you will have to face them if you want to create a stable, healthy, and joyful relationship.

Bipolar disorder takes away so many dreams from a couple when it's not successfully managed. It may be that your dreams have been consistently trampled by the whims of this illness, but there is still hope. One way to face the future of your relationship is to get a clear picture about the realities of that future. You may want things to work out perfectly, where your partner is suddenly cured and your lives are what you dreamed they would be, but it may be more effective to know what you're truly up against, so that you can face your future with a clear head. The more accepting you are of the realities of this illness and how they may affect your relationship in the future, the easier it will be to either help your partner find stability or make the decision that you no longer want to stay in the relationship.

The material in this chapter will help you look at the big picture of your relationship and figure out what you need to do to move forward and create the relationship you have always wanted. Facing all the realities of bipolar disorder at once may be a lot to handle, but keep in mind that reading something doesn't mean you have to put it into effect immediately. Read through the ideas in this chapter, think about what you want to do first, and then file the other ideas away for the future.

The Past Hurts

Let go of the past. It hurts too much anyway, and there is nothing you can do to change it. This doesn't mean that it's okay for past behaviors to continue; it just means that you let them go and start over with your new treatment plan. What your partner did while ill is something you have to forgive and forget. If they're willing to try a new treatment plan and work with you on this issue, give them the benefit of your trust and love so that they know they are safe in the relationship as they try to heal. This will probably be hard on you. What your partner has done may still be terribly painful, and you may feel it isn't possible to forgive. It may seem as though you are expected to be without feelings, but that is not what this is about. This is about new beginnings. Your partner needs a new beginning and you do too.

Let your partner know that their bipolar disorder–influenced behavior is forgiven and then move on. Let your partner know that you're proud of them for trying a new treatment plan and that you want to work together to make sure the future is much more stable than the past. It can be done and it starts with you.

Acceptance and Loss

You may have lost a lot because of bipolar disorder. It helps if you can mourn the ending of your earlier dreams for your relationship and create new ones. The first chapters talked about getting real with bipolar disorder and learning to treat it first in your relationship. This is a heavy burden for some people. This may not be your idea of a good relationship. (No kidding!) But it's a reality and it's one you must think about clearly, intelligently, and thoroughly.

It takes a lot of acceptance to stay with someone who will have bipolar disorder throughout life. The illness will not go away and this is a fact you have to accept. If you're still hoping that things will right themselves magically and you will have a totally normal relationship in the future, this is not realistic. Bipolar disorder will always need to be managed with medications and a holistic treatment plan. It's possible and you and your partner can do it, but you have to face facts. Your partner needs to do the same.

It's time to accept that your relationship has been impacted by a treatable, but serious and often difficult, lifetime illness. In many ways, this is very sad. It affects your plans, children, future generations, finances, and lifestyle. It's okay to feel sad and lost when you face this reality. It's also okay to accept it and make a decision to do what it takes to create a life that is filled with joy and happiness, despite bipolar disorder.

Letting Go

There comes a time when there is just too much to handle, and you just have to let it go. If you want to stay with your partner, work on your treatment plan, and create a more stable relationship, you will have to let go of what you thought your relationship would or should look like or how you thought your world should be. Finding meaning in what has happened to you in your relationship may give you strength for the future, but it can also take up all of your time. Try to focus on the present. Thinking of the past can drain all of your energy.

Can you embrace your partner for who they are now? Not for who you thought they were when you fell in love. Not for what you think they should be, but as someone with a serious but treatable illness. It may be that the treatment plan in this book will make significant changes in your relationship. To help the new plan work, try to let go of the past and any mistakes, hospital visits, money problems, sexual misconduct, and angry fights it might include.

Start new with a program that works. It will take time, but you can both change on a daily basis. Bipolar disorder is an illness, not your life. There are no guarantees, but with diligent effort, appropriate psychiatric treatment, and a holistic approach to healing, your partner can have a good chance at getting better. Try to let them get better peacefully. If you continually demand explanations for past behaviors, especially if they were totally controlled by bipolar disorder, change will be more difficult. Can you feel all of the pain of the past, think about it, and then let it go? Let go and move forward. Say to yourself, *That is the past. I live in the present and prepare for the future.*

Some things can't be repaired: Your partner may have committed unforgivable acts when sick. Their behavior may have hurt you to the bone, yet you're still here. But how are you here? Do you hold past behaviors over your partner's head? Or are you able to let go of what happened? The solution is to make it very, very clear to your partner that you're willing to move forward together, if they are willing to work on a treatment plan together with you. If your partner is willing, then take those past hurts, put them on a little boat in your mind, and let them set sail. You're done with them. Some things can't be repaired. So don't try. Forgive, forget, and move on—if you can. This may be easier said than done, but you can choose to give it a try.

Your Partner Won't Change

What if no matter what you say or do, your partner says you're attacking them and that you just need to leave them alone? What if your partner simply refuses to make any changes? This can be a terribly frustrating and frightening position to be in. But it's true that no one is forcing you to stay in your relationship. If you know your partner is this way and there is not much you can do to change it, then it's up to you whether to accept this behavior from your partner or to decide that you will leave. Maybe your partner tells you that bipolar disorder is none of your business or that they want to deal with things in their own way. Maybe you will do all of the work in this book for yourself, and your partner will do none of it. This can happen, especially if your partner is controlled by the illness. You can't force someone to do anything. You can only take care of yourself.

There are many people with this illness who either deny they have it and refuse prescribed medications or feel that medications are all that they need. They feel this way even when the evidence strongly indicates that they need a lot more help than they are receiving. This is common behavior for some people with bipolar disorder and is not something your partner is doing to upset you. Sometimes the illness is so strong they can't accept help.

If your partner will not talk to you about bipolar disorder, you have a decision to make. You really can't change someone, but you can make it clear what you need from the relationship. If this means talking about bipolar disorder and working together on a treatment plan, then do the work yourself and approach your partner once you have a treatment plan ready. If you still meet resistance, the future is up to you. Can you live with this for the rest of your life together?

The facts are that some people will consistently struggle. Whether this is due to choice or because the illness is too strong, it may be that your partner can't change as much as you would like them to. Don't try to force change. If you have created a plan and your partner won't or can't use it, and after six months or more little has changed, that is when you will have to make decisions about your own life. Do you stay or do you go?

Your Partner May Be Too Ill to Change (at This Time)

Your partner may be too ill right now to work on a holistic treatment plan with you. The solution is to do what you can, make the changes you need to make, and go on from there. You may be amazed to discover that simply by making just a few changes in the way you relate to your partner regarding bipolar disorder, you can help your partner get better so that they can make some significant changes themselves. One option you have is to give this time, in the hope that gradual positive changes eventually will lead your partner to become more open to implementing further changes. There is a lot of work for you in this book. Use the time to work in your journal, find supportive help, and make the decisions about what you need. When you have done this work, start to involve your partner slowly.

Your Partner's Family Won't Help

It's always shocking to people when someone is sick and their family members either don't see that they're sick or refuse to help when it's obvious that they need help. Your partner's family members may be very unhelpful or in denial. Or they may feel that everything is your responsibility because you're the one in the relationship. Others may say that you're being overemotional. You have a few options. You can try to educate your partner's family (and friends). You can teach them what triggers bipolar disorder and help them see that they play a part in this illness. You can suggest that your partner live with them for a while. You can make sure they come to the hospital. You can also involve them in your treatment plan and use the same skills you learned in the first chapters to respond to them instead of reacting. It helps if you understand that many of your partner's family members may have untreated mental illness as well. Mental illness does run in families.

Your other option is to turn to others and give your partner's family a very limited role to play in your new treatment plan. If your partner's family sabotages your work, then you must make a choice. It's a hard choice, but it's one that has to be made. You can tell them that they either have to join you or leave you alone, but they can no longer undermine the work you're doing.

One effective tool is to teach yourself how to talk with your partner's family. For example, your partner's family may say, "He's not sick, he's just creative. You need to give him some space." Or, "She doesn't have an illness. She's just a sensitive person. You're just trying to cause problems. Why can't you accept her for how she is?" They may also continually bail your partner out of difficult situations or lend money after the mood swings have caused a financial disaster. Here is a suggestion on how you can talk with your partner's family if they are causing you trouble:

Your patient but very firm response: "I know you love your child (brother, sister, etc.). You have the right to your own opinions, but as I'm the one who lives with them every day, it's time for me to make some decisions on my own. Whether you like what is going on or not, the truth is that your relative has been diagnosed with an illness that has very distinct and clear symptoms. All of the people who have bipolar disorder have the same symptoms. This isn't something I've made up. It has nothing to do with being creative, though many people with bipolar disorder are very creative. It has nothing to do with being sensitive, though that's also a symptom of the illness. I need your help with this. Every time you help them after a mood swing, you're allowing the behavior to continue. You must see that there is a very definite pattern to their behavior. I know that you love them and it's time for us to work together or for you to leave us alone so that they can get better. We're going to try the new treatment plan in this book and I would love for you to join us in this new project. What do you say?"

If the family is unresponsive or if your partner continues to run back to their family for help when sick and shuts you out, you then have to decide whether you will put up with this behavior and for how long. Once you decide this, create a plan to take care of yourself and let your partner's family take over. Yes, this is hard, but you have to think of *your* future.

People Will Say the Wrong Thing

People are people. They often don't make sure the brain is in gear before they run their mouths. Have you heard people make statements like the following when you tell them about your partner's illness? *My father had bipolar disorder, but he shot himself.* Or *My cousin has bipolar disorder, but we don't know where she is.* These things are not said to be cruel; people just don't think. Let it go, and if someone continues to talk to you in this manner, then stay away from them. You can say, "What you just said doesn't help my situation in any way, you know." It may also be possible to get a good laugh from some of the dumb things people say and share them with your partner. Laughter eases pain quite a lot.

Medication Side Effects

Many people with bipolar disorder take medications successfully with few side effects. Then there are those who experience many side effects and have to keep trying new medications. Some people can't tolerate medications at all. In other words, medications can really create a lot of problems for your partner. It's important that you understand that the pills your partner takes are not innocuous, as you read in chapter 4. They are serious drugs that change your partner's brain chemistry and affect the body.

It makes sense that there will be side effects just as there are side effects with any other major drug treatment, including chemotherapy for cancer. Few people think of drug treatment for bipolar disorder as chemotherapy, but that is exactly what it is. It's easier to accept the side effects of cancer chemotherapy because they are so well-known and because they may be life-saving. In contrast, side effects from bipolar disorder medications are often not fully explained or they are discounted. Doctors may not talk enough about the side effects with you, and they may say that your partner just needs to adjust to the medications. It's hard to hear this when your partner is sleeping fourteen hours a day and has gained fifteen pounds in one month. It's hard to accept this when the person you love can't have an orgasm. It's hard to accept this when your partner simultaneously throws up and has diarrhea from a medication that is supposed to keep them stable. It's understandable that your partner would want to quit taking medications that seem to make them more ill than bipolar disorder itself. But there has to be a compromise.

Talk with your partner about trying your new treatment plan so that they may, at some point, be able to take smaller doses of the medications (which will mean fewer side effects). Medications are something you need to get a handle on, sooner rather than later. Just as you have to accept bipolar disorder in your relationship, your partner needs to accept that they will need certain medications, possibly for the rest of their lives, depending on what symptoms cause them the most trouble.

You can help by educating yourself about the medications for this illness so that you can be an advocate for your partner especially if they are overmedicated and can't speak for themselves. Some side effects are to be expected. And often, just as with chemotherapy for cancer treatments, side effects must be tolerated to save one's life. But side effects where your partner can't lead a normal life don't have to be accepted blindly. If your partner has given the medications the time that the doctors suggested and is still having problems, it's then time to see the doctor again and get some help. It's entirely appropriate to be proactive and assertive in discussing any medication issues with your partner's doctor. It is also very reasonable to ask what other medications are available as alternatives should the side effects become significant. But remember, it's not safe to simply stop taking medications because the side effects are too strong. This is one of the most common reasons that people with bipolar disorder relapse.

Help your partner get support from their health care team if the drugs are causing too many side effects, but make sure they don't simply stop taking them. Going off medications too quickly or without a doctor's help can cause serious problems. Do things sensibly and slowly. Try to create a relationship with your partner's doctor so that you can discuss medications and your new treatment plan honestly. Be future oriented with all that you do, especially when it comes to medications.

Stopping Medications

Another problem you may face is that your partner either refuses to take medications or stops them once they start to feel well. This can be a huge issue in your relationship, especially if your partner gets manic while off medications. First, you should know that it's very common for someone who feels better to think they don't need medications. It's also normal for someone who is starting a manic episode to feel they're cured.

The only way to prevent this behavior from happening is for you and your partner to create a plan that keeps your partner on medications. This includes writing down the thoughts and feelings your partner first has when they start to feel they're well enough to stop the medications. These thoughts and feelings must be recorded on your symptom lists so that you both are aware of when the symptoms start and what triggers them. It also means that you have a health care professional's number on your "What Works" list to call if you feel your partner is getting sick because they stopped their medications. It may be that you will have to tell your partner that you can be with them only if they continue to take the medications that prevent them from becoming sick. It's up to you.

Untreated Bipolar Disorder Always Causes Problems

My partner went off his medications. He feels he doesn't need them. I told him he has to leave if he's not on medications. He'll call and beg me to take him back, and when I do, a few weeks later he'll tell me he doesn't love me anymore. He makes up things about me and says I stay with him because I like being with sick people. He's totally unreasonable when he's off his meds and gets sick, and I have no idea how he is going to feel toward me from day to day.

When your partner is not treating their bipolar disorder, there will be problems. It may take some time, but problems will show up. This illness will not just go away because your partner wants it to. When your partner is untreated, it affects your life and all of the people around your partner as well, especially children. You need to get clear and set boundaries about what you will and will not tolerate regarding untreated bipolar disorder, and then you have to stick to what you say.

When Enough Is Enough

You may be at the point where you feel you can't take this any longer. Your partner may have been sick for years, refusing help no matter how many times you've told them that for you to be in the relationship, you need them to be stable. Of course, your new treatment plan can help with this, but you also have a few other options. You can take a break. You can talk with your partner's doctor about your options. You can let other family members or friends take care of things for a while. You can tell your partner's family that they need to help more. Give yourself some breathing space so you can think outside of the crisis. Give the treatment plan a chance to work, and then decide when enough is enough.

Only you can decide how long you should stay in a relationship that isn't working. You have to set a time limit on how long you are willing to wait for your partner to change. Maybe you have spent years trying to help someone who refuses your help. When do you decide that it's time for you to leave and find a more stable relationship? No one can answer this question except you, yourself.

If you feel you're fighting a losing battle every single day, and you know that nothing is going to change, then you have to be very honest with yourself and decide what you need to do for yourself. You have only one life in this body. What do you want your life to look like? You do have a choice— even if it's a *very* difficult one.

Children Will Listen

It's important that even during a crisis you stay aware of the effects that your partner's bipolar disorder may be having on your children. Younger children simply don't have the maturity to understand that an illness is causing their parent to behave in a strange way. They simply feel scared. Protecting your children always comes first, even if this means a temporary separation from the ill partner until control can be reestablished. Here are steps you can take to protect, educate, and involve your children.

Talk with your children: You don't have to hide your partner's illness from your children. If they're very young but are showing signs that they're upset and they know that something is going on, gently explain that sometimes people get sick and need to be helped by a doctor. Once they are old enough to understand, tell them the truth and involve them in your treatment plan. If your partner goes to the hospital, don't lie and say that they're visiting grandma or away on a business trip. It's very unlikely that your children are not aware of what is going on, at least on some level. It will be less scary for them if they know that their parent has an illness that is treatable and that they can help.

If you're not sure what to do, get some professional advice, but be aware that even a very young child can be perceptive. Don't overwhelm children with your feelings, but don't shut them out either. It's okay for a child to see you in pain once in a while. Let them know they can help you and support you while at the same time making sure you allow them to continue to be children. Ask them about their fears and worries and take them seriously.

They see your partner get sick, so talk with them realistically. It's a good idea to tell the truth and say that mom or dad is sick and is getting help. You don't have to go into details, unless the child is old enough to understand.

Crisis: Although you are probably overloaded with your own fears and worries when your partner is in the hospital, there are many things you need to be aware of regarding your children and their issues. Your children may be very frightened. They may think their parent is going to die. Children can become very upset when they witness out-of-control manic or psychotic behavior, and they always need to be protected from physical and psychological harm. You need to honestly reassure them that their parent is safe because they're in the hospital. If your partner is gone and is not safe, then you must reassure the children that you're there and that you will take care of them. Explain that illness happens sometimes and that there is help for your partner.

It's also a good idea to have mental illness out in the open as an illness instead of being hidden away as something frightening. Talk about cancer and diabetes and then explain to your child in an age-appropriate way that their parent has an illness that has symptoms that can be strange and scary. The whole point is to make sure your children feel safe.

You may not feel right in your relationship with your partner when they're ill, but your children must feel safe in their relationship with their parents. Remember, it's your partner who is in crisis, but it's also their parent. The bottom line is that children must always be protected. They come before you and your partner. They are children and can't always speak for themselves.

Genetic risk: Another important topic for you to discuss with your partner and your other family members is the genetic risk your children have of developing bipolar disorder. When one parent has bipolar disorder, there is a 15 to 30 percent chance that a child will develop the illness (Papolos and Papolos 1999). This is a very serious issue when you have or are thinking of having children. It doesn't mean you have to be scared. It means you have to be aware and honest with family members. It's so easy to think, *It won't happen to me*, but it has already happened to your partner's parents, so don't be naïve. This also makes it very important for you and your partner to watch for any early warning signs of mood swings in your children.

The average age of onset for bipolar disorder is twenty-three, although late-adolescent onset is fairly common. Bipolar disorder can occur as early as six years old or as late as fifty (Hales and Yudofsky 1999). Note that most kids living in a home where one person has bipolar disorder are subject to significant stresses, and their reactions to this stress must be distinguished from the early signs of emerging bipolar disorder.

SIGNS OF POSSIBLE BIPOLAR DISORDER IN CHILDREN

1. Poor sleep.

2. Marked depression. In children this is most commonly seen when they become withdrawn and socially isolated. Irritability is also associated with depression in kids, as in an inability to be soothed when upset.

3. Mania in children primarily is evident in the following behaviors and symptoms: extreme irritability or even violence, agitation, decreased need for sleep, and pronounced restlessness.

Bipolar disorder that begins in adolescence looks much the same as the illness seen in adults. In almost all cases, one of the most important warning signs is the onset of noticeable sleep disturbances. Have you talked about this subject with your partner? If you have children, it's time to have this discussion. There is increasing evidence that early recognition and treatment of bipolar disorder can make a significant difference in the overall outcome in a person's life, so it's very important to be alert to the early signs that a child or adolescent is showing possible symptoms.

Children are one of the main reasons it's so important for you and your partner to find a treatment plan that works. The toll that a parent's untreated bipolar disorder takes on children is too high. The illness needs to be stabilized so that your children can have a healthy and supportive living environment. Otherwise, it will be hard to distinguish their stressful reactions to your partner's illness from their own issues, especially if they are teenagers.

When Bipolar Disorder Is Too Severe

Some people with bipolar disorder don't get better. They may have a dual diagnosis (bipolar disorder and significant alcohol or another type of drug abuse) that complicates the illness. They may refuse treatment or not respond to treatment. Their depression may be so strong that they can't function and there is nothing you can do to help them. Maybe your partner is violent or uncooperative. Maybe your partner is in jail because of what they did during a mood swing. And maybe you just can't take it anymore.

There comes a time when you have to take care of yourself, your life, your future, and your children. Have you reached that point? Maybe reading this book is a last effort to see if your partner can change. But, at some point, you will have to face the hard truth about your partner and their chances for recovery and stability. No one can do this for you. Sometimes you have to make terribly difficult and sad decisions.

Protect Yourself

Although this topic was covered in chapter 11, it bears repeating here. If you're married, know your rights in your state. If your partner has debt and continues to create debt because of bipolar disorder, you may one day be responsible for that debt. Do what it takes to protect yourself. Do it in a kind way and do it calmly, but make the changes needed to remove your finances from the mess your partner may have created or might create in the future.

You don't want to file for bankruptcy or lose your credit rating because of your partner's illness. If money really is a problem, don't buy houses, cars, or other large items together. As stated in chapter 11, don't keep bank accounts or credit cards in both of your names. Don't go into business with your partner or support an idea you think will not work. Think of yourself first when it comes to your future. This is not being selfish. This is being realistic and mature.

When Your Partner Gets Well

In some relationships, when a partner who has been ill for many years finally gets better, the partner who was once a caretaker has a difficult time adjusting to the fact that the once-ill partner now has strength, a self, and a life. This may be hard for you to believe. If you have struggled together for years to help your partner find stability, doesn't it make sense that you would both be overjoyed when it happens? It may seem as if this should not be hard for you—of course you want your partner to get better—but thinking about something intellectually and actually going through it are different matters.

The fact is, your relationship will change when your partner starts to get well. The truth is, as twisted as this may sound, some relationships do better when one partner is ill. The roles are clearly defined and there is a caretaking system in place that is familiar and safe. When the ill partner gets better, everything changes. Whatever terms you came in on, or have lived with over the years, are no longer valid. It will be a new relationship, and you both will have to adjust. There will be new roles to play, and you may find time on your hands that you have absolutely no idea how to use. Be ready for this. Joyous recovery can be short-lived when people are stuck in their old roles.

Always Ask the Tough Questions

When you're faced with something about bipolar disorder that seems confusing and you're unable to make a decision, ask yourself the following tough questions to find answers to your dilemma: *Can I deal with this for six more months? If things don't improve in a year, what am I going to do? How long am I willing to wait for the treatment plan to work? If my partner refuses to work with me, am I going to stay in the relationship? Does my partner's illness affect our children, and do I need to do something to protect the children? What are my legal rights? Will my partner harm me or someone else?*

These questions force you to see that your participation in this relationship is a choice. If you ask yourself these questions every time you're faced with a bipolar disorder issue, you will at least know how you feel about it. This will help you make more stable and future-oriented decisions.

REALITY CHECK

Ultimately, you may have to make some very sad and very difficult decisions regarding your relationship. There are many hard truths about bipolar disorder that you may not want to face. Maybe you have lived in crisis for so long you haven't had the chance to examine what your future will look like realistically, if you stay with your partner. What do you need to do to create the life you want?

Facing the hard truths about bipolar disorder may open a door to recovery. Knowing the reality of this illness can at least help you be honest with yourself about what you face as a couple. Use this knowledge to strengthen your treatment plan and then work together to achieve stability.

CHAPTER FIFTEEN

How to Create Laughter and Joy in Your Relationship

It's okay for you to have fun when your partner is ill.
This will help you have fun together in the future.

It may be very hard for you to have fun if your partner is often sick. It may be that you haven't had any fun in your relationship in a very long time. Many relationships where one partner has unmanaged bipolar disorder are often completely under the control of bipolar disorder and its symptoms. The good news is that it's never too late to change. Fun can be created. It doesn't have to be spontaneous. It can be planned and practiced until it becomes second nature. This is a very important part of your new holistic treatment plan. Every "What Works" list should include ideas on what to do for fun. Anyone who has experienced heartache knows that laughter really does provide relief from pain. Even if this relief lasts just for a moment, it starts the healing process and helps you find yourself again, despite the stress and grief in your relationship caused by your partner's bipolar disorder.

This chapter will give you some tips on how to add laughter and joy to your everyday life. It will help you plan at least one evening a week where your entire focus is on pleasure. This may seem impossible right now if your partner is ill, but look at this as a way to help your partner get better. Placing some distance between your partner and bipolar disorder can be a wonderful part of healing. This is not about ignoring the difficult realities of living with this illness. It's about affirming life and finding balance. It's about having fun along the way while you make changes and start your new treatment plan.

What is your partner's favorite thing to do? Perhaps bipolar disorder has stopped your partner from doing what they love. This can certainly be a result of all of the symptoms they experience. Mania may cause your partner to do the things they think they love to do, and yet the behavior often seems unfocused and over the top. Anxiety or psychosis may make it impossible for your partner to concentrate on anything for very long. Depression may eliminate your partner's desire to do most things, so it's only natural they would completely stop doing what they love.

How can your partner start doing the things they love again? This is where you can make a big difference. You can help your partner get back into doing the things they loved to do before they became ill. Maybe you have also stopped doing what you love because your partner has been ill. If this is the case, the process starts with you. It's time for you to get back to doing what you love.

Do What You Love

Using your journal, answer the following question: *What do I really love to do?* And then write about the last time you did what you love and how you want to start doing it again. You may have stopped doing what you love to take care of your partner. It's normal for you to do this, but your spirit needs laughter and joy, and doing what you love fills you up so that you will have more to give your partner when they need your help.

Write how you are going to do what you love this week. Set a goal with a timeline and take the first step. You need to do this step first, before you help your partner do the same. You will then use your example to help your partner do what they love. One of the best ways to do this gently and supportively is to create a bipolar-free zone in your relationship.

The Bipolar-Free Zone

How do you help someone who is ill do what they love? How do you get someone who is depressed to laugh? These are tough questions. But there are some answers. The first step is to create a time when you and your partner can be together without talking, thinking, or worrying about bipolar disorder. This is called the bipolar-free zone. You can create a bipolar-free zone so that you and your partner can just be together as a couple and do the things that couples do. At first, it can take place once a week. Or it can be an hour each night or more. It's up to you.

There has to be some laughter and joy for a relationship to grow and survive, and you need to create a place where laughter and joy can bloom. Talk to your partner about creating this bipolar-free zone and pick a specific time when you can both be together, free from bipolar disorder. Then you can plan your evening to do something that you and your partner love to do. If your partner is resistant, use the tools you learned in the first chapters of this book to respond to their concerns. Here's an example of what you can say:

I know that you've been sick and that our relationship has had troubles. But we have the treatment plan now, and part of that treatment plan is to add laughter and joy to our lives. I want to spend one night a week alone with you just for fun. We can learn something new together like how to make root beer or we can watch a funny movie or we can do something you love to do.

There are rules for these fun evenings. We won't talk about the past. We won't talk about our relationship. We'll simply have fun and then go to bed. We don't have to analyze or discuss what we do. We're just going to do it. I need you to do this with me. I want to connect with you and have fun again. You don't have to be well to do this, and you don't have to be enthusiastic about it; you just have to say yes, and I will take care of the rest.

Bipolar disorder may have caused you both to overanalyze everything. By talking with your partner and letting them know you are making changes, you can separate yourselves from the control that bipolar disorder has over your relationship. Decide that, for at least a few hours, you will take your lives back. At first, this will not be easy, but keep doing it. Soon it will become second nature and your partner may be amazed to realize they can still have fun—even when they're sick. This may start a healing chain reaction where your partner has a taste of what it feels like to feel better, and they will want more.

EXERCISE: The "Do What You Love" Evening

You can plan this evening in your journal. The first step is to answer the same question for your partner that you answered yourself: *What does my partner really love to do?* Once you have that answer, write down all of the ways your partner used to do this activity. It may be cooking, going to movies, rock climbing, traveling, singing, crafts, or working on the car. You will know what your partner likes. Write about what your partner was like before they got sick. How did they do what they love? Did it take special tools, supplies, or a specific location? Write down what you will need to prepare for this evening. You may have to modify things a bit, but you can still re-create the activity your partner used to love by surrounding them with the objects and tools used for doing what they loved to do in the past.

You will then plan an evening completely around this activity. Your partner may resist you at first, but keep trying. If they're depressed, you have to break through the depression with action, and one of the best ways to do this is by helping them do something they love. Here is an example of an evening planned around a person who loves to cook and watch movies.

Getting ready: Tell your partner that the kitchen and dining area are off-limits. You will then clean these areas and set a beautiful table with candles and flowers. You will choose a recipe that your partner loves to cook and then buy all of the ingredients. Make sure that this is a simple yet interesting recipe. You will prepare all of the ingredients. Have all of the ingredients and pans ready for your partner to use. If your partner is not feeling well, often it's the preparation that feels overwhelming. This is important to remember for any activity you do with your partner. If you take care of the preparation, they will be able to do what they love without becoming stressed.

Choose a fun movie that you know your partner loves. It's okay to watch something you have seen before. Just make sure it is uplifting, fun, and maybe even romantic. Have it ready to go. Clean the viewing area and add some flowers and candles to the room. Play some good music when you cook and dine. If you are having dessert, buy something ready-made and eat it while you watch the movie.

Cooking together: Tell your partner you want to watch them cook. Get involved and ask questions. This will make your partner feel needed and appreciated and can help them connect once again with doing something they love. Your goal this evening is to recreate the feelings that your partner feels when happy. They will forget that this is possible when they're sick, but you are going to remind them. As your partner cooks, you do the cleaning, so there is little to do after the dinner. Once again, it's often the mess and obligation that keeps people from doing what they love.

Eating together: Remember that this is a bipolar-free zone. Have some ideas about what to talk about before you even start eating. This is not about bills, hospitals, medications, or illness. This evening is about your relationship. Tell some jokes or funny stories. This is your time to bond together as a couple and not as a caretaker and an ill person. If your partner has trouble and can focus only on their worries, gently remind them that this is a bipolar-free zone, and you can discuss the issue tomorrow. Tonight, you just want to be together.

After dinner: Remember the excitement you felt when you first got together? Can you capture that again? Talk about the time when you met each other. Sit next to each other and hold hands. Start the movie and enjoy it and each other's company.

After the movie, do something loving like taking an aromatherapy bath together, or lying in bed, holding hands and talking, before you go to sleep. There are no rules, except the rule that this is a bipolar-free zone for the entire evening. You goal is to provide a safe place for you and your partner to feel good again. You can protect them for at least one evening from worrying about the illness.

Believe it or not, a simple evening spent like this can work like compound interest—a small investment can return huge rewards. When you use bipolar-free evenings as a part of your treatment plan, you are reprogramming your partner's brain to accept health. Hope is a healer and if your partner can feel just one stress-free evening of fun, they may want more.

An Evening of Fun (at Least) Once a Week

You and your partner really can have fun together, even when your partner is sick. This will help your partner learn to separate themselves from the symptoms of bipolar disorder and will help you both to get some breathing space away from the illness. Here are some suggestions for the bipolar-free evening:

- Go to a used bookstore.

- Eat outside at a restaurant.

- Make popcorn and set up the room with candles and get comfortable.

- Take time to be together intimately, but not sexually. Do something funny in bed.

- Read aloud to each other from something silly.

- Play the "You're great" game. You tell your partner why they are great and then they tell you why you are great. Do this for at least five minutes each.

- See if you can make each other laugh. (How long has it been since you laughed together?)

- Even if your partner is in the hospital, you still need to laugh for the sake of your own health. This will strengthen you for the hospital visits.

- Go see a play where all the actors are kids.

- Go to a petting zoo.

- Go to a playground and do what kids do: swing, seesaw, go down a slide.

- Do something dumb.

- Go to a pool and swim with kids.

- Do anything together that takes your mind off your troubles.

- Think outside of the bipolar disorder box and try not to be so serious about everything!

Now, what ideas do you have about what you and your partner can do? Write them in your journal and start to think of how you will plan the bipolar-free evening. Of course, there will be times when all of this will seem impossible, but bipolar-free fun times can happen if you create your new treatment plan and take things slowly. If your partner is in the hospital, you can spend a bipolar-free evening with a friend. This is important for your mental health, and it will provide you with practice for when your partner comes home.

Laugh about the Serious Things

You may think there's nothing funny about psychosis and, initially, there isn't at all. In fact, it was the scariest thing I ever saw when my partner got sick. But once he was in the hospital for a while, I was able to find humor in what he was saying. It was so obviously not him saying those things. He made what he thought were jokes and would laugh as though he was a stand-up comedian. Then he would put his hand on his heart and say the Pledge of Allegiance in a language all his own. It was funny and it helped me a lot to laugh. I knew he was safe in the hospital and it was easier for me to drive back home and laugh over what he had said than it was for me to cry in fear and desperation as I had when he first got sick.

It's okay for you to laugh and feel joy when someone you love is very ill. Don't be ashamed or embarrassed to see your friends or to have a moment when you're not thinking about your partner. You really do need a break from the stress. Time off will make you more able to deal with the reality of your partner's illness and it will help you stay well mentally, as well as physically. This may seem too difficult to do, but there is a strong technique you can use until you are ready to actually feel laughter and joy more naturally. This technique is called *acting as if.*

Acting as If

"Acting as if" is a powerful tool you can teach your partner, but you must first learn the technique yourself. It's interesting that so many songs tell us to act as if we are well. We are told to put on a happy face, walk on the sunny side of the street, sing in the rain, and smile even if our heart is breaking. Why? Because it can change who you are. Just as a negative thought, whether true or not, affects how you feel about yourself and the world, a happy thought, whether true or not, can trick your brain into thinking that things are better than they are. And the miracle is that, when you act as if, something happens and things suddenly *do* feel better than they had been feeling.

This is not about being unrealistic about your life. It's about accepting your present situation and deciding you're going to act as if things are okay anyway. When you walk down the street, smile. When you see friends and family, act as though you are the strong person you want to be. Be honest with your feelings and feel your pain, but if it's appropriate, act as though you will be okay. Because you will be okay in the future. Why not just act like it now?

Once you learn how to do this, you can help your partner. Acting as if is one of the most powerful tools your partner can use to treat depression. They may feel sick, worthless, hopeless, and miserable, but if they can just stand up, pull their shoulders back, and put a smile on their face, they will change the way they look at the world and the way others interact with them. Acting as if things are better than they are means that your partner accepts the truth that the illness makes them feel a certain way, but they have decided to act as though they are well in spite of the disorder.

Here is how this works: Your partner feels too depressed to work. There are projects that need to be done, but even thinking about doing them seems impossible. When your partner acts as if, they make a conscious decision to bypass the bipolar disorder feelings and get something done anyway. Once they make the decision to act as if the project is possible, they simply stand up and say to themselves, *My brain doesn't want to do this. Bipolar disorder doesn't want me to do this. I know the illness is controlling me. But for now I'm going to say no to that and act as if I'm well. I'm going to start with the first step of the project and take it from there. Bipolar disorder can't do this, but I can.* (And when the bipolar thoughts start to take over, your partner can say, *I hear you, but I'm acting well today, so you can just go away.*) And they keep on going. Acting as if takes a lot of practice, but it works. Eventually, it will no longer be an act. The mood swing will end and your partner can feel joy naturally.

This works really well if your partner can do this when you're enjoying your bipolar-free evening. They may not want to participate at first, because it's one of the symptoms of bipolar disorder not to do what you love doing, but they have to act as if. They have to make themselves laugh. They have to remind themselves that it's natural and healthy to feel joy again. Laughter and joy are like muscles. You and your partner have to exercise these muscles every day. Acting as if can strengthen your relationship if you do it together on a regular basis.

REALITY CHECK

Your partner may be too ill to create a bipolar-free zone with you at first. You may do all of the planning and all of the suggesting and they will just sit there. Just keep trying until you see a change. If your partner is too ill, or refuses to experience happiness and joy with you, then you must find it for yourself to stay strong and stable. You don't need another person's permission to feel happy. It really is okay to mix your pain and fear with laughter and joy. Then you will be able to enjoy your own life, if and when your partner gets better. There is no need for you to change your life to one of misery just because your partner is ill. Get on with your life the best you can, and laugh and have fun in honor of your future together.

A Final Thought

Many of the techniques in this book take some time to get started. The beauty of adding laughter and joy to your relationship is that you can start immediately. You can get started today. In fact, you can get started right now and then help your partner do the same. Close this book and find something to make yourself laugh. Woo hoo! Remember something funny. Remember something wonderful about your partner. Think of all of the joy you have experienced in life and remind yourself that it can happen again. You now have the tools to make it happen. You have a new treatment plan that can work to help you recognize, modify, and hopefully prevent your partner's major bipolar disorder symptoms. Your relationship has the opportunity to be happy, healthy, stable, and filled with joy.

This book can help you through the many ups and downs you and your partner will experience as you create a more stable relationship. Read it often to find what you need at certain moments. Remember to always treat bipolar disorder first. And, most importantly, remember that laughter and joy are your first option when things get really tough. They will give you the peace of mind you need to move on and face your problems with strength. You can both do it.

APPENDIX

Quick Reference Guide to Medications

Note: To the best of our knowledge, doses and side effects listed below are accurate. However, this is meant as a general reference only and should not serve as a guideline for prescribing medications. Brand names are registered trademarks.

This appendix covers in detail the medications used to treat bipolar disorder. This is for your general information. It's a good idea to read through this material once and then go over it again with a highlighter, noting all of the medications your partner has used and is currently using. This knowledge will help you ask informed and fact-based questions about your partner's medication treatment.

Mood Stabilizers

Lithium

Lithium is the drug with the best track record in preventing recurrences of episodes. It is a naturally occurring element and is the only psychiatric drug proven to substantially reduce the incidence of suicide. Lithium is used to treat mania and bipolar depression and is used to reduce recurrences of mania and depression.

Lithium generally takes about seven to ten days to start working.

Lithium is a very dangerous drug if taken in an accidental or intentional overdose. In the event of an overdose, seek immediate medical attention.

GENERIC AND BRAND NAMES AND TYPICAL ADULT DAILY DOSES

Lithium carbonate: Lithotabs, Eskalith, Lithonate, Lithane, Carbolith, Lithobid, Duralith

Lithium citrate: Cibalith

Eskalith and Lithonate are the most commonly prescribed, and the typical dosage is 600 to 2400 mg per day.

THERAPEUTIC BLOOD LEVELS

What matters with lithium treatment is not the dose, per se, but the blood level (which is carefully monitored). A lithium level between 0.8 and 1.2 mEq/l (mEq/l is the technical designation for what is commonly called the lithium level) is generally thought to be in the therapeutic range for treating mania. Once the manic episode is resolved, it is common practice to lower the dose to establish a blood level somewhere between 0.6 and 0.8 mEq/l. Blood levels above 1.2 are associated with significant side effects, and levels above 2.0 can be dangerous.

It is necessary to periodically check lithium blood levels. This is done frequently during the first weeks of treatment and when there are significant changes in dosage. Once a person is stabilized on lithium for several months, lithium levels will be checked less often (e.g., three to four times a year).

LABORATORY TESTS

Prior to starting treatment with lithium, laboratory tests are required to establish baseline measures of the functioning of certain body systems. A complete blood count, an ECG (EKG), kidney function tests (BUN, creatinine, and urinalysis), thyroid tests, and tests of calcium and electrolyte levels are required. The ECG (EKG) and the thyroid and calcium tests should also be repeated periodically during treatment. A pregnancy test is optional.

SIDE EFFECTS

Common side effects: These include nausea or heartburn, muscle tremors or weakness, decreased sex drive, lethargy and drowsiness (which may impair the ability to safely drive an automobile), difficulty concentrating, weight gain, increased thirst and increased frequency of urination, and rash or acne.

Less common side effects: These include loss of balance, double vision, vomiting, diarrhea, slurred speech, and trembling. These side effects should be reported to your doctor.

Rare side effects: Rare, potentially dangerous side effects include soreness of the mouth, throat, or gums; severe rash or itchiness; swelling of the neck or face; severe nausea, vomiting, weakness, fever, or flu-like symptoms; and marked increase in thirst and very frequent urination. If any of these side effects occur, immediately contact your doctor.

ADDICTION POTENTIAL

Lithium is not habit forming.

INTERACTIONS WITH OTHER MEDICATIONS

The medications with which lithium most commonly has adverse interactions are the following.

- diuretics
- calcium channel blockers
- ACE inhibitors
- nonsteroidal anti-inflammatory pain medications such as ibuprofen
- theophylline

SAFETY DURING PREGNANCY AND BREASTFEEDING

Lithium is generally considered to be safe for use during pregnancy. However, there is a slight risk of a rare birth defect (Ebstein's anomaly, a heart defect) if lithium is taken during the first trimester. This defect occurs in 0.1 to 0.2 percent of fetuses exposed to lithium. A woman who is taking lithium and is planning to get pregnant or thinks that she may be pregnant should contact her doctor.

Breastfeeding is not recommended when taking lithium.

Anticonvulsant Mood Stabilizers

Anticonvulsants are medications originally developed to treat epilepsy. It was only by accident that it was discovered that some anticonvulsants also have the ability to treat mania. In addition, the anticonvulsant Lamictal has antidepressant actions and can be used to treat bipolar depressive episodes. It is also FDA approved for use to prevent recurrence of depressive episodes.

Research evaluating the ability of anticonvulsants to help prevent recurrences of mania and bipolar depression is not yet conclusive. Depakote and Tegretol likely help prevent recurrences of mania, and Lamictal likely reduces the recurrence of bipolar depression.

Anticonvulsants generally take around seven to ten days to start working. One exception is Depakote: if high doses of Depakote are administered, effects can be seen in four days.

GENERIC AND BRAND NAMES AND TYPICAL ADULT DAILY DOSES

divalproex	Depakote	750–1500 mg
carbamazepine	Tegretol	600–1600 mg
oxcarbazepine	Trileptal	1200–2400 mg
lamotrigine	Lamictal	50–500 mg

THERAPEUTIC BLOOD LEVELS

Blood levels of Depakote and Tegretol must be periodically monitored (especially during the initial weeks of treatment) to check the levels of medication present in blood. Those treated with Tegretol must have periodic and ongoing monitoring of Tegretol levels. Generally, once a person is stabilized on Depakote, blood level monitoring is not necessary.

Depakote	50–125 mcg/ml
Tegretol	4–12 mcg/ml

The optimal blood level for Trileptal has not been established, and it's not necessary to monitor blood levels of Lamictal.

LABORATORY TESTS

Pretreatment laboratory tests are required for Depakote, Tegretol, and Trileptal. Specific tests depend on which drug is used but often include complete blood count, platelets, electrolytes, cholesterol, triglycerides, liver function tests, ECG (EKG), and pregnancy test. Because Depakote can cause polycystic ovaries in prepubertal girls, periodic imaging with a sonogram is sometimes used to detect the early stages of this condition. After puberty the following symptoms may signal the onset of polycyctic ovaries: abnormal hair growth on the chest or face and/or irregular menses.

Pretreatment laboratory tests are generally not required for Lamictal.

SIDE EFFECTS

Common side effects: Each anticonvulsant has specific side effects. Those most commonly seen with most of the anticonvulsants are drowsiness and lethargy, mild dizziness, unsteadiness when standing or walking, difficulty concentrating, blurred vision, dry mouth, muscle tremors, nausea or heartburn, weight gain (in all drugs except Lamictal), changes in menstrual cycle, and decreased sex drive.

Less common side effects: These include infertility problems (seen in women under the age of twenty who were treated with Depakote) and menstrual irregularities, changes in hair (such as hair loss or changes in hair texture), and rash or itching. These should be reported to a doctor.

Rare side effects: Rare, potentially dangerous side effects include skin rash (mild rashes are fairly common, but a rash that is severe and rapidly increases in severity, especially with Lamictal or Tegretol, should be reported to your doctor immediately); confusion; yellow tint to skin or eyes; severe problems with balance and dizziness; soreness of mouth, throat, or gums; tending to bleed or bruise easily; and severe nausea, vomiting, and abdominal pain. *If these effects occur, contact your doctor immediately.*

ADDICTION POTENTIAL

Anticonvulsants are not habit forming.

INTERACTIONS WITH OTHER MEDICATIONS

Anticonvulsants can interact adversely with the following medications. Interactions vary depending on the specific anticonvulsant.

- birth control pills (especially with Tegretol; may occur with Topamax, a medication that does not treat bipolar symptoms but is commonly prescribed to bipolar patients to reduce weight gain)

- anticoagulants

- aspirin (moderate to high doses)

- cimetidine (Tagamet)

- antibiotics (especially with Tegretol)

- calcium channel blockers

- propoxyphene (Darvon; especially with Tegretol)

- antidepressants (high doses)

- antacids (may affect the absorption of some anticonvulsants)

Anticonvulsant mood stabilizers are often prescribed for patients who are also taking antidepressants. Generally there are no problems with interactions unless the antidepressant doses are high.

SAFETY DURING PREGNANCY AND BREASTFEEDING

There is a risk of birth defects when taking anticonvulsants during pregnancy (especially the first trimester). This can happen with all anticonvulsants taken for bipolar disorder, except Lamictal. Most psychiatrists do not prescribe these medications during pregnancy.

Breastfeeding is not recommended when taking anticonvulsants.

Antipsychotics

Antipsychotic medications were first developed to treat psychotic symptoms such as hallucinations. The first such drugs were found to be effective in reducing psychotic symptoms, but they were notoriously "dirty" drugs, causing significant side effects. Since the mid-1990s, new antipsychotics have been developed and marketed. These newer-generation medications are not free from side effects, but they are considerably safer and better tolerated. The newer drugs are commonly referred to as *atypical antipsychotics.*

Although atypical antipsychotic medications are highly effective in treating psychotic symptoms, it has been found that they are also good treatments for mania, agitation, and aggression. The antipsychotic Seroquel also treats bipolar depression. Thus, these medications are currently being widely used to treat bipolar disorder, even in individuals who have no psychotic symptoms.

Atypical antipsychotic medications used to treat mania can begin to reduce severe agitation within a few hours to a few days. However, the onset of effects when treating more pronounced manic symptoms is similar to that seen with mood stabilizers such as lithium and anticonvulsants (seven to ten days or longer).

GENERIC AND BRAND NAMES AND TYPICAL ADULT DAILY DOSES

olanzapine	Zyprexa	5–20 mg
risperidone	Risperdal	4–10 mg
quetiapine	Seroquel	150–600 mg
ziprasidone	Geodon	60–160 mg
aripiprazole	Abilify	15–30 mg
asenapiner	Saphris	10–20 mg
iloperidione	Fanapt	12–24 mg
lurasidone	Latuda	40–80 mg
paliperidone	Invega	3–12 mg
clozapine	Clozaril	300–900 mg

A note about clozapine (Clozaril): This older-generation antipsychotic medication, which is used occasionally to treat bipolar disorder, has significant side effects (e.g., dry mouth, constipation, sedation, seizures, excessive salivation, blurred vision, nausea, heartburn, and weight gain) and has been associated with a serious blood disorder, agranulocytosis, which causes soreness of the mouth, throat, and gums and a high fever. Agranulocytosis can be fatal. Thus, Clozaril is never considered to be a first-line medication choice. However, despite the problematic side effects, Clozaril is an important medication that can often successfully treat those rare people who have not responded to first-line mood stabilizers.

The following information regarding antipsychotics pertains to the atypical antipsychotics (except Clozaril).

LABORATORY TESTS

Periodic monitoring of cholesterol, triglycerides, and blood glucose is strongly recommended. Abnormalities in these lab measures can be seen with all atypical antipsychotics but are less common with Geodon, Abilify, Saphris, and Latuda.

SIDE EFFECTS

Common side effects: These include drowsiness and lethargy (can occur with all except Abilify); weight gain (can occur with all—however, minimal with Geodon and unlikely with Abilify); nausea, vomiting, and heartburn; stuffy nose; mild dizziness, and changes in cholesterol, triglycerides, or blood glucose.

Less common side effects: These include constipation; decreased sex drive; breast tenderness, liquid discharge from breasts (can occur with high doses of Risperdal); rash; severe sunburn when exposed to even moderate amounts of sunlight; muscle rigidity; tremor; rash; blurred vision; and abnormal, involuntary movements of the mouth and tongue and sometimes head, neck, and hands (rare). These effects should be reported to your doctor.

Rare side effects: Rare, potentially dangerous side effects with antipsychotics include soreness in mouth, throat, and gums; moderate to severe nausea, vomiting, and flu-like symptoms; yellow tint to skin or eyes; seizures; high fever (especially if accompanied by muscle stiffness); confusion; extreme restlessness; unusual bruising or bleeding; severe rash; and frequent urination or loss of bladder control. *If these occur, immediately contact your doctor.*

ADDICTION POTENTIAL

Antipsychotics are not habit forming.

INTERACTIONS WITH OTHER MEDICATIONS

Antipsychotics can interact adversely with the following medications. Interactions vary depending on the specific antipsychotic.

- levodopa (antipsychotics can decrease effectiveness of levodopa)

- amphetamines

- anticonvulsants (can decrease antipsychotic blood levels)

- digoxin (may increase blood levels of digoxin and the antipsychotic)

- warfarin (antipsychotic may increase warfarin blood levels)

- antacids (may interfere with the absorption of the antipsychotic)

SAFETY DURING PREGNANCY AND BREASTFEEDING

Atypical antipsychotics are generally considered to be safe during pregnancy.

Antipsychotic medications are secreted in breast milk. Since these are recently developed medications, there is inadequate information regarding whether it's safe to breastfeed while taking antipsychotics.

SPECIAL CONCERNS

- Avoid exposure to extreme heat (e.g., saunas).

- Grapefruit juice may interfere with the effects of the drug.

- Excessive cigarette smoking may interfere with the effects of the drug.

- Avoid direct exposure to sunlight (since some antipsychotic medications can increase the likelihood of severe sunburns).

Antidepressants

Antidepressants are FDA approved for treating major depression (i.e., unipolar depression); in addition all antidepressants (except Wellbutrin) are effective in treating severe anxiety, panic attacks, and obsessive-compulsive disorder (OCD).

It usually takes two to six weeks for antidepressants to take effect.

It cannot be stressed enough that the use of antidepressants in bipolar I can provoke manic episodes (in psychiatry this effect is known as *switching*) and can cause increased frequency of manic and depressive episodes (this effect is often referred to as *cycle acceleration*). In addition, antidepressants are generally ineffective in treating bipolar depression in people with bipolar I. They can be used in bipolar II, but with caution, and only if other treatments have been ineffective. When used, they must be prescribed along with an antimanic agent (e.g., lithium). Antidepressants can provoke hypomania, but of greater concern is the possibility that long-term antidepressant treatment may cause cycle acceleration in bipolar II patients. Antidepressants are a well-known cause of rapid cycling (e.g., experiencing four or more full-blown episodes a year). Among antidepressants, the MAOIs (Nardil and Parnate) have the best track record in terms of effectiveness, although they are rarley used in the United States. Also effective are Wellbutrin and some other antidepressants such as Prozac and Zoloft. All carry some risks of switching, but this is much less likely if given alongside a mood stabilizer. The antidepressant Effexor and older-generation antidepressants like Elavil are very prone to cause rapid cycling and cycle acceleration.

Please note that not all health care professionals are aware of this information. It simply can't be stated often enough that antidepressants in bipolar disorder treatment must be handled by a skilled health care professional who understands these medications' direct effect on bipolar disorder mood swings. It is never indicated for a person with bipolar disorder to be on an antidepressant without some form of antimania medication. *There are no exceptions.* If your loved one is on an antidepressant, it is essential that they discuss this issue with their prescriber.

GENERIC AND BRAND NAMES AND TYPICAL ADULT DAILY DOSES (FOR MORE COMMONLY USED ANTIDEPRESSANTS)

trazodone	Desyrel, Oleptro	50–400 mg
fluoxetine	Prozac, Sarafem	20–80 mg
bupropion	Wellbutrin	150–400 mg
sertraline	Zoloft	50–200 mg
paroxetine	Paxil	20–50 mg
venlafaxine	Effexor	75–350 mg
nefazodone	generic only	100–300 mg
fluvoxamine	Luvox	50–300 mg
mirtazapine	Remeron	15–45 mg
citalopram	Celexa	10–60 mg
escitalopram	Lexapro	5–20 mg
duloxetine	Cymbalta	20–80 mg
atomoxepine	Strattera	60–120 mg
vilazodone	Viibryd	10–40 mg
desvenlafaxine	Pristiq	50–400 mg
phenelzine	Nardil	30–90 mg
tranylcypromine	Parnate	20–60 mg
selegiline	Emsam (patch)	6–12 mg

LABORATORY TESTS

Laboratory tests are not required for antidepressants.

SIDE EFFECTS

Common side effects: These include nausea and heartburn; energized or anxious feelings (this typically subsides within one to two weeks); headaches; sedation (primarily with Remeron and Desyrel); difficulty falling asleep (often subsides in a few weeks); muscle tremor; rash; and sexual dysfunction. Note that depression itself can significantly reduce sex drive, and not all forms of sexual dysfunction among depressed people are caused by antidepressants. Occasionally antidepressants may decrease sex drive, but the most common sexual side effect is inorgasmia, or difficulty achieving an orgasm despite adequate arousal. Drug-induced inorgasmia can occur in 25 to 30 percent of people treated with antidepressants (sexual side effects are very rare with Wellbutrin). Antidepressants do not cause erectile dysfunction (i.e., impotency). Weight gain is another side effect common with antidepressants, especially with Remeron and Paxil (with other antidepressants, weight gain can occur in up to 10 percent of people, but the weight gain typically does not occur until the person has been taking the drug longer than six months).

Rare side effects: Rare, potentially serious side effects of antidepressants include soreness of mouth, throat, or gums; severe rash; seizures; unusual bruising or bleeding; severe nausea, vomiting, and flu-like symptoms; severe agitation or restlessness; a yellow tinge to skin or eyes; dark-colored urine; a rapid shift into mania or hypomania; and racing thoughts. If these effects occur, contact your doctor immediately.

ADDICTION POTENTIAL

Antidepressants are not habit forming.

INTERACTIONS WITH OTHER MEDICATIONS

Interactions between antidepressants and other medications vary depending on the antidepressant. The following should not be taken with antidepressants.

- 5-HTP (dietary supplement)

- MAOIs

- cimetidine (Tagamet)

- Saint-John's-wort

SAFETY DURING PREGNANCY AND BREASTFEEDING

Most experts agree that some new-generation antidepressants (e.g., Prozac, Zoloft, Effexor, Wellbutrin, and Luvox) are safe for use during pregnancy. Note that Cymbalta, Strattera, Lexapro, Celexa, nefazodone, Pristiq, Viibryd, and Remeron have only recently come to market and there is inadequate data to evaluate safety during pregnancy. These newer antidepressants are associated with the same rate of birth defects as that found in the general population (i.e., in pregnant women who are not taking medications). In contrast, the antidepressant Paxil has been associated with increased risk of cardiac defects and should not be used during pregnancy. High doses of Desyrel should not be used during pregnancy.

Antidepressants are secreted in breast milk, but the amounts are extremely low. Most experts agree that it is safe to breastfeed while taking newer-generation antidepressants. Among antidepressants, Zoloft has the lowest level secreted in breast milk.

SPECIAL CONCERNS

If you have been taking antidepressants for a period of six weeks or more, abruptly stopping the medications can result in withdrawal symptoms (this can occur with any of the antidepressants with the exception of Prozac). Withdrawal symptoms include nausea, stomach upset, nervousness, and flu-like symptoms. Withdrawal symptoms are very unlikely if you have been taking the medication for less than six weeks. And withdrawal symptoms can be avoided almost 100 percent of the time by reducing the dose gradually. When your doctor thinks it is time to discontinue antidepressants, they will likely instruct you on how to gradually discontinue (this often will be done over a period of several weeks).

Antianxiety Medications

Benzodiazepines

Benzodiazepines are a class of antianxiety drugs also commonly referred to as minor tranquilizers.

Benzodiazepines are used to treat acute anxiety, agitation, and insomnia during episodes of mania. They are also used to treat anxiety disorders (such as panic disorder, post-traumatic stress disorder, and generalized anxiety disorder). In the treatment of mania, benzodiazepines are generally used only for the first few days of treatment, to reduce agitation; ideally, these drugs are not used beyond a few weeks.

These drugs take effect within thirty to sixty minutes.

GENERIC AND BRAND NAMES AND TYPICAL ADULT DAILY DOSES

diazepam	Valium	4–30 mg
clonazepam	Klonopin	0.5–4.0 mg
lorazepam	Ativan	2–6 mg
alprazolam	Xanax	1–4 mg

TYPICAL ADULT NIGHTTIME DOSES (FOR BENZODIAZEPINES USED TO AID IN SLEEP)

temazepam	Restoril	15–30 mg
triazolam	Halcion	0.25–0.5 mg
zolpidem	Ambien	5–10 mg
zaleplon	Sonata	5–10 mg
eszopiclone	Lunesta	1–3 mg

LABORATORY TESTS

No laboratory tests are required for benzodiazepines.

SIDE EFFECTS

Common side effects: These include drowsiness, dizziness, forgetfulness, and slurred speech.

Less common side effects: These include confusion, nervousness, rash, and loss of balance and falls.

ADDICTION POTENTIAL

Of the classes of drugs used to treat bipolar disorder, benzodiazepines are the one class that can be abused. There is significant risk of addiction for people with a prior personal or family history of alcoholism or other forms of serious drug abuse.

INTERACTIONS WITH OTHER MEDICATIONS

When taking benzodiazepines, any other type of medication that causes drowsiness or impaired alertness and reaction time can be potentially dangerous, especially if one has to drive an automobile. Alcohol should not be consumed when taking benzodiazepines.

SAFETY DURING PREGNANCY AND BREASTFEEDING

Benzodiazepines typically are not to be used during pregnancy.

Benzodiazepines are secreted in breast milk and should not be used when breastfeeding.

SPECIAL CONCERNS

If benzodiazepines are being taken on a regular basis, the body develops a tolerance for the medication. When this happens, typically the drugs continue to work to reduce anxiety. The problem is that, when there is tolerance, if you abruptly stop the medication there can be withdrawal symptoms. Withdrawal symptoms usually include nervousness, agitation, and difficulty falling asleep. On occasion, withdrawal can result in seizures. This needs to be taken very seriously. If you have been taking a benzodiazepine on a daily basis for more than six weeks, and especially if the dose is moderate to high, withdrawal reactions are a very real risk. You should never abruptly stop taking the medication without first consulting with your doctor. It is also a good idea to be especially careful to monitor your supply of the medications so that refills can be requested in a timely fashion. Many people find it helpful to keep at least a two-day supply on hand in the event that it takes longer than usual for a prescription to be refilled.

Other Medications

Calcium Channel Blockers

Calcium channel blockers are medications that are often used to treat certain cardiovascular diseases. Two of these drugs have been found to be effective in the treatment of mania and possibly as a treatment to prevent the recurrence of mood episodes. The calcium channel blockers used in psychiatry are verapamil and nimodipine.

These drugs are used for people who cannot tolerate lithium, for rapid cycling bipolar, and during pregnancy (verapamil is considered to be the safest mood-stabilizing medication for the treatment of bipolar disorder during pregnancy). Like most other mood stabilizers they generally take seven to ten days to begin reducing symptoms.

Nimodipine is used occasionally to treat mania. This medication looks promising in terms of efficacy; however, it is very expensive.

GENERIC AND BRAND NAMES

verapamil	Calan, Isoptin
nimodipine	Nimotop

Older-Generation Antipsychotics

As noted above, newer-generation, atypical antipsychotics have been developed during the past fifteen years. The newer drugs are considerably safer and have significantly fewer side effects than older-generation antipsychotic medications. We are simply mentioning these older medications here as a point of information, since in rare instances some people may be treated with these drugs. Brand names of older antipsychotics include Thorazine, Mellaril, Serentil, Moban, Trilafon, Loxitane, Stelazine, Prolixin, Navane,

Orap, and Haldol. Of these, the drug most likely to be used these days is Haldol (often to treat the very severe agitation seen in some types of mania).

Anticholinergic Medications

This class of medications is used occasionally to combat side effects of some antipsychotic drugs (side effects such as muscle rigidity or spasms, restlessness, and tremor). The brand names of anticholinergic medications include Cogentin, Akineton, and Artane. Anticholinergic drugs have their own set of side effects including constipation, blurred vision, dry mouth, difficulty beginning urination, and (occasionally) memory loss, confusion, and delirium.

Over-the-Counter Drugs

OMEGA-3 FATTY ACIDS

Omega-3 fatty acids are not effective in treating severe episodes of mania or depression. Their role appears to be in reducing the severity of episodes and possibly having a positive impact on preventing recurrences. Unfortunately, however, their effect is minor, although omega-3 fatty acids are safe to take and offer additional health benefits. Studies have found that people treated with omega-3 fatty acids must take these dietary supplements on a daily basis and over a prolonged period of time. The main sources of omega-3 fatty acids are fish and shellfish, and presumably adding more fish to your diet may be a way to enrich levels of these molecules in the brain. However, all of the studies that have had positive results have used dietary supplement capsules (available from health food stores). The three types of omega-3 fatty acids are LNA (derived from seed and nut oils, principally from flaxseed oil), EPA (from fish oil), and DHA (also from fish oil). Most studies have demonstrated that EPA is the most effective type of omega-3 fatty acid in treating mood disorders. LNA has difficulty getting into the brain (the brain is protected by what is known as the blood-brain barrier, and LNA cannot cross the blood-brain barrier). Thus, for use to treat mood disorders, one must get omega-3 from fish oil. The dosage that has been shown to have some impact on mood is 500 to 1000 mg twice a day.

SAM-E

SAM-e (S-adenosylmethionine) is found in most living cells. It is thought to be necessary for carrying out a number of important intracellular chemical reactions. SAM-e has been used in Europe for more than twenty years as a treatment for depression. A number of studies have shown it to be equally effective when compared to prescription antidepressants. Most notable is the virtual lack of side effects. However, it has not been well supported in studies of the treatment of bipolar disorder. Additionally, it is not useful for treating mania and has, in fact, been found to switch people with bipolar depression into states of mania. Doses for the treatment of depression range from 400 to 1600 mg per day, although recent investigations indicate that often higher doses (1200 to 1600 mg per day) may be necessary for effectively reducing depressive symptoms. In general, SAM-e poses risks in treating bipolar disorder (e.g. provoking manic episodes). It is strongly recommended that for bipolar disorder SAM-e be taken *only* with close observation by your treating prescriber.

SAINT-JOHN'S-WORT

Saint-John's-wort is a dietary supplement that has been found to have antidepressant properties. There are two big problems: (1) Saint-John's-wort has significant and potentially dangerous interactions with some prescription drugs. It should never be taken unless it is monitored by a health care professional. (2) Like SAM-e, Saint-John's-wort can provoke mania in people suffering from bipolar disorder.

Resources

Books

Fast, Julie A., and John Preston. 2006. *Take Charge of Bipolar Disorder: A Four Step Plan for You and Your Loved Ones to Manage the Illness and Create Lasting Stability.* New York: Hachette/Warner Wellness.

————. 2008. *Get It Done When You're Depressed: 50 Strategies for Keeping Your Life on Track.* New York: Penguin/Alpha Books.

Preston, John, John O'Neil, and Mary Talaga. 2010. *A Consumer's Guide to Psychiatric Drugs: Straight Talk for Patients and Their Families.* New York: Pocket Books.

Websites

Julie A. Fast's official website is www.JulieFast.com.

Dr. John Preston's official website is PsyD-fx.com.

www.Sharecare.com
    Julie A. Fast and Dr. John Preston are bipolar disorder experts on Sharecare, an interactive Q&A platform designed to greatly simplify the search for high-quality healthcare information and answer the

world's physical and mental health questions, allowing people to get quality answers, provided by trusted experts. Search under Julie A. Fast and John Preston to find their pages.

www.BpHope.com

Julie A. Fast is a columnist for *Bp Magazine*. BpHope.com offers much-needed information for anyone affected by bipolar disorder through forums, blogs, and *Bp Magazine* articles.

www.HealthyPlace.com

Julie A. Fast is a mood disorder specialist on HealthyPlace, a trusted and comprehensive website including information on all aspects of bipolar disorder and related psychological conditions. HealthyPlace includes the latest information on bipolar disorder treatments, online psychological tests, and an active mental health support community.

Mental Health Organizations

The National Alliance on Mental Illness
Nami.org

The Depression and Bipolar Support Alliance
www.DBSAlliance.org

References

Akiskal, H. S., M. L. Bourgeois, J. Angst, R. Post, H. Moller, and R. Hirschfeld. 2000. Re-evaluating the prevalence of and diagnostic composition within the broad clinical spectrum of bipolar disorders. *Journal of Affective Disorders* 59, Suppl 1:S5-S30.

Bowden, C. L. 2003. Rapid cycling disorder. *Medscape Psychiatry and Mental Health* 8(1): www.medscape.com.

Hales, R. E., and S. C. Yudofsky, eds. 1999. *Essentials of Clinical Psychiatry.* Washington, D.C.: American Psychiatric Press, Inc.

Judd, L. L., H. S. Akiskal, and P. J. Schettler. 2003. A prospective investigation of the natural history of the long-term weekly symptomatic status of bipolar II disorder. *Archives of General Psychiatry* 60:261-269.

Judd, L. L., and H. S. Akiskal. 2003. The prevalence and disability of bipolar spectrum disorders in the US population: re-analysis of the ECA database taking into account subthreshold cases. *Journal of Affective Disorders* 73(1-2):123-131.

National Institute of Mental Health. 2003. Bipolar Disorder. www .nimh. nih.gov.

———. 2011. "Systematic Treatment Enhancement Program for Bipolar Disorder (STEP-BD)." Accessed July 19, 2011. http://www.nimh.nih. gov/health/trials/practical/step-bd/index.shtml.

Papolos, D., and J. Papolos. 1999. *The Bipolar Child.* New York: Broadway Books.

Julie A. Fast is a leading bipolar disorder specialist and a critically acclaimed national speaker, family coach, and sought-after media source. She has been featured in *US Weekly, Self Magazine,* and on national radio, and is a bipolar expert for www.sharecare.com. She blogs at www.juliefast.com and is coauthor of Take Charge of Bipolar Disorder and *Get It Done When You're Depressed.* She lives in Portland, OR.

John D. Preston, PsyD, ABPP, is professor emeritus at Alliant International University in Sacramento, CA, and a bipolar expert for www.sharecare .com. He is author or coauthor of over twenty books addressing psychotherapy, psychiatric medication treatment, and neurobiology, including the *Handbook of Clinical Psychopharmacology for Therapists.* He has presented continuing education conferences internationally. He lives in Shingle Springs, CA.

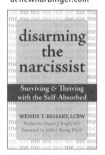